THE BEDFORD SERIES IN HISTORY AND CULTURE

Experiencing the Thirty Years War

A Brief History with Documents

Related Titles in
THE BEDFORD SERIES IN HISTORY AND CULTURE

Street Life in Renaissance Rome: A Brief History with Documents
Rudolph M. Bell, *Rutgers University*

Religious Transformations in the Early Modern World: A Brief History with Documents
Merry E. Wiesner-Hanks, *University of Wisconsin–Milwaukee*

The German Reformation and the Peasants' War: A Brief History with Documents
Michael G. Baylor, *Lehigh University*

The Prince by Niccolò Machiavelli
Translated, Edited, and with an Introduction by William J. Connell, *Seton Hall University*

The Scientific Revolution: A Brief History with Documents
Margaret C. Jacob, *University of California, Los Angeles*

Utopia by Sir Thomas More
Edited with an Introduction by David Harris Sacks, *Reed College*

The Saint Bartholomew's Day Massacre: A Brief History with Documents
Barbara B. Diefendorf, *Boston University*

The Trial of Mary Queen of Scots: A Brief History with Documents
Jayne Elizabeth Lewis, *University of California, Irvine*

Louis XIV and Absolutism: A Brief Study with Documents
William Beik, *Emory University*

The Enlightenment: A Brief History with Documents
Margaret C. Jacob, *University of California, Los Angeles*

England's Glorious Revolution, 1688–1689: A Brief History with Documents
Steven C. A. Pincus, *Yale University*

THE BEDFORD SERIES IN HISTORY AND CULTURE

Experiencing the Thirty Years War

A Brief History with Documents

Hans Medick

Göttingen

Benjamin Marschke

Humboldt State University

BEDFORD / ST. MARTIN'S Boston ◆ New York

For Bedford/St. Martin's

Publisher for History: Mary V. Dougherty
Director of Development for History: Jane Knetzger
Senior Editor: Heidi L. Hood
Executive Editor: Elizabeth M. Welch
Production Supervisor: Victoria Sharoyan
Senior Marketing Manager: Paul Stillitano
Editorial Assistant: Laura Kintz
Project Management: Books By Design, Inc.
Cartography: Mapping Specialists, Ltd.
Permissions Manager: Kalina K. Ingham
Text Designer: Claire Seng-Niemoeller
Cover Designer: Marine Miller
Cover Art: bkp, Berlin/Kupferstichkabinett, Staatliche Kunstsammlungen, Dresden, Germany/Herbert Boswank/Art Resource, N.Y.
Composition: Achorn International, Inc.
Printing and Binding: RR Donnelley and Sons

President, Bedford/St. Martin's: Denise B. Wydra
Presidents, Macmillan Higher Education: Joan E. Feinberg and Tom Scotty
Director of Marketing: Karen R. Soeltz
Production Director: Susan W. Brown
Associate Production Director: Elise S. Kaiser
Manager, Publishing Services: Andrea Cava

Manufactured in the United States of America.

8 7 6 5 4 3
f e d c b a

For information, write: Bedford / St. Martin's, 75 Arlington Street, Boston, MA 02116 (617-399-4000)

ISBN 978-0-312-53505-6

Acknowledgments

Acknowledgments and copyrights are continued at the back of the book on pages 194–96, which constitute an extension of the copyright page. It is a violation of the law to reproduce these selections by any means whatsoever without the written permission of the copyright holder.

Foreword

The Bedford Series in History and Culture is designed so that readers can study the past as historians do.

The historian's first task is finding the evidence. Documents, letters, memoirs, interviews, pictures, movies, novels, or poems can provide facts and clues. Then the historian questions and compares the sources. There is more to do than in a courtroom, for hearsay evidence is welcome, and the historian is usually looking for answers beyond act and motive. Different views of an event may be as important as a single verdict. How a story is told may yield as much information as what it says.

Along the way the historian seeks help from other historians and perhaps from specialists in other disciplines. Finally, it is time to write, to decide on an interpretation and how to arrange the evidence for readers.

Each book in this series contains an important historical document or group of documents, each document a witness from the past and open to interpretation in different ways. The documents are combined with some element of historical narrative—an introduction or a biographical essay, for example—that provides students with an analysis of the primary source material and important background information about the world in which it was produced.

Each book in the series focuses on a specific topic within a specific historical period. Each provides a basis for lively thought and discussion about several aspects of the topic and the historian's role. Each is short enough (and inexpensive enough) to be a reasonable one-week assignment in a college course. Whether as classroom or personal reading, each book in the series provides firsthand experience of the challenge—and fun—of discovering, recreating, and interpreting the past.

Lynn Hunt
David W. Blight
Bonnie G. Smith
Natalie Zemon Davis

Preface

In no period of early modern European history has war had a deeper impact than in the thirty years between 1618 and 1648. By the time the Thirty Years War ended, the fighting and violence had devastated the lands of central Europe, killed at least five million people, and produced far-reaching changes in European politics, society, and culture. When contemporaries themselves labeled the conflict the "Thirty Years War" soon after it ended, they signified it as a war that surpassed all wars in its scope of suffering and devastation. Through the cultural memory of later generations, this image of the Thirty Years War as a devastating "Great War" has continued into the twenty-first century.

Now, as then, intertwined religious and political issues are at the root of major conflicts in the world. Until recently, however, historians concentrated on the momentous long-term consequences of the Thirty Years War, an approach that overlooks the actual participants in this transformative conflict. As its title indicates, *Experiencing the Thirty Years War* strives for a broader understanding of the war by focusing on the actions, suffering, and perceptions of those who lived it. While it treats the war's enormous impact on European and world history, it highlights the human experience to provide students with a complete picture of the war—and hence the opportunity to draw parallels and contrasts between it and other wars, including those of today.

The book opens with an introduction that supplies a clear, concise overview of the Thirty Years War and its meaning for contemporaries and later generations. After explaining the war's origins, the introduction examines its stages and significance. Cross-references to related documents orient students to the core of the book, its rich collection of written and visual primary sources. Included are essential texts such as the key peace treaties, but the bulk of the collection consists of what historical anthropologists term *ego-documents*, personal accounts in which individuals write about what seems important in their lives, both in their ordinary existence and in extraordinary situations such as wartime. Thus the sources bring to the fore the everyday dimensions of the Thirty Years War, as it was experienced and understood by contemporaries from all ranks of society. Many of the documents have never before been published, and most of them have been translated into English here for the first time.

To aid students' analysis of the sources, each source opens with a headnote that provides historical context and biographical information about the author. Explanatory footnotes appear where useful to support students' understanding of the events described. At the end of the book, students and instructors will find a chronology of the era of the Thirty Years War, a list of questions suitable for discussion or for writing assignments, and a selected bibliography with suggestions for further reading.

A NOTE ABOUT THE TEXT AND TRANSLATION

This book is the collaboration of a German historian and an American historian. Hans Medick selected most of the documents and contributed the headnotes to each source and the introductions to most of the chapters. Benjamin Marschke undertook the difficult balancing act of translating the seventeenth-century German texts into English that is understandable to twenty-first-century students but also historically accurate. Both wrote the introduction to the book and composed the appendixes.

ACKNOWLEDGMENTS

We had a great deal of help in researching and producing this work. John Mangum, now with the San Francisco Symphony, was a fellow traveler in Hans's 2003 graduate seminar at the University of California, Los Angeles, where we first began to translate and analyze these documents. Hans discussed the work's emerging shape and contents in a 2008 graduate seminar at Washington University in St. Louis. There he received much encouragement from his students and colleagues to go forward with the project, which he gratefully acknowledges. Andrea Holland, one of Ben's undergraduate students at Humboldt State University, read and fact-checked the entire manuscript. Thomas Kossert, doctoral student at the University of Göttingen, contributed a valuable text (Document 39) along with helpful advice. Bernd Warlich, of Volkach, supplied many useful suggestions. We also thank Lynn Hunt, advisory editor for the Bedford Series in History and Culture, for supporting this project and our editors at Bedford/St. Martin's for their guidance. Developmental editor Elizabeth M. Welch patiently and perspicaciously accompanied us throughout the editorial process. We thank Beth and her colleagues Mary Dougherty, Heidi Hood, Laura Kintz, Andrea Cava, Nancy Benjamin, and Barbara Jatkola for their constantly helpful and constructive work in improving our book. Many thanks as well to Theodore Rabb, whose foundational work helped to inspire this volume, and to the other outside readers for their candid and helpful critiques, which led to countless improvements of the manuscript: Dan Beaver, Pennsylvania State University; Marc R. Forster, Connecticut College; Neal Galpern, University of Pittsburgh; Sigrun Haude, University of Cincinnati; Randolph C. Head, University of California, Riverside; and Terence V. McIntosh, University of North Carolina at Chapel Hill. Finally, we thank the many individuals who helped us find and allowed us to reproduce documents, along with their institutions, especially the Institute Deutsche Presseforschung at the University of Bremen, the Herzog August Bibliothek in Wolfenbüttel, the Württembergische Landesbibliothek in Stuttgart, the Heeresgeschichtliche Museum in Vienna, and the Thüringer Universitäts- und Landesbibliothek in Jena.

Hans Medick
Benjamin Marschke

Contents

Maps and Illustrations

PART ONE

Introduction: The Thirty Years War in Experience and Memory

In the spring of 1618, Protestants in the kingdom of Bohemia furiously protested the Holy Roman Emperor's attempts to curtail their hard-won religious freedoms. The Protestants had started to build new churches; the regents of the Catholic emperor would not tolerate this and had begun to close them again. Tensions boiled over when two regents of the emperor tried to dissolve the assembly of mainly Protestant representatives who had gathered in the Bohemian capital of Prague. In the early morning of May 23, two hundred representatives from this assembly marched in protest to the royal castle. A dozen of these Bohemian nobles pushed their way inside the castle and trapped the two imperial regents and their secretary in the council room. When the officials would not listen to their grievances, the Bohemians threw them out of a window. This "defenestration" (from the Latin for "out of the window") touched off the Thirty Years War (1618–1648), which eventually involved almost every major power in Europe. By the time the war ended, the fighting and violence had devastated the lands of Central Europe, killed at least five million people, and produced far-reaching changes in European politics, society, and culture.

At the time, however, the rebelling Bohemian nobles viewed the Defenestration of Prague as a strictly limited and rightful act of resistance aimed primarily at defending their traditional political and religious rights. They had no idea that their violent deed would set off a chain reaction of armed conflict that would last thirty years and later be called Europe's "first world war" of the modern era.[1]

THE ORIGINS OF THE THIRTY YEARS WAR

The Defenestration of Prague was indicative of the tense religious, political, and social situation that had been developing for decades in Central Europe. The principal battleground of the Thirty Years War was the Holy Roman Empire, centered on what is now modern Germany but also including Bohemia (now the Czech Republic), the Spanish Low Countries (now Belgium), and parts of eastern France and northern Italy (see Map 1). Since the middle of the sixteenth century, the position of Holy Roman Emperor had been filled by members of the Austrian Habsburg dynasty. The Austrian Habsburgs also controlled a number of other major territories in Central Europe through their personal rule as the archdukes of Austria and the elective kings of Hungary and Bohemia. The Habsburg dynasty had split into Austrian and Spanish lines with the abdication of Emperor Charles V in 1555/1556. Charles had left to his son, Philip II, the Spanish Habsburg territories, which included the Netherlands, Italy, and the Spanish colonies in the New World. He had left to his brother, Ferdinand I, the Austrian Habsburg territories, including Hungary and Bohemia.

Several of the positions held by the Austrian Habsburgs, including that of Holy Roman Emperor, were not hereditary but rather elective, meaning that the Habsburgs had to stand for election at each succession. The Holy Roman Emperor was elected by seven imperial *electors*, three archbishops and four territorial princes: the archbishops of Mainz, Cologne, and Trier, and the rulers of the Palatinate, Saxony, Brandenburg, and Bohemia. To ensure an orderly succession, it was customary for the sitting Habsburg ruler to have his successor named and elected well in advance of his death.

Due to this complex political configuration,[2] the Holy Roman Empire was not a sovereign state in the modern sense, but rather a kind of federal institution in which different levels of sovereignty overlapped. The territorial princes of the empire, and especially the electors, liked to think of themselves as independent, and they fervently defended their independence against perceived incursions by the Habsburgs, who in turn demanded the deference and obedience they thought was due them as emperors. As in other early modern European monarchies, it was customary that the *estates*—representatives of the elites, typically noblemen and important townsmen—meet at a *diet*, or assembly, to consult or negotiate with the monarch, especially regarding extraordinary taxes but also on other matters related to the fundamental structure of the empire.

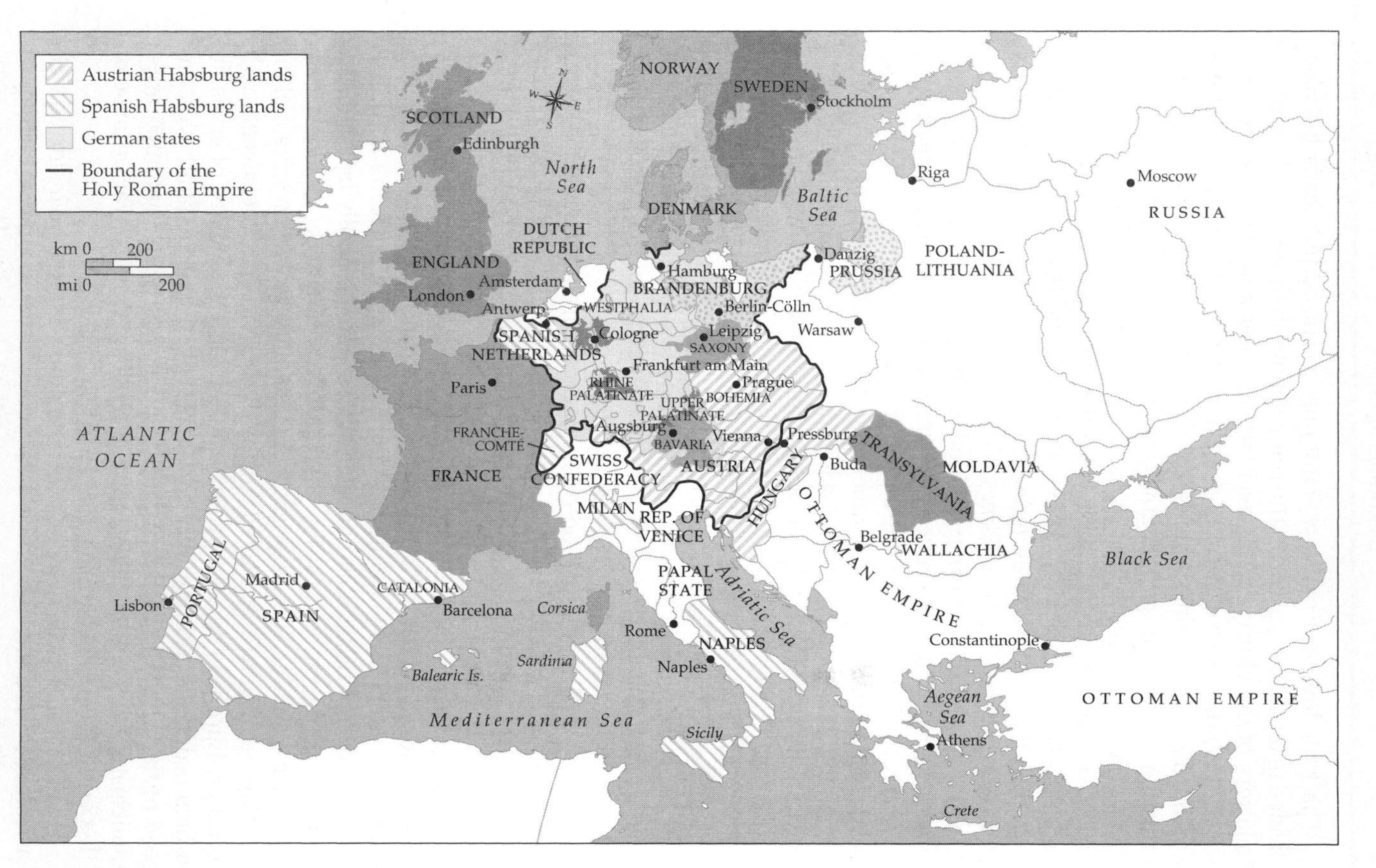

Map 1. *Europe at the Time of the Thirty Years War*

The Holy Roman Empire was not only fractured politically but also divided in terms of religion. In the reformations of the sixteenth century, followers of the church reformer Martin Luther and, a few years later, those of Huldrych Zwingli and John Calvin broke away from the Catholic Church. Soon leading princes of the empire joined the Lutheran Reformation out of a desire to follow their religious convictions, to assert their political independence, or to seize the Catholic Church's properties within their realms. Later on, other princes adopted Calvinism, including the electors of the Palatinate (1561) and Brandenburg (1613). Together, the new doctrines, or confessions, of Lutheranism and Calvinism are known as Protestantism.

Thus the empire became divided religiously between those who remained loyal to the Catholic Church and those who rejected its authority in favor of Lutheranism or Calvinism. The War of the Schmalkaldic League between the emperor and the Lutheran princes broke out in 1546 and ended in 1552 with the Treaty of Passau, which was confirmed at the imperial diet in Augsburg in 1555 (Document 6). As a temporary solution, until the issue of the "divided religion" could be resolved, the so-called Religious Peace of Augsburg recognized and tolerated the establishment of Lutheranism and the confiscation of Catholic Church property in Lutheran territories. Calvinism was not mentioned in the Peace of Augsburg, but it was tacitly tolerated in the same way as Lutheranism.

These complex political and religious configurations lent themselves to tensions and disputes, which were exacerbated by social and economic conflicts and crises.[3] In the context of a general economic slump that started in the 1580s—brought on by long-term changes in social structures, in the economy, and in climate—popular revolts and political rebellions sparked by increased taxes became more common in the late sixteenth century. Economic conflicts between peasants and their lords, between the nobility and the princes, and especially between the princes and the emperor also erupted more frequently.

These economic, political, and religious tensions and conflicts often overlapped or were intertwined, and by the beginning of the seventeenth century, European society was gripped by a general sense of crisis, in which order and stability were fundamentally threatened and even the end of the world seemed imminent.[4] Indeed, early on contemporaries anticipated the coming catastrophe of the Thirty Years War because of this growing sense of crisis.

Even as the Thirty Years War began, other Europeans inside as well as outside Germany recognized its potential to become a conflict of incomparable proportions and uncontrollable brutality. As early as 1621,

Figure 1. *The Comet of 1618 over Heidelberg*
This 1635 copper etching by Matthaeus Merian shows the comet of 1618 over the city and castle of Heidelberg, the capital of Elector Palatine Frederick V (and elected king of Bohemia). The position of the comet is that of a day in November 1618 at dawn. From Johann Philipp Abelin, Matthaeus Merian, *Theatrum Europaeum* [1617–1628] (Frankfurt 1635), p. 119. Herzog August Bibliothek Wolfenbüttel, Sign. A: 70.A Hist.2.

an official in London ominously wrote, "There is nothing in comparison of those hideous fires that are kindled in Germany, blown first by the Bohemians, which is like[ly] to be a war without end."[5]

One could even say that contemporaries, because of this very sense of crisis, predicted the Thirty Years War before it happened. Thus the comet that appeared in the night sky with increasing brightness from September to November 1618 (see Figure 1), shortly before the war actually broke out, was widely understood to be an astrological sign: an omen of impending conflict and calamity.[6] In retrospect, many contemporaries, such as the shoemaker Hans Heberle (Document 4) and the town councilor Andreas Kothe, judged the comet to be a harbinger specifically of the Thirty Years War. Kothe wrote:

> In the year 1618, sometime in November, a large comet was seen in the sky. . . . [It] appeared thirty nights in a row. Thus one can easily infer [what it meant], since the German war in the [Holy] Roman Empire lasted for thirty years and ended by the grace of God in the year 1648 in November. . . . If [I] had known that it was supposed to indicate a thirty-year-long war, I would have conducted my affairs differently.[7]

THE COURSE OF THE THIRTY YEARS WAR

Based on the conduct of the war and the issues in contention, the Thirty Years War can best be understood as having three phases.[8] The first phase of the war lasted from the Defenestration of Prague (Document 3) to the Edict of Restitution of 1629 (Documents 7–9) and the intervention of Protestant Sweden in 1630. This first phase was characterized by repeated Catholic imperial triumphs. At issue were the attempts of the Habsburgs to centralize their control of the Holy Roman Empire and to roll back Protestantism, as embodied in the overreaching Edict of Restitution, which outlawed Calvinism and reclaimed Catholic Church properties confiscated by the Lutherans. The second phase, 1630–1635, initially was characterized by Swedish Protestant victories and a dramatic expansion of the war in terms of its geographical spread, the size of the armies involved, and the degree of devastation and human suffering. During this phase, it became clear that the Catholic imperial side could not hope to change significantly the imperial political structure or to roll back Protestantism. The beginning of a willingness to compromise was evidenced by the Peace of Prague in 1635 (Document 54). The third phase of the war began with the Peace of Prague and the direct involvement of France in the war in Central Europe. This phase witnessed the widespread devastation of the countryside, the decimation of the population, and the destruction of agriculture, commerce, and industry. The war reached a diplomatic and military stalemate, and the major belligerents were financially exhausted. After years of negotiations, the war officially ended in 1648 with the Peace of Westphalia (Document 58), although it took two more years to demobilize the armies and actually bring the war to an end.

Phase 1: The Bohemian Rebellion, the Intervention of Denmark, and the Triumph of the Emperor, 1618–1630

Under Emperor Matthias (r. 1612–1619) and his chief adviser, Cardinal Melchior Khlesl, the Habsburg monarchy at first attempted to defuse the growing political and religious tensions in Central Europe by taking a conciliatory approach to religious issues (Document 9). Their immediate priority was to better control the institutions of the Holy Roman Empire and to centralize the governance of their own lands, not to impose religious conformity or suppress Protestantism. Matthias thus granted concessions to Protestants and even guaranteed religious freedom in some of the Habsburgs' lands. He continued, if somewhat begrudgingly, the policies of his predecessor, Emperor Rudolf II, who in his Letter of Majesty in 1609 had granted significant religious liberties to his Protestant Bohemian subjects.

In June 1617, Matthias's cousin and heir apparent, the future emperor Ferdinand II (r. 1619–1637), was elected king of Bohemia. Ferdinand was a religious hard-liner, and his moves to restrict the rights of Protestants in Bohemia ultimately led to the Defenestration of Prague. The Bohemian Estates, led by Protestant nobles, then proceeded to form an army and rise up against Habsburg rule.

When Matthias died in March 1619, he was succeeded by Ferdinand. Ferdinand was elected Holy Roman Emperor in August 1619, but earlier that month the Bohemian Estates had nullified his election as king of Bohemia. In his place, they elected one of the foremost Protestant political figures in the Holy Roman Empire: Frederick V, elector of the Palatinate, who was a Calvinist. In November 1619, he was crowned Frederick I, king of Bohemia. Frederick is often referred to as the Winter King because his reign lasted only during the winter of 1619–1620.

The Winter King had high hopes of rallying an array of allies against the Habsburgs, but he and the Bohemian "rebels" (as they were called by the Catholic imperial side) soon found that they were largely left to defend themselves. As the elector of the Palatinate, Frederick was a leading member of the Protestant Union, the Protestant alliance within the Holy Roman Empire formed in 1608 (Document 1). However, this loose alliance excluded any territories that had not been part of the original treaty of 1608. Thus the other members of the Protestant Union would not support Frederick as king of Bohemia. Frederick, who was married to Elizabeth Stuart, daughter of King James I of England, also hoped to parlay his dynastic ties into direct assistance, but this came to naught. On the other side, the Habsburg emperor Ferdinand II could count on support from the Spanish branch of the Habsburg dynasty and from the Catholic League, the Catholic alliance within the Holy Roman Empire (Document 2).

Diplomatically isolated, Frederick and the Bohemian rebels were quickly militarily overwhelmed by Catholic imperial forces. At the Battle of White Mountain in November 1620, an army of the Catholic League, consisting of 27,000 men under Johann Tserclaes, Count of Tilly, smashed a Bohemian army of 15,000 men and effectively ended the war in Bohemia. At the same time, troops recruited by Duke Maximilian of Bavaria and his allies in the Catholic League invaded Frederick's Upper Palatinate territories bordering Bohemia. In a parallel action, Spanish Habsburg troops, from their base in the southern Netherlands (modern Belgium), invaded Frederick's Rhine Palatinate territories in western Germany (see Map 2 on pages 10–11).

Thus the Winter King was deposed, not only as king of Bohemia but also as elector of the Palatinate. He fled to the Protestant Netherlands, where he spent most of the rest of his life in exile. In Bohemia, Emperor Ferdinand reestablished himself as king. He tried and executed many of those who had opposed his rule, redistributed the estates of opposing Protestant nobles to loyal Catholic followers (including the future commander in chief, Albrecht von Wallenstein), and forcibly imposed Catholicism. In the Palatinate, Duke Maximilian of Bavaria was granted Frederick's Upper Palatinate territories and Frederick's electoral title.

The Catholic imperial side seemed to be triumphant, but the war continued for several reasons. First, pockets of resistance in the Upper and Rhine Palatinate held out against the Catholic forces for years, and Protestant armies retreated into Lower Saxony (northern Germany), where they were pursued by Catholic imperial forces. Second, in 1621 Spain and the Netherlands renewed their war, which in many ways paralleled the Thirty Years War in Germany. The Protestant Netherlands had first revolted against Catholic Spanish Habsburg rule in the 1560s, and their war of independence would continue intermittently until 1648, when Dutch independence from Spain was finally granted as part of the Peace of Westphalia. In 1609, after decades of fighting, Spain and the Netherlands had signed a twelve-year cease-fire. Spain's intervention in the Rhine Palatinate was motivated in part by a desire to gain a better strategic position against the Dutch before the expiration of the cease-fire between the two countries in 1621. Third, although the war in Germany seemed to be coming to a close by 1624, it was renewed in 1625 when a new actor appeared on the Protestant side: Denmark.

Denmark's entry into the war in 1625 did little to reverse the poor fortunes of the Protestants, however. King Christian IV of Denmark entered the war because he felt threatened by the progress of the Catholic imperial forces. The Danish king held extensive territories in northern Germany, and as a Lutheran ruler he was alarmed by the impending collapse of the Protestant side.

Unfortunately for the King of Denmark, he had to face not only Tilly's Catholic League army but also a new Catholic imperial army that had been raised for the emperor by Albrecht von Wallenstein (Documents 51–53). Wallenstein was a loyal follower (and creditor) of the emperor. In 1625, Ferdinand appointed Wallenstein imperial commander in chief, or *generalissimo*, awarded him a duchy taken from a Bohemian Protestant, and made him Duke of Friedland. Wallenstein proved to be not only an able military leader but also a highly successful (and profitable) military contractor. Because the emperor could not pay for another army, Wallenstein used his own credit to raise a new imperial army. He was allowed to support his army by having his soldiers "live off the land"—that is, by collecting extraordinary taxes and extorting "contributions" from civilian populations, regardless of whether they were enemies, neutrals, allies, or even loyal Habsburg subjects (Documents 29–31). After several battlefield victories, Tilly's and Wallenstein's armies overran the territories allied with Christian IV in northern Germany and even occupied parts of Denmark itself. In 1629, the Danish king was forced to make peace with Ferdinand and withdraw from the war.

In 1629, as before in 1624, it once again appeared that the war in Germany was nearing its end and that it would result in a Catholic imperial triumph. Nonetheless, the war continued. Outside Germany, Spain's war against the Netherlands was going calamitously, which gave the Protestant side in Germany new hope and reinforced their unwillingness to accept defeat. At the same time, the political problems within the French monarchy were resolved by the late 1620s, and Cardinal Richelieu emerged as the new policymaker for King Louis XIII. Although Richelieu was a Catholic clergyman who sought to suppress Protestantism in France, in international relations he was fervently anti-Habsburg. Thus France went to war against the Austrian Habsburgs in northern Italy in 1628 and supported the Protestants in Germany, especially Sweden's involvement there, which inaugurated a new phase of the war.

Phase 2: The Intervention of Sweden and the Protestant Resurgence, 1630–1635

It was at this point that the emperor, confident of victory, made two important decisions that he would later be forced to reverse. First, in 1629, Ferdinand issued the Edict of Restitution (Document 7), and second, in 1630, he dismissed his generalissimo, Wallenstein. The Edict of Restitution specifically demanded the return of all Catholic properties that had been seized by Protestant rulers since the Peace of Passau in 1552, and it proclaimed an end to the unofficial tolerance of Calvinism that had been in place for decades. Generally, the edict was significant

Map 2. *The Central European Theater of the Thirty Years War*

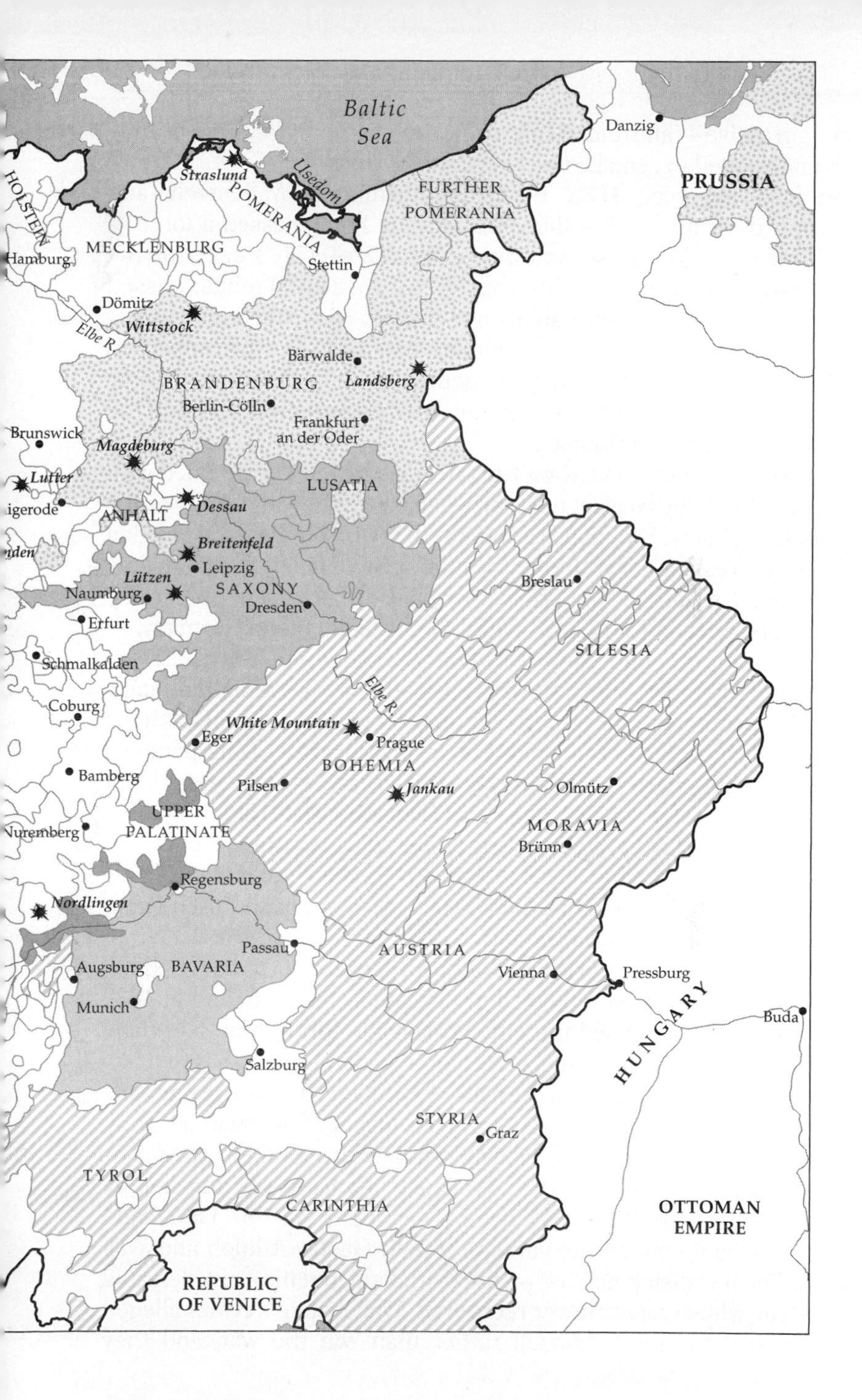

Baltic
Sea
Danzig
PRUSSIA
Straslund
Usedom
POMERANIA
FURTHER
POMERANIA
HOLSTEIN
MECKLENBURG
Hamburg
Stettin
Dömitz
Wittstock
Elbe R.
Bärwalde
Landsberg
BRANDENBURG
Berlin-Cölln
Frankfurt
an der Oder
Brunswick
Magdeburg
Lutter
LUSATIA
Dessau
ANHALT
Breitenfeld
Leipzig
Lützen
Naumburg
SAXONY
Dresden
Erfurt
Breslau
SILESIA
Schmalkalden
Elbe R.
Coburg
White Mountain
Prague
Eger
BOHEMIA
Bamberg
Pilsen
Jankau
Olmütz
UPPER
PALATINATE
MORAVIA
Brünn
Regensburg
Nordlingen
Passau
AUSTRIA
Augsburg
BAVARIA
Vienna
Pressburg
HUNGARY
Munich
Buda
Salzburg
STYRIA
Graz
TYROL
CARINTHIA
OTTOMAN
EMPIRE
REPUBLIC
OF VENICE

as an aggressive—and ultimately overreaching—declaration of how Ferdinand wanted to remake the Holy Roman Empire.

The following year, 1630, Ferdinand dismissed Wallenstein and disbanded his army. By that time, Wallenstein had amassed a force of 130,000 men, which was several times the size of Tilly's army or the Danish army. Wallenstein and his army thus were a great military asset, but they were also a political liability and danger. His extortion of goods and money to supply and pay his soldiers had alienated the emperor's allies as well as his enemies, and the generalissimo's outsize economic and military power was increasingly regarded as a political threat to the authority of the emperor himself.

Meanwhile, in June 1630, King Gustav Adolph of Sweden landed with an army on the Baltic coast of northern Germany. The king had recently concluded the Polish-Swedish War (1626–1629), through which Sweden had become dominant over the eastern Baltic Sea. He felt threatened by the prospect of a Catholic imperial victory in Central Europe, especially given the presence of Catholic imperial forces in northern Germany.

Sweden's intervention caused profound changes in the course of the Thirty Years War. First, the Swedish king's spectacular military successes soon reversed the hitherto uninterrupted series of Catholic imperial victories. Second, despite the relative brevity of his personal involvement, the charismatic king became by far the most prominent and popular Protestant leader of the war (Documents 47–50).

At the Battle of Breitenfeld in September 1631, Gustav Adolph and a Swedish Protestant army of more than 40,000 men annihilated Tilly's Catholic imperial army of more than 30,000 men (see Map 2). The king then took the strategic initiative and in 1632 carried the war deep into the mostly Catholic territories of southern Germany. Duke Maximilian of Bavaria was forced to flee from his capital, Munich, and in 1632 the Swedish army occupied the city. Protestants throughout Germany rejoiced and rallied behind Gustav Adolph's leadership.

Because of these military reversals, Ferdinand found it necessary to reinstate Wallenstein. Wallenstein again managed to raise an army within a few months, but he cautiously refrained from taking any major military action. In November 1632, Wallenstein's army was attacked by Gustav Adolph at the Battle of Lützen (Documents 44–46). One could say that this battle ended the careers of both Gustav Adolph and Wallenstein. The Swedish king died on the battlefield, but his army defeated Wallenstein, whose career never recovered. Wallenstein's critics alleged that he aimed to enrich himself rather than win the war, and they accused him of pursuing his own political goals. Wallenstein's clandestine and independent attempts at diplomacy with the Swedes threatened to undermine the emperor's authority, and in early 1634 Wallenstein was condemned by a secret imperial tribunal. Officers from his own army assassinated him and several of his most trusted advisers in February of that year (Documents 51–53).

Although Sweden remained in the war until its end, without the charismatic and military leadership of Gustav Adolph, the Swedish Protestant side again lost the strategic initiative to the Catholic imperial side. At the Battle of Nördlingen in September 1634, a Catholic imperial army smashed the principal Swedish Protestant army, which spelled the end of Swedish leadership of the Protestant side.

Phase 3: The Peace of Prague, the Intervention of France, and the Long Stalemate, 1635–1648

By 1635, the Swedish Protestant alliance had collapsed, and the Catholic imperial side was exhausted. It again appeared as if the war might come to an end. The emperor and most of the Protestant princes of Germany, including Sweden's principal German ally, the elector of Saxony, agreed to the Peace of Prague, which basically called for a return to the prewar situation (Documents 54–56).

Once again, however, the war continued. Anything other than a Habsburg defeat was unacceptable to Cardinal Richelieu of France. Consequently, the French declared war on the Spanish Habsburgs in 1635 and also directly entered the war in Central Europe. France had hardly been neutral before then. It had subsidized the Swedish Protestant side for years, and French troops had fought the Habsburgs in northern Italy and had been active periodically in the Rhineland.

The French military initially performed poorly, but Sweden was able to renew its efforts with financial support from France. The conflict continued, essentially devolving into a military and diplomatic stalemate. Although both sides continued to hope for a miraculous military victory, even the major battles in the last phase of the war did little to influence the war's outcome—neither side was capable of landing a knockout blow. On the contrary, the fighting became increasingly aimless as the commanders and soldiers on both sides were forced to focus less on military objectives and more on simply ensuring their own survival. They did this by quartering, or housing, themselves with civilian populations still able to provide money and supplies, or by simply plundering the areas in which they stayed or through which they moved. Both sides generally abandoned any military strategy, except to deny the enemy the ability to "live off the land," either by depriving them of access to plunderable areas or by devastating such areas before the enemy could reach them.

Changes in leadership brought little in the way of willingness to compromise. Emperor Ferdinand II died in 1637 and was succeeded by Ferdinand III. Richelieu died in 1642 and Louis XIII in 1643, and they were succeeded by Cardinal Mazarin and Louis XIV, respectively. Like Richelieu, Mazarin was convinced that France was financially and politically stronger than Habsburg Spain or Austria and could hold out longer than either in what seemed to be a struggle for European, and even world, supremacy.[9] Indeed, the Spanish Habsburgs were defeated in the Low Countries by the Dutch and in Italy by the French, and in Spain they faced revolts sparked by increased taxes and troop levies. For their part, the Austrian Habsburgs had given up any hope of winning the war and of imposing their will on the Holy Roman Empire, but they also refused to admit defeat and end the war on unfavorable or humiliating terms. By the mid-1640s, however, France was also straining under the burden of new taxes imposed to finance the war. As peasant revolts and tax protests became more frequent, Mazarin became more willing to accept a compromise peace with the Habsburgs.

There had already been many abortive attempts to end the Thirty Years War, but the negotiations that would ultimately end the war began in July 1643 and dragged on for five more years. Hundreds of Catholic and Protestant diplomats met in the cities of Münster and Osnabrück in Westphalia (see Map 2). The fighting—and, worse, the quartering of troops with civilians—continued during the negotiations. Indeed, the question of how to pay and demobilize the armies became a central point of contention. As difficult and expensive as it was to raise an army, it was even more difficult and expensive to disband one.

Even the official conclusion of the Peace of Westphalia in 1648 did not mean an end to the war (Documents 58 and 59). Hundreds of thousands of soldiers still occupied and plundered Central Europe, and the demobilization and payment of the armies was not settled until June 1650. Even when the soldiers were gone, those who had lived through three decades of war and knew little else could hardly believe that the war was finally over (Documents 60–62).

THE SIGNIFICANCE OF THE THIRTY YEARS WAR

The importance of the Peace of Westphalia can hardly be overstated. In many ways, the settlement of 1648 resolved some of the contentious issues in the history of Europe since the Reformation, and it set the stage for developments in Europe up to the present.[10]

The Religious and Political Significance of the Thirty Years War and the Peace of Westphalia

In terms of religion, the Peace of Westphalia largely reinforced the compromise that was in place before the Thirty Years War had started, as codified by the Peace of Augsburg in 1555 (Document 6). It thereby institutionalized the multireligious coexistence that continues to characterize Germany until the present. The settlement of 1648 brought a few changes, however. Most obviously, the religious settlement's *normative date* was updated to 1624. That is, conversions and seizures of church lands that occurred before 1624 were officially accepted (including the Habsburgs' actions in Bohemia in the early 1620s), but changes instituted after 1624, including the harsh changes imposed by the 1629 Edict of Restitution (Document 7), were voided. Moreover, Calvinism, which had not been mentioned in the settlement of 1555 but which had come to be tacitly accepted by the beginning of the Thirty Years War, was officially recognized. Finally, although rulers were still free to change their own religion, they were not allowed to impose their religion on the communities over which they ruled. In the case of such a change on the part of the ruler, the religion practiced by his subjects in their communities should be the same as it had been in 1624, even if that meant reversing any changes that had taken place since then.

In political terms, the Peace of Westphalia established a new theoretical and systematic basis for international relations. Visions of universal rule and world domination—as they had been upheld and were pursued during the war by the Spanish and Austrian Habsburgs, by Sweden, and by France—were abandoned. Instead, rulers were forced to accept the existence of other equally legitimate sovereign rulers. The European "system of states" thus established in 1648 remained the theoretical norm (if not always the reality) for relations between European states well into the twentieth century and can be seen as the foundation of modern international law.[11] The "conference system" of diplomacy, modeled on the negotiations that had taken place in Münster and Osnabrück, also became the norm for international relations in Europe and the world.

The Peace of Westphalia was immeasurably important for political developments within Germany as well. Historian Johannes Burkhardt has conceived of the Thirty Years War as a "war of state formation," rather than a war among states, and this process of state formation reached an important turning point with the settlement of 1648.[12] The system of German states it inaugurated followed a "third" path of political development unlike that of the rest of Europe. In Germany, there was neither "one state" governed by one monarch (like France) nor a "multiple-state" arrangement without any central authority (like early modern Italy).[13] Instead, one could say that Germany developed a "double statehood," which involved the simultaneous development of political institutions on both the imperial and territorial levels.[14] From this perspective, the Peace of Westphalia was neither a setback for the political development of Germany nor the beginning of the end of the Holy Roman Empire, but rather a "completion and new orientation" of this uniquely bilevel system of politics in Central Europe.[15]

The Thirty Years War and the Peace of Westphalia also resulted in far-reaching military and political changes. This war had been the heyday of the "military enterpriser," as the spectacular example of Wallenstein illustrates.[16] By the end of the war, however, most military contractors had been squeezed out or brought to heel by their royal employers, and armies were essentially de-privatized. In other ways, the expedients used in the long and financially draining war simply became the norm after the war, which resulted in increased centralization of military and political power, and even a "monopoly of violence." Although most of the armies were ultimately disbanded after the war, many rulers continued to maintain standing armies during peacetime. They were able to support these armies—and, in fact, needed to do so—because they continued to collect extraordinary taxes without the acquiescence (and often despite the resistance) of representative bodies. These extraordinary taxes were modeled on the coerced contributions of wartime, and the tax collectors themselves had often been trained in the military apparatuses of the Thirty Years War. These developments fed on one another as they had during the war, so that the more a ruler expanded his military, the more taxes he could collect, and the more taxes he collected, the more he could expand his military.[17] Thus wartime absolutism, induced by the imperatives of waging war and financing armies, led to peacetime absolutism. The ruler's ability to run the government without any interference from representative bodies, supported by (and supporting) a standing army, became a hallmark of Europe's "age of absolutism," which is usually regarded as beginning only with the Peace of Westphalia.[18]

Experiencing the War

Breaking the Thirty Years War down into phases based on military developments is one important way to study the war's long-term impact on politics and diplomacy. To appreciate the war's impact on ordinary people's lives, however, historians require a different approach—the historical-anthropological analysis that informs this book. *Historical anthropology* is an approach that puts the actions, sufferings, experiences, and perceptions of people and individuals from both the lower and higher ranks of society into the center of the historian's attention and research. In applying this approach to the Thirty Years War, historians examine specific wartime experiences of both soldiers and civilians and explore how these experiences affected their everyday lives. The methodological tool used to achieve this experiential perspective is the ego-document. *Ego-documents* are personal accounts in which individuals write about what seems important in their lives, both in their everyday existence and in extraordinary situations such as wartime. The Thirty Years War inspired a wide variety of such documents. Many ego-documents were written with the purpose of trying to describe the indescribable, as it was often expressed, and to record personal testimonies of unique experiences during the war.

The traditional religious interpretation of the events of the Thirty Years War, which dominated historical writing since the nineteenth century, measured religious identity and religiosity by their influence on political-military developments. This approach has been cast into doubt in the last decade.[19] When viewed from the historical-anthropological perspective, the unresolved religious conflicts of that time seem to have developed their own dynamic during the war. Symbolic and physical violence against religious opponents, whether in the destruction of their sacred objects and symbols, in the occupation and use of their religious space, or even in forced conversion or expulsion from their homes, was an important and constant aspect of the war.[20] The documents presented in Part Two, chapter 2, of this book present an up-close historical-anthropological perspective on the religious dimensions of the violence of the Thirty Years War.

The significance of civilian-military relations in the war also takes on new meaning when viewed from a historical-anthropological perspective. The ego-documents in chapters 3 and 4 demonstrate a wide spectrum of civilian-military relations. The civilians represented in these documents were not merely passive victims of the war. Civilians suffered, but they also acted. Civilian resistance against military violence took forms ranging from the physical violence of hard-pressed peasants who fought against plundering soldiers (Document 17 and Figure 2) to the sophisticated "soft power" of the nuns who pacified the Swedish occupiers of their cloister with sweet delicacies (Document 24). Although military violence against civilians, including sexual violence against women (Documents 21–24), dominated many situations, there were often possibilities for negotiation, such as the give-and-take regarding the quartering of soldiers and the collection of "contributions," and even civilians' payment of the military for protection, called a *salvaguardia*, even though such arrangements frequently proved precarious or ineffective. Civilian-military arrangements reflected the social reality of the time, and they offered various advantages and disadvantages for people of different statuses and ranks on both sides. Not only did officers enjoy much greater benefits from contribution and quartering arrangements than did common soldiers (Document 30), but the burdens of such arrangements were also unevenly distributed among civilians, so that privileged elites and officials were often exempted from paying a share that fully corresponded to their wealth. In addition, civilian-military arrangements offered the opportunity for further discrimination and exploitation of minority groups. For instance, Jews, who did not enjoy common legal rights, were more heavily burdened than Christians in the Thirty Years War's "economy of violence" (Documents 31 and 32).

As the documents in chapter 5 reveal, disease and famine dominate many recollections of the war as a terrible catastrophe. Although plague and starvation were usually not the direct results of military violence, they were consequences of the war, whether because contagious diseases were spread by moving armies, because the unbendingly harsh demands of the armies resulted in a scarcity of food, or because military violence disrupted or destroyed agricultural production. Even in these desperate situations, people tried to exercise some precarious human agency. They attempted to optimize their chances of survival, even if this meant consuming all of their food reserves to prevent them from falling into the hands of enemy soldiers (Document 37) or, as an extreme measure, resorting to cannibalism (Document 38).

The Thirty Years War is known as a "war of extremes" in popular memory and in historical scholarship primarily because of the mass killings that occurred in battles and massacres. In reality, however, relatively few spectacular battles took place during the war, which was characterized instead by long sieges and small-scale engagements (Documents 39 and 40) as well as quartering with civilians, requisitioning supplies, and plundering the countryside.[21] Nevertheless, massacres

Figure 2. *The Revenge of the Peasants*

Engraving No. 17 from a series of 18 images by Jacques Callot, *Les Grandes Misères et les Malheurs de la Guerre* (*The Great Miseries and Misfortunes of the War*), Paris, 1633.

such as the one at Magdeburg in 1631 (Documents 41–43 and Figure 3) and battles such as the Battle of Lützen in 1632 (Documents 44–46) became "defining events,"[22] which for centuries were closely tied to the memory of the war.[23] The recollections of the participants in and witnesses of these events are often fairly sober assessments, even if they were written down immediately after the events occurred. Some protagonists and observers, including Wallenstein after the Battle of Lützen (Document 45) and Prince Christian II of Anhalt-Bernburg after the destruction of Magdeburg (Document 43), immediately attempted to ascribe world-historical significance to the events they had participated in or witnessed. This is especially evident in Wallenstein's letter, written immediately after the Battle of Lützen. Although Wallenstein was still uncertain of the death of his worthy opponent, Gustav Adolph (see Figure 4, page 22), he reported the battle as being of "such a fury as no one has ever seen or heard" and "[fought] with the greatest resolution in the world."

Contemporary print media were of the utmost importance in the transformation of specific happenings into "defining events." Soon after these events took place—whether they were battles, massacres, or the deaths of leading protagonists of the war, such as Gustav Adolph and Wallenstein—their significance was defined, argued, and established in pamphlets, broadsheets, and newspapers (Documents 47–53). Often this was a contentious process in which the opposing sides tried to pursue and publicize their own specific interests. In fact, the Thirty Years War was the first war in the modern world in which the print mass media played a decisive role by publicly commenting on and defining the events. The press may even have played an active role in actually waging the war, as some contemporaries and later historians have claimed.[24]

In assessing the significance of the Thirty Years War, one should also ask about the loss of human life, as well as the destruction and regeneration of economic resources. Since the nineteenth century, historians have repeatedly debated these questions. Generally in these debates, a negative interpretation, which judges the war a catastrophe, stands against a revisionist interpretation, which questions how thoroughly disastrous the demographic, economic, social, and cultural consequences of the war really were.[25] A common weakness of both interpretations is their "balance-sheet perspective."[26] They assess the war's significance and consequences based on the sum balance of losses in population and the destruction of material resources at the end of the war, compared with the situation at the beginning of the war. As for all

Figure 3. *A View of the Catastrophe of Magdeburg*
This engraving by Daniel Mannasser of Augsburg was published in 1631. It shows the city being besieged and bombarded by Tilly and Pappenheim's army from the perspective of the besiegers and ultimate victors, whose troops stand in the foreground, to the right.

wars, such a perspective on the Thirty Years War obscures wide variations in different regions and localities and also great variations in time. The war was a complex process of socioeconomic, political, cultural, and religious developments and changes, which occurred quite differently in various areas of Europe and in the various phases of the war. A static balance-sheet perspective overlooks this crucial variety among different groups of society in their experience of the war. Nevertheless, balance-sheet interpretations have rendered valuable data and estimates, which clearly show that the Thirty Years War was "the most

destructive conflict in European history."[27] A cautious estimate is that the war directly or indirectly caused 5 million civilian deaths in the Holy Roman Empire, which amounts to 20 percent of the prewar population. To put this proportion in perspective, the population loss for the whole of Europe during World War I (1914–1918) is estimated at 27 million, which amounted to 5.5 percent of the prewar population, and the death toll during World War II in Europe (1939–1945) is estimated at 33.8 million, which was 6 percent of the prewar population.[28] Judged from this aggregate data, the Thirty Years War was indeed the most destructive war in modern European history.

The War in Cultural Memory

It is precisely in their often emphatic assertion that what they witnessed and lived through was a unique experience that the people who wrote the personal accounts presented in Part Two of this book laid claim to their commemorative and admonitory function for the generations to come. However, the reservoir of memory of the Thirty Years War was by no means confined to *communicative memory*—that is, the memory of the people who lived through the war or its immediate aftermath. Their collective communicative memory came to be inscribed in the long-term *cultural memory* of Central Europe in a multitude of forms: in monuments, in memorial practices, and not least of all in literary and scholarly texts.[29] Among the monuments are the many local places of remembrance, such as the spectacular battlefield monument at Lützen, where King Gustav Adolph died in 1632,[30] and the large cannonball with a fiery tail that was hung from the ceiling in the Nikolai Church in Leipzig in 1666 as a commemoration of the siege and bombardment of the city in 1636.[31] There are also ongoing memorial practices, such as the Augsburg Peace Festival, in which Augsburg Protestants have celebrated annually—since 1650, without interruption—the restoration of religious parity in 1648.[32]

Opposite: Figure 4. *King Gustav Adolph in the Battle of Lützen*
In this oil painting of 1634 by the Dutch artist Jan Asselijn (1610–1652), the battle is portrayed as a typical clash between cavalry, with Gustav Adolph on horseback featured prominently with drawn sword and feathered hat on the right side, close to the center. The picture captures the moment in which the king was being shot at and wounded for the first time in the battle by a foot-soldier poised standing on the left side.

One of the main channels through which remembrance of the Thirty Years War has been transmitted is its representation in poetry, literature, plays, and songs, as well as in pamphlets, images, and historiography. In each case, the images and narratives of the war were reinterpreted in keeping with the discourses and the problems of the times when they were written. For example, participants in the eighteenth-century Enlightenment regarded the catastrophe as a result of unreasonable and "unenlightened" behavior and they enthusiastically referenced the accomplishments of the Peace of Westphalia. This differed fundamentally from the partisan religious interpretations of the war by Catholics and Protestants that began circulating in the eighteenth century and culminated in the nineteenth century. In such interpretations, the war was invoked as a period of extreme barbarism and violence, but also as a time shaped by sacrifice and heroism on both sides.

Seen in this way, the Thirty Years War became a cornerstone of divergent national and political foundational narratives.[33] The political and religious discord of the war was seen as a foil against which the nineteenth-century success in unifying Germany shone all the more brightly. Until the development of the academic discipline of history in the second half of the nineteenth century, and for some time thereafter, these otherwise diverging historical recollections shared the view of the Thirty Years War as an extreme historical case and as a negative example of a war with the greatest possible number of civilian casualties. It became, at least in the German-speaking societies of Central Europe, a "superlative of horror,"[34] the standard by which to measure later wars. Not until World War I did the Thirty Years War relinquish its status as the "Great War." Even then, it did not do so completely.

The cultural memory of the Thirty Years War gained new meaning in the twentieth century as the "Age of Extremes" of violence and war, as it has been called by the late Eric Hobsbawm, one of the most insightful historians of Europe.[35] During and following World War II in Europe, the image of the seventeenth-century war acquired a new, if limited, currency when the twentieth-century world wars were conceived together as a "second Thirty Years War" (1914–1945). It may seem strange that this formulation remained confined to the perspectives of the political and intellectual elite and a few professional historians.[36] However, unlike the Thirty Years War itself, which from its beginning was perceived by contemporaries as one long and continuous configuration of events and has also been remembered in this way, the concept of a "second Thirty Years War" was not based on the perceptions and experiences of contemporaries and thus failed to establish any resonance in popular memory. As Hobsbawm cast a retrospective glance at his lifelong experience and work as a historian in the twentieth century, he formulated the problem this way:

> Looking back on the thirty-one years from the assassination of the Austrian Archduke in Sarajevo [in 1914] to the unconditional surrender of Japan [in 1945], they must be seen as an era of havoc comparable to the Thirty Years' War of the seventeenth century in German history. And Sarajevo . . . certainly marked the beginning of a general age of catastrophe and crisis in the affairs of the world. . . . Nevertheless, in the memory of the generations after 1945, the Thirty-one Years' War did not leave behind the same sort of memory as its more localized seventeenth-century predecessor. This is partly because it formed a single era of war only in the historians' perspective. For those who lived through it, it was experienced as two distinct though connected wars, separated by an "inter-war" period without overt hostilities.[37]

Thus the "shadow image" (in German, *Schattenbild*) of the Thirty Years War, as evoked by the German poet Friedrich Schiller around 1800 in a famous trilogy of plays devoted to Wallenstein,[38] still set the standard in the twentieth-century "Age of Extremes." The cultural memory of the Thirty Years War was not eclipsed by the world wars of the twentieth century, and attempts to regard them as ultimate and to characterize all previous wars as lesser conflicts proved fruitless. It remains to be seen whether the Thirty Years War will continue to be a point of reference in the twenty-first century, a time when the power of the media and the ubiquity of images of war increasingly overlay and interfere with the reality of ongoing wars, as well as with the historical memory of them.

The cultural memory of the Thirty Years War was not eclipsed by the world wars of the twentieth century, and attempts to regard these as ultimate and to characterize all previous wars as lesser conflicts were overreaching. It remains to be seen whether the Thirty Years War will continue to be a point of reference in the twenty-first century, a time when the power of the media and the ubiquity of images increasingly overlay and interfere with the reality of ongoing wars, as well as with the historical memory of them. However, what seems certain from the following documents is that they will move their readers to appreciate the Thirty Years War from the perspective of those who experienced it.

NOTES

[1] Immanuel Wallerstein, *The Modern World-System II: Mercantilism and the Consolidation of the European World Economy, 1600–1750* (New York: Academic Press, 1980), 23.

[2] A penetrating overview and analysis of the institutional, political, jurisdictional, and religious tensions and dynamic of the Holy Roman Empire in the century preceding the Thirty Years War and during the war itself is provided by Joachim Whaley, *Germany and the Holy Roman Empire, Volume 1: From Maximilian I to the Peace of Westphalia, 1493–1648* (Oxford, U.K.: Oxford University Press, 2012).

[3] Sheilagh Ogilvie, "Germany and the Seventeenth-Century Crisis," *Historical Journal* 35, no. 2 (1992): 417–41.

[4] Theodore K. Rabb, *The Struggle for Stability in Early Modern Europe* (New York: Oxford University Press, 1975).

[5] James Howell, letter to his father, March 20, 1621, in James Howell, *Epistolae Ho-Elianae: Familiar Letters Domestic and Forren . . . Partly Historicall, Political, Philosphicall, upon Emergent Occasions*, 3rd ed. (London: Humphrey Moseley, 1655), vol. 1, sec. 2, 74. Howell was a courtier, diplomat, and later clerk of the Privy Council. This judgment of the ensuing German wars continued to occupy Howell's perceptions. One year later, while in Antwerp, he wrote to the Viscount of Colchester on May 1, 1622, "It is fear'd this German war will be as the Frenchman saith, de longe balaine, long breath'd, for there are great powers on both sides, and they say the king of Denmark is arming." Ibid., vol. 1, sec. 2, 85.

[6] On the contemporary context in which comets were perceived and explained, see Sigrun Haude, "Zorn und Schrecken, Buße und Gnade: Diskurse in astrologischen Schriften des 17. Jahrhunderts" ("Rage and Terror, Atonement and Mercy: Discourses in Astrological Texts of the Seventeenth Century"), in *Die Sterne lügen nicht: Astrologie und Astronomie im Mittelalter und in der Frühen Neuzeit* (*The Stars Do Not Lie: Astrology and Astronomy in the Middle Ages and in the Early Modern Period*), ed. Christian Heitzmann (Wolfenbüttel: Herzog August Bibliothek, 2008), 188–89.

[7] Andreas Kothe, *Die Chronik des Ratsherrn Andreas Kothe: Eine Quelle zur westfälischen Geschichte im Zeitalter des Dreißigjährigen Krieges* (*The Chronicle of the Councilor Andreas Kothe: A Source Regarding Westphalian History in the Time of the Thirty Years War*), ed. Franz Flaskamp (Gütersloh: Flöttmann, 1962), 25–26.

[8] See especially Ronald G. Asch, *The Thirty Years War: The Holy Roman Empire and Europe, 1618–1648* (New York: St. Martin's Press, 1997), and Thomas A. Brady, *German Histories in the Age of Reformation, 1400–1650* (Cambridge, U.K.: Cambridge University Press, 2009), 375–76.

[9] On the Thirty Years War as a struggle between the Habsburgs and the French Bourbon monarchy for universal rule, see Johannes Burkhardt, *Der Dreißigjährige Krieg* (*The Thirty Years War*) (Frankfurt: Suhrkamp, 1992), 30–62.

[10] This point is made by Johannes Burkhardt in his important study *Vollendung und Neuorientierung des frühmodernen Reiches, 1648–1763* (*Completion and New Orientation of the Early Modern Empire, 1648–1763*), Gebhardt Handbuch der deutschen Geschichte (Gebhardt Handbook of German History) 11 (Stuttgart: Klett-Cotta, 2006), 25.

[11] Burkhardt, *Vollendung und Neuorientierung*, 27–28.

[12] Johannes Burkhardt, "Der Dreißigjährige Krieg als frühmoderner Staatsbildungskrieg" ("The Thirty Years War as an Early Modern War of State Formation"), *Geschichte in Wissenschaft und Unterricht* (*History in Scholarship and Instruction*) 45 (1994): 487–99.

[13] Burkhardt, *Vollendung und Neuorientierung*, 29; Barbara Stollberg-Rilinger, *Das heilige Römische Reich Deutscher Nation vom Spätmittelalter bis 1806* (*The Holy Roman Empire of the German Nation from the Late Middle Ages until 1806*), 3rd ed. (Munich: Beck, 2007), 88–89.

[14] Burkhardt, *Vollendung und Neuorientierung*, 28–29. On the Holy Roman Empire, see also the essays collected in Jason Philip Coy, Benjamin Marschke, and David Warren Sabean, eds., *The Holy Roman Empire, Reconsidered* (New York: Berghahn Books, 2010).

[15]Burkhardt, *Vollendung und Neuorientierung*, passim; Stollberg-Rilinger, *Das heilige Römische Reich*, 87.

[16]Fritz Redlich, *The German Military Enterpriser and His Work Force: A Study in European Economic and Social History*, 2 vols. (Wiesbaden: F. Steiner, 1964–1965).

[17]Jeremy Black, *A Military Revolution? Military Change and European Society, 1550–1800* (Basingstoke, U.K.: Macmillan Education, 1991).

[18]See, for example, the remarkable work by Rudolf Vierhaus, *Germany in the Age of Absolutism* (Cambridge: Cambridge University Press, 1988). As a counterpoint, see the cogent qualifying remarks by Peter H. Wilson in *Europe's Tragedy: A History of the Thirty Years War* (London: Allen Lane, 2009), 807–12. Wilson warns against too-broad assumptions and stresses that among the consequences of the war were not only the "new order" of absolutist states but also a considerable amount of unsettling "state destruction."

[19]See, for example, Wilson, *Europe's Tragedy*, 9–10; and Peter H. Wilson, "On the Role of Religion in the Thirty Years War," *International History Review* 30 (2008): 473–514.

[20]Johannes Burkhardt's well-argued claim that there was a relativization of the "confessional reading of events" by contemporaries in the course of the war prompts the questions, which and whose "confessional reading," and which "events"? Burkhardt, "War der Dreißigjährige Krieg ein Religionskrieg?" ("Was the Thirty Years War a War of Religion?"), in *Der Dreißigjährige Krieg*, 128–43, here 134.

[21]This point is made by, among others, Geoff Mortimer, *Eyewitness Accounts of the Thirty Years War, 1618–48* (Basingstoke, U.K.: Palgrave, 2002), 38–44.

[22]Wilson calls the sacking and destruction of Magdeburg a "defining event" of the Thirty Years War. Wilson, *Europe's Tragedy*, 470.

[23]For the Battle of Lützen, see Maik Reichel and Inger Schuberth, eds., *Gustav Adolf, König von Schweden: Die Kraft der Erinnerung, 1632–2007* (*Gustav Adolf, King of Sweden: The Power of Memory, 1632–2007*) (Dößel: Janos Stekovics, 2007). For the massacre at Magdeburg, see Hans Medick, "Historical Event and Contemporary Experience: The Capture and Destruction of Magdeburg in 1631," *History Workshop Journal* 52 (2001): 25–48.

[24]Johannes Burkhardt, "Krieg und Frieden als Medienereignis" ("War and Peace as Media Event"), in *Der Dreißigjährige Krieg*, 225–34; Wolfgang Behringer, "Veränderung der Raum-Zeitrelation: Zur Bedeutung des Zeitungs- und Nachrichtenwesens während der Zeit des Dreißigjährigen Krieges" ("Change in the Space-Time Continuum: On the Significance of the News and Information Media during the Time of the Thirty Years War"), in *Zwischen Alltag und Katastrophe: Der Dreißigjährige Krieg aus der Nähe* (*Between Everyday and Catastrophe: The Thirty Years War from Up Close*), ed. Benigna von Krusenstjern and Hans Medick, 2nd ed. (Göttingen: Vandenhoeck and Ruprecht, 2001), 57, 75.

[25]On the history of this debate, see Theodore K. Rabb, "The Effects of the Thirty Years' War on the German Economy," *Journal of Modern History* 34 (1962): 40–61. As a more recent example of the negative interpretation, see Jürgen Kuczynski, "Der Dreißigjährige Krieg" ("The Thirty Years War"), chap. 2 in *Geschichte des Alltags des deutschen Volkes* (*History of the Everyday Life of the German People*) (Cologne: Pahl-Rugenstein Verlag, 1980). As an extreme example of the revisionist interpretation, see Sigfrid Henry Steinberg, *The "Thirty Years War" and the Conflict for European Hegemony, 1600–1660* (London: Edward Arnold, 1966).

[26]In German, *bilanzierende Sichtweise.* The term was introduced and criticized by Rudolf Schlögl in *Bauern, Krieg und Staat: Oberbayerische Bauernwirtschaft und frühmoderner Staat im 17. Jahrhundert* (*Peasants, War, and State: Upper Bavarian Agriculture and the Early Modern State in the Seventeenth Century*) (Göttingen: Vandenhoeck and Ruprecht, 1988), 15.

[27]Wilson, *Europe's Tragedy*, 787.

[28] Ibid., table 7, 787. Wilson's chapter "The Demographic Impact" contains a critical assessment of the data available from regional or local historical research on the differences and similarities of population movements in the various regions and localities of the Holy Roman Empire during the Thirty Years War. Ibid., 786–95.

[29] For a full discussion of the distinction between "communicative memory" and "cultural memory," see Jan Assmann, "Communicative and Cultural Memory" in *A Companion to Cultural Memory Studies*, ed. Astrid Erll and Ansgar Nünning (New York: Walter de Gruyter, 2008), 109–18. For the background of this distinction, see Birgit Neumann and Martin Zierold, "Cultural Memory and Memory Cultures" in *Travelling Concepts for the Study of Culture*, ed. Birgit Neumann and Ansgar Nünning (Boston: Walter de Gruyter, 2012), 225–48.

[30] See the images of the monument designed by the famous Prussian architect Karl Friedrich Schinkel in Reichel and Schuberth, *Gustav Adolf*, 164 and 205–7.

[31] See Hans Medick, "The Thirty Years' War as Experience and Memory: Contemporary Perceptions of a Macro-Historical Event," in *Enduring Loss in Early Modern Germany: Cross Disciplinary Perspectives*, ed. Lynne Tatlock (Leiden: Brill, 2010), 43–49.

[32] Johannes Burkhardt and Stefanie Haberer, eds., *Das Augsburger Friedensfest: Augsburg und die Entwicklung der neuzeitlichen europäischen Toleranz-, Friedens- und Festkultur* (*The Augsburg Peace Festival: Augsburg and the Development of the Modern European Culture of Tolerance, Peace, and Celebration*) (Berlin: Akademie Verlag, 2000).

[33] See Kevin Cramer, *The Thirty Years' War and German Memory in the Nineteenth Century* (Lincoln: University of Nebraska Press, 2007).

[34] In German, *Superlativ des Entsetzens*, a phrase used in a critical distancing from such views by Bernhard Erdmannsdörffer, *Deutsche Geschichte vom Westfälischen Frieden bis zum Regierungsantritt Friedrichs des Großen, 1648–1740* (*German History from the Peace of Westphalia to the Succession of Frederick the Great, 1648–1740*) (Berlin: Baumgärtel, 1892), 1:102.

[35] Eric Hobsbawm, *Age of Extremes: The Short Twentieth Century, 1914–1991* (London: Michael Joseph, 1994).

[36] See Medick, "The Thirty Years War as Experience and Memory," 47ff.

[37] Hobsbawm, *Age of Extremes*, 52.

[38] Friedrich Schiller, prologue to *Wallenstein*, in *Werke und Briefe* (*Works and Letters*), ed. Fritjof Stock (Frankfurt: Deutscher Klassiker Verlag, 2000), 4:16.

PART TWO

The Documents

1

Sense of Crisis, Sense of Time

Political and religious tensions were building in early-seventeenth-century Europe. There was frustration on all sides that the temporary settlement established by the Peace of Augsburg in 1555 was becoming unenforceable and unsustainable, and there was anxiety that the institutions and traditions of the Holy Roman Empire appeared to be breaking down. The proclamations of the Protestant Union in 1608 (Document 1) and the Catholic League in 1609 (Document 2) expressed and further intensified these tensions and concerns.

Religious fear of an impending apocalypse, which was shared by all social groups across Central Europe, magnified this sense of barely constrained conflict. As the Thirty Years War began, contemporaries understood that the tensions and anxieties of the past decades were finally being unleashed. Already in its opening stages, people from all walks of life recognized—and were inspired to write about—the war as something far beyond the normal scope of armed conflict.

Tensions and Preparations before the War

1

The Protestant Union

1608

The Holy Roman Empire suffered an unprecedented political breakdown in 1608 when the delegates at the imperial diet failed to agree on a concluding statement. A major point of contention was Emperor Rudolf II's intervention in the Protestant imperial free city of Donauwörth in Bavaria at the end of 1607. This was highly problematic not only for religious reasons—the emperor had ceded control of the Protestant churches in Donauwörth to the Catholic Church—but also for political ones. By refusing to consult with the local imperial institutions, Rudolf had overstepped his authority.

Within days of the end of the failed diet, several Protestant princes met to form an alliance for mutual defense. The significance of this Protestant Union as a political institution or a military alliance is easily overestimated. Only approximately half of the Protestant principalities in the empire ultimately joined the alliance, and some of the most important, such as Saxony, never did. The alliance had no institutions of its own, and it continued to rely on the political structure of the empire.

This proclamation of a Protestant alliance within the Holy Roman Empire was both a symptom and a cause of the growing diplomatic and religious tensions in Central Europe in the years leading up to the Thirty Years War. Especially noteworthy is the justification of the alliance as a restoration of long-standing traditions, a form of political rhetoric that was typical in early modern Europe. The signatories professed their continued obedience and loyalty to the empire, even while complaining of its inadequacy (or unwillingness) to protect them. Indeed, the Protestant Union claimed that the new alliance was intended to support the empire.

From Hanns Hubert Hofmann, ed., *Quellen zum Verfassungsorganismus des Heiligen Römischen Reiches Deutscher Nation, 1495–1815* (*Sources regarding the Constitution of the Holy Roman Empire of the German Nation, 1495–1815*) (Darmstadt: Wissenschaftliche Buchgesellschaft, 1976), 150, 151, 152–53.

In the Holy Roman Empire of the German Nation of our dear fatherland, out of the especially stalwart care of our dear forefathers, a general peace and unity were well established . . . and if anyone, whoever it was, should act or undertake anything against it, then against such illegitimate violence and distress the estates of the Holy Roman Empire . . . should really be obligated to stand by each other and lend a hand. Such [obligations] . . . have in part been lamentably misunderstood and in part been overstepped with hostile and violent actions and in many ways outrageously violated, so that one cannot have confidence in any reliable help. Now for many years the appeals of obedient estates for such help, as assiduously and as much as they held to it, have not been granted, in direct violation of the constitution of the empire. Instead they were put off from one meeting of the imperial regions and deputations to another, and the situation in more than one place has become more worrisome and dangerous than ever before. Therefore it is to be feared that if these things continue to be seen in such a way and are not corrected with God's help, then in this situation, some [powers] outside and some within the Holy [Roman] Empire will not let this opportunity pass, and they will increase in many ways their aggressive and outrageous actions. Thereby they will foment one disturbance after another in the beloved Fatherland to overrun and wage war on the peace-loving and obedient estates of the empire. They will throw the entire ancient, worthy constitution of the empire into disorder, and destroy that towards which we have worked so long. From this there is nothing to expect except an ultimate disturbance of all good order, government, and prosperity, and the downfall of all peace-loving spirit in the Holy [Roman] Empire, and also the loud clamor of the general arming for war in the region, in secret and in the open.

[. . .]

Thus, we, the undersigned electors and estates of the Holy [Roman] Empire, in timely consideration and contemplation of all of that and to prevent such problems, and also for other serious and considerable reasons, as mentioned above, and not at all against the [Holy] Roman Emperor's Majesty, our most graceful lord, to whom we all owe the most submissive and dutiful obedience . . . also not against, to the disadvantage, or to the burden of any other person, and even less to break up the constitution of the Holy [Roman] Empire, but much more to reinforce it, and for the better maintenance of peace and unity in the empire . . . have concluded the following:

[. . .]

In case one of us or our subjects are attacked by enemy forces . . . then the threatened and damaged party should immediately, upon his notification of the other allies, it is specifically agreed, be aided and helped out of the entire situation.

2

The Catholic League

1609

Barely a year after the creation of the Protestant Union, a group of Catholic princes formed their own confederation. This alliance was instigated by and centered on Duke Maximilian of Bavaria, who hoped to counter both the Protestants and the Habsburgs. Ultimately, dozens of Catholic bishoprics, imperial free cities, and principalities joined the Catholic League.

Like the proclamation of the Protestant Union, the proclamation of this alliance justified itself by citing the impending dangers and growing political and religious tensions of the early seventeenth century. Just as the Protestants had done, the Catholics lamented the failure of the empire to ensure peace and tranquillity, even as they formed an alliance that was aimed at curbing its power. They publicly pledged to support the empire, yet they underhandedly excluded the emperor from their new confederation.

It is to be known, that for some time happenings in the Holy [Roman] Empire of the German Nation have proven themselves to be very worrisome and dangerous. The beneficial imperial statutes and constitutions, especially those regarding the maintenance of peace, tranquillity, and unity, and the religious and secular peace,[1] not only have been drawn

[1] This is a reference to the Peace of Augsburg of 1555 (Document 6).

From Hanns Hubert Hofmann, ed., *Quellen zum Verfassungsorganismus des Heiligen Römischen Reiches Deutscher Nation, 1495–1815* (*Sources regarding the Constitution of the Holy Roman Empire of the German Nation, 1495–1815*) (Darmstadt: Wissenschaftliche Buchgesellschaft, 1976), 153–55.

into lamentable misunderstanding but also have been broken many times by obvious violent incursions and actions. Therefore, it is to be feared to the utmost that if these things continue to be observed to happen, then little by little such manifest actions will occur in the empire by which the peace-loving and obedient Catholic estates of the empire will be violated and overwhelmed by the unruly others. From that certainly nothing is to be expected other than the elimination of the one true, redeeming, old Catholic faith and in connection with this the suppression of all regular propriety, laws, and imperial statutes.

. . . Attentive to the necessity, and for better implementation and execution, of the Holy [Roman] Empire's statutes, of its beneficial and most precious religious and secular peace, and its concluding enforcement orders, and not in any way contrary to it, we therefore have now and forever agreed to the following union.

First, this union of ours is only intended for the defense and preservation of the true Catholic faith and for the propagation of common peace, of tranquillity and prosperity, for the deterrence of worrisome danger, and then, as said above, for the implementation of the resolutions of the Holy [Roman] Empire, for its religious and secular peace, and the other worthy old traditional customs of the empire.

[. . .]

Now, in the future, if one of us confederates is violently attacked and manifestly assaulted, hurt, and aggrieved by someone else, contrary to the secular and religious peace and to the imperial constitutions and resolutions, as well as contrary to venerable customs of the empire, or to the consequences resulting thereof, under whatever supposed pretense this might occur; if in this situation the orderly access to law or to the other procedures in the empire would be barred and delayed and no help would be possible without obvious danger to himself, then the violated and aggrieved party in such a difficulty should make it known in due course to the head of the confederation. The head of the confederation should then without hesitation appeal amicably to the offender or to him, to whom the assaulting party is subject,[2] to halt his [the offender's] plans so that the offended is maintained in his rights. Should this not be successful and should an amicable resolution not be possible, the aforementioned head of the confederation should then, having taken the advice of the members of the confederation, immediately undertake the necessary defense through the united help of the confederation.

[2] In most cases, this would be the emperor or an elector.

1618: Spectacular Action and an Omen of War and Doom

3

WILHELM, COUNT VON SLAVATA

The Defenestration of Prague

1618

Wilhelm, Count von Slavata (1572–1652),[1] *and Jaroslav, Count von Martinitz (1582–1649),*[2] *were the two imperial regents in Bohemia, who, together with their secretary, Philipp Fabricius,*[3] *were thrown out of a window of the royal castle in Prague on May 23, 1618.*

This incident, known as the Defenestration of Prague, followed a heated meeting with a delegation sent by the Bohemian Estates. Two hundred representatives of the estates had marched to the castle to protest new imperial policies that violated their religious rights as Protestants, as well as their political rights as estates. The Defenestration of Prague is often portrayed in political historiography as the spectacular beginning of the Thirty Years War. It was, the nineteenth-century Catholic Czech-Austrian

[1] Slavata, a staunch Roman Catholic and leader of the Counter-Reformation in Bohemia, was president of the Bohemian chamber from 1612 to 1618 and as such responsible for the revenue and debts of the Bohemian crown. After fleeing the country in 1620, he returned in 1621, once the Bohemian uprising was over, and continued his career in the service of the emperor. From 1628 to 1652, as chancellor of the Bohemian court, he was the most powerful person in Bohemia.

[2] Martinitz fled the country in 1618. Like Slavata, he returned in 1621 and continued his career in the service of the emperor. He became the highest judge of the land and marshal of the Bohemian court, and in the pursuance of his career, he managed to multiply his landed estates.

[3] Fabricius, whose original family name was Philipp Platter, served as secretary of the Bohemian chancellery. After the defenestration, he fled to Vienna and was the first to report the news to the emperor. Upon this, he was ennobled and granted the title Baron von Rosenfeld and Hohenfall. (*Hohenfall* means, literally, "High Fall.") He remained in Vienna in service of the emperor.

From "Wilhelm Graf von Slavata," in Adam Wolf, ed., *Geschichtliche Bilder aus Österreich* (*Historical Images from Austria*) (Vienna: Braumüller, 1878), 1:324–26.

historian Anton Gindely wrote, "the catastrophe, which was the beginning and the cause of all the following tribulations."[4]

In this excerpt from Slavata's memoirs, which were written several years later, he describes the famous incident in the third person. An ardent Catholic, Slavata explains that he and his colleague, Martinitz, along with their secretary, Fabricius, were meant to be killed but were miraculously saved by divine intervention. The reason for their soft landings may have had more to do with contemporary fashion and the cool weather, as they were wearing long, heavy coats that cushioned the impact. Additionally, the wall outside the palace window was not vertical, but inclined slightly outward, so the three officials slid down rather than falling freely.

Although Slavata insisted that the event was unprecedented, there had been a defenestration in Prague before, and the rebels of 1618 consciously followed this historical example. On July 30, 1419, followers of Jan Hus, an influential religious reformer who had been burned at the stake as a heretic four years before, stormed the town hall in Prague to free their imprisoned co-religionists and threw seven Catholic town councilors out of the window. Another defenestration almost happened in 1609 during the controversy that arose over the Letter of Majesty, in which Emperor Rudolf II promised the Protestant estates of Bohemia freedom of religion.

It will be necessary that I describe in somewhat greater detail how the two counts happened to be thrown out of the window, and in what a wonderful way God Almighty protected them. In the entire empire, in all the kingdoms and principalities of Christians, it has since been regarded as wrong and punishable that Bohemian people from the two upper estates [the nobility and clergy] committed such a shameful crime and, unheard of in the chronicles of the world, pitilessly ejected from the window into a deep ditch two regents of His Majesty and the highest authorities in Bohemia. Although they had answered in all mildness all the malicious imputations which were put to them, and though they had sufficiently protested against the barbaric proceeding, the others, in their perverse wickedness, would hear nothing of order, truth, and justice, and instead they violently seized the counts and insolently attacked them. First four of the lords and one knight (namely Wilhelm von Lobkowitz,

[4] Anton Gindely, *Geschichte des dreissigjährigen Krieges*, vol. 1, *Geschichte des Böhmischen Aufstands* (*History of the Thirty Years War*, vol. 1, *History of the Bohemian Uprising*) (Prague: Tempsky, 1869), 275.

Albrecht Smiricky, Ulrich Kinsky, Litwin von Rican, and Paul Kaplir) grabbed hold of Count von Martinitz, held him firmly by the hands, led him to the already open window, and screamed, "Now we will deal with our religious enemies appropriately." The two counts thought that they would be taken out of the chancellery and arrested; however, when Martinitz recognized the manner of his impending death, he called in a loud voice, "Because I must die for God, His Holy Catholic faith, and His Royal Majesty, I will happily suffer it all, only please bring me my confessor, so that I can confess my sins." One of the lords told him as an answer, "We'll still bring you a villainous Jesuit." Then Count Martinitz, greatly aggrieved and heartfully repenting his sins, began to pray: "Jesus, Son of the Living God, have pity on me, Mother of God, pray for me." The aforementioned persons lifted him up off the floor and threw him, with his rapier and dagger, but without his hat, which was torn from his hands, headfirst out the window into the depth of the ditch around the castle. However, while falling he never stopped calling the names "Jesus, Mary," and he fell to the earth so gently, that it was as if he was just sitting down. Through his prayers to the Virgin Mary and the protection of God, the terrible fall did not harm him, despite his heavy physique. . . .

Now when Count Slavata saw what happened to Count Martinitz, his true friend and dear colleague, he could easily conclude that the same would happen to him. With his hands raised up to heaven, he asked in the name of God and His merciful will that he be allowed to confess his sins; afterward they could kill him, however they wished. But they screamed, "We don't want to bring the villainous Jesuit here. You've confessed enough." And when Count Thurn[5] said to them in German, "Noble lords, there's the other one," they seized Count Slavata, lifted him up off the floor, and ejected him, with his cloak and sword, headfirst out the same window. Still in the window he made the sign of the Holy Cross across his breast and with a contrite heart said, "*Deus propitius esto mihi peccatori*" [Lord, have mercy on me, sinner]. When he grasped the window with his right hand and held on a little bit, one of them hit his fingers with the hilt of his dagger, so that he fell out. His hat, on which there was a beautiful band with golden roses and diamonds, remained in the chancellery. They tore off the gold chain with the cross of black enamel while they were throwing him out, and so it remained

[5]Heinrich Matthias, Count von Thurn (1567–1640), military leader of the Bohemian Protestants. After the Battle of White Mountain in 1620, he served as a diplomat and general on the Protestant side in the Thirty Years War.

in their hands. Count Slavata hit the stone ledge of the lower window, hit his head on a rock when he fell to the ground, and then tumbled into the bottom of the ditch. Because he had blood in his mouth, he began to cough like someone suffocating and then lay still, half-dead. Count Martinitz had decided to help him in any way possible, and because he was afraid that the people in the window might shoot at them, he pretended to be weaker than he was and rolled down to Count Slavata. Although he injured himself on the left side with his rapier and dagger in doing so, he unwrapped his . . . cloak from around his head, and he wiped away the blood that was coming out of his [Slavata's] mouth with his handkerchief. From a small silver case, which was enveloped by his handkerchief, he immediately took balm, smeared it under the nose and on the temples of the unconscious lord, and with God's help got him upright again. He thereby told him to patiently bear the pain. Slavata repeated reverentially his earlier prayer: "*Deus propitius esto mihi peccatori*" [Lord, have mercy on me, sinner].

4

HANS HEBERLE

The Comet of 1618 as a Sign of the Times and a Bad Omen

1618

In the belief systems and historical understandings of early modern Europe, a comet was regarded as a sign of future wars, epidemics, and political calamities. A comet appeared first in September 1618 and reached its maximum brightness in October and November of that year, but remained visible until the beginning of 1619. In the context of the

From Gerd Zillhardt, ed., *Der Dreißigjährige Krieg in zeitgenössischer Darstellung: Hans Heberles "Zeytregister" (1618–1672). Aufzeichnungen aus dem Ulmer Territorium. Ein Beitrag zu Geschichtsschreibung und Geschichtsverständnis der Unterschichten* (*The Thirty Years War in Contemporary Portrayals: Hans Heberle's "Time Register" (1618–1672). Records from the Territory of Ulm. Regarding the History Writing and Historical Understanding of the Lower Classes*) (Ulm: Kommissionsverlag W. Kohlhammer, 1975), 85–87, 93–94.

tensions of the late 1610s, this comet was widely interpreted as an omen of impending doom, as indicated by the abundance of material written about it. One could almost say that in their predictions of the future, these contemporary writers "invented" the Thirty Years War before it even began. Hans Heberle's description of the comet in his chronicle reveals its great significance at the time. Heberle, a cobbler with no formal education, lived in the countryside around the city of Ulm. The appearance of the comet, and the associated apocalyptic expectation that the end of the world was near, caused him to begin writing his chronicle, in which he fastidiously recorded the happenings of the Thirty Years War.

Time Register [title page]

This is a little book of diverse histories and true things,
also of many conditions in the final state of this oppressive, miserable,
sad, terrible, wrong, and disdainful world. The stories have been
happening to us daily and they are still in full swing. What caused me
to write this brief history, one can simply read for oneself in the
introduction. Everything described diligently and in the
minutest detail by Johannes Heberle, shoemaker
in Neenstetten.[1]
Anno Domini, Year 1618

Anno Domini 1618, a great comet appeared in the fall in November. To see the thing was terrible and strange, and it moved me and changed my disposition so that I started to write, because I thought that it would mean something big would happen, as then really did happen, enough reports of which the reader will find here. . . .

Anno 1618, a great comet appeared in the form of a great and terrible rod through and by which God threatened us mightily because of our sinful lives, which we fully deserved and continue to deserve daily. The same comet was seen from the fall into the spring. What it meant and what would follow thereafter causes one to cry hot tears, as we would sadly experience and have so experienced over and over again from anno 20 until anno 30, which cannot be described well enough, though

[1] Neenstetten is approximately 12½ miles (20 km) north of Ulm.

this little book diligently tries to do so.[2] Also in this year the great and widely known marketplace in Plurs in Graubünden was destroyed.[3]

Anno 1619, Ferdinand II became the [Holy] Roman Emperor, under whom a great persecution happened through war, unrest, and the spilling of the blood of Christians, as the examples will show well enough. First he started a big war in Bohemia, which he then oppressed and subjugated under his religion, then in the following years the land of Braunschweig, the land of Mecklenburg, the land of Leineberg, Friesland, the land of Brandenburg, the land of Pomerania, Gotland, Austria, Moravia, the countryside above the river Entz, Silesia, the Palatinate of Heidelberg, yes, almost the whole of Germany, was conquered, all of which I hardly can describe and explain.[4]

[2] Heberle rewrote the introduction to his chronicle from a retrospective perspective in 1630 or soon thereafter.

[3] In September 1618, a landslide destroyed the village of Plurs, then located in the canton of Graubünden in Switzerland. The village is now known as Piuro and is located in northern Italy.

[4] Remember that Heberle wrote this in 1630, when the emperor seemed triumphant.

5

The Siege and Capture of Pilsen and the Comet

1618

The astronomy-minded author of the pamphlet excerpted here reported on the siege and capture of the Bohemian city of Pilsen (see Map 2, pages 10–11). Since October 1618, Pilsen had been besieged by the troops of the Bohemian Estates, commanded by the Count of Mansfeld.[1] *Following weeks of fighting, the city was finally taken on November 21. The author, who was part of the besieging force, connects the comet that first appeared in September but reached its maximum brightness in October and November to dire prophecies for the future not only of Pilsen and Bohemia but also of the entire world.*

On the second day after this engagement, on the 9th or 19th of October,[2] in the night a corporal woke me up, and indicated to me a very terrible comet, which was at first only a third as large as it later would be. I also had our captain awoken, who then had the others awoken. It was about dawn. We were without a clock, but according to the burning of the fuses [with which the soldiers kept track of time] it was about three o'clock. The hourglasses that some had with them were consulted

[1] Ernst II (ca. 1580–1626), Count of Mansfeld, was a classic mercenary captain of the Thirty Years War. Starting in August 1618, he fought as a general of artillery for the army of the Bohemian Estates. Two years later, however, at the decisive Battle of White Mountain, he refused to fight in the Bohemian army under the newly elected king, Frederick V, elector of the Palatinate, and gave as the reason that he and his troops had not been paid.

[2] In early modern Europe, it was common to give dates using both the ancient Julian calendar and the newer Gregorian calendar. In this case, the comet appeared on October 9 according to the Julian calendar and on October 19 according to the Gregorian calendar.

From Warhaffter Bericht von der Belaegerung und mit gestuermter Hand Eroberung der Stadt Pilsen inn Behem. *Von einer unpartheyischen Person, so selbsten darbey gewesen, soviel ihm moeglich, erstlich in Behmischer Sprach zusammen geschrieben: Jetzt aber auß dem Behmischen Original getreulich verteutscht . . .* (*True Report of the Siege and the Taking by Storm of the City of Pilsen in Bohemia. From an Impartial Person, who was there himself, who wrote it first in Bohemian, as much as possible. But now from the Bohemian Original accurately translated into German . . .*) (Prague, 1619), 28–29.

as well. If one went by the fuses burning, the hourglasses, and the movement of the stars, then it was two thirty. Mars had just risen a little bit before. Thereafter came his temporary companion [the comet], which was to the south. I didn't have any instrument at hand and was without a telescope, but I found the comet immediately. In itself the body of the comet was as large as Canicula or Sirius,[3] and in color and especially in tint it was like Saturn. Later it changed itself, and the tail was toward the northwest, directly over the city, so that one of the observers said, "Brothers, it wants to sweep Pilsen away." It was on the horizon then, and later it became even larger and could be seen by day, which was terrible, not only because of its size, like all [heavenly] bodies, but also because of the tail, which drove some with peripatetic hearts insane. . . .

Anyone who can read the portentous signs of nature will easily understand what this will mean. We are on the threshold of a great reformation, God help us that it is the Judgment Day, otherwise it is going to be grim.

[3] The Dog Star, Sirius, was also referred to as Canicula at that time.

2
A Religious War?

The Thirty Years War has often been referred to as the last of the religious wars. This characterization is problematic for several reasons. On both sides of the religious divide, rulers made decisions based on secular dynastic interests, international relations, and constitutional politics. These factors were arguably just as significant as religion in shaping the war's beginning, course, and outcome. Catholic France's support of the Protestant side and entry into the war in 1635 is only the most obvious example of this. At the grassroots level, from the beginning of the war the line between the Catholic and Protestant powers was blurred by the confessional heterogeneity and diversity of the populations and armies on both sides and completely distorted by soldiers' equal-opportunity plundering of civilians regardless of religion. Finally, the Thirty Years War was not the last war fought over religion. In the eighteenth, nineteenth, and twentieth centuries, religion played an important role in many European wars, to say nothing of the religious underpinnings of several conflicts thus far in the twenty-first century.

That said, contemporaries pointed to the confessional divide between Catholics and Protestants as the most obvious and provocative reason for confrontation before, during, and after the Thirty Years War. Not even the most secular analysis of the war can ignore the importance of confession in political allegiances and diplomatic alignments. Religious points of contention were often pursued even to the detriment of a ruler's secular interests.

This chapter presents documents that illustrate the extent to which the Thirty Years War was a religious conflict. They include not only official pronouncements that identified "the religious problem" and tried to impose solutions, but also countervailing opinions and common people's perceptions of such pronouncements. Included as well are several documents that illustrate episodes of grassroots religious violence during the war. These episodes reveal that contemporaries were affected as much by the symbolic violence of attacks on sacred objects and spaces as they were by the physical violence against people and the killing of persons for reasons of faith. They understood and remembered these incidents, even those in which violence was moderated or avoided, as being about religion and confessional identity.

Confessional Politics before and during the War

6

The Religious Peace of Augsburg

1555

This famous document, commonly known as the Peace of Augsburg, is actually the concluding statement of the imperial diet held in Augsburg in 1555. It confirmed and expanded the Treaty of Passau, which in 1552 had ended the War of the Schmalkaldic League (1546–1552). That war, though often identified as one of the first "religious" civil wars in early modern Europe, had, like all the wars that would follow, as much to do with politics and diplomacy as it did with religion.

The Schmalkaldic League had been formed in 1531 as an alliance of Lutheran princes and cities to counter the anti-Protestant and politically centralizing agenda of the Holy Roman Emperor Charles V (r. 1519–1556). In 1546, the emperor went to war against the Schmalkaldic League. Although he was militarily victorious, Charles suffered a diplomatic defeat, and he was forced to acknowledge Protestantism and the decentralized nature of the empire.

The Peace of Augsburg is significant for many reasons. It was an attempt to create a system in which Catholicism and Protestantism could coexist in peace, although it was an explicitly temporary solution and still looked forward to an ultimate reconciliation of the "divided religions."

From *Abschied Der Römischen Königlichen Maiestat, und gemeiner Stende, auff dem Reichstag zu Augsburg, Anno Domino MDLV aufgericht . . .* (*Concluding Statement of His [Holy] Roman Imperial Majesty and the Common Estates, Established at the Imperial Diet in Augsburg, in the Year of Our Lord 1555 . . .*) (Mainz: Franciscum Behem, 1555), 3r–4r, 6v–7v, 9r. Available as a digital facsimile at Bayerische Staatsbibliothek at Munich, http://daten.digitale-sammlungen.de/bsb00001441/image_1.

The system it created was characterized by the phrase cuius regio, eius religio, *"whose reign, his religion," meaning that every prince in the empire was free to select for himself and his subjects either Catholicism or Lutheranism. Significantly, the agreement did not mention Calvinism. The Peace of Augsburg preserved a fragile peace in Central Europe until 1618, but the exclusion of Calvinists planted the seeds of further conflict.*

And the specially delegated councilors of the electors, also some princes and estates of the Holy [Roman] Empire, appeared obediently before Us [Charles V], some of them in person and some of them through their plenipotentiaries [deputies]. And We, with them, at first reminded ourselves which points were most important to deal with, and in which form the consultation was to take place. It was found immediately, as it had been at some previously held imperial diets, that it was the issue of the divided religion that had led for some time to all kinds of nasty problems, incidents, and disagreeableness in the empire of the German Nation. Among the other lamentable, unsettled, and urgent issues of the Holy [Roman] Empire, this is once again the most prominent, the most pressing, and the most important point that remains unsettled and that at the same time is most important to resolve for all estates.

[. . .]

So, because of the aforementioned concerns and their pressing urgency, it was considered expedient, helpful, and necessary by the estates, envoys, and ambassadors, and it was reported to Us in submission, that the final treatment of this issue of religion be postponed to another time.

And in keeping with the article of the peace treaty, in order to bring about, to develop, and to maintain general peace and security in the German Nation, and so that electors, princes, and estates can face one another in good faith, and so that further harm, damage, and ruin may be prevented, the Imperial Majesty, Our Dear Brother and Lord,[1] and they, the estates of the empire, shall debate and negotiate in beloved peace on the other multifarious urgent issues of the Empire of the German Nation, at the still ongoing imperial diet or at another time, so much more thoroughly, securely, and productively.

[1] This is a reference to Charles V's brother Ferdinand, who after the Peace of Augsburg effectively took over the administration of the empire. He became Emperor Ferdinand I when Charles abdicated in 1556.

[. . .]

And that such peace apply to the divided religion is necessitated by the great need of the Holy [Roman] Empire of the German Nation, for the aforementioned and indicated reasons. In order to establish, uphold, and maintain the religious peace more firmly between Our [Holy] Roman Imperial Majesty and the electors, princes, and estates of the Holy [Roman] Empire of the German Nation, His Imperial Majesty and the electors, princes, and estates in their domains, lands, and jurisdictions, shall not attack, harm, or violate in a violent manner, or in any other way oppress, burden, or disadvantage, through mandates or in some other form, any estate of the empire because it adheres to the . . . [Lutheran] Augsburg Confession, faith, liturgy, rules, and ceremonies. Their belongings, property (movable and immovable), land, people, jurisdiction, authority, dignity, and legal rights should be left in peace and tranquillity. The disputed religion should not be reconciled other than through Christian, amicable, and peaceful means and ways, and through Christian understanding and agreement, all in keeping with imperial and royal dignity, princely honor, true words, and the enforcement of the secular peace.

Likewise, the subjects who adhere to the Augsburg Confession, regardless of when and how they converted or how they changed their residences, shall take the same stance toward the religion, faith, liturgy, rules, and ceremonies of Our [Holy] Roman Imperial Majesty and the electors, princes, and other imperial subjects, ecclesiastical and secular, including their colleagues and other clerical subjects, who adhere to the old [Catholic] religion. Their belongings, property (movable and immovable), land, people, jurisdiction, authority, dignity, legal rights, rent, interests, and tithes shall not be troubled, and they shall be allowed to peacefully and tranquilly use, enjoy, and follow these things unhindered and shall be faithfully helped to do so. No one shall act or otherwise plan to do harm to another, but instead in all ways content himself versus the others according to the pronouncements of the Holy [Roman] Empire's laws, statutes, and resolutions, as well as the rules of the established secular peace.

All others, who do not adhere to the aforementioned two religions, are not included in this peace, but rather are entirely excluded.

[. . .]

And though an agreement on religious and confessional matters shall be sought in earnest and in appropriate ways, it is evident that without an enduring peace, it cannot come to a Christian, amicable agreement on religion. So We and the others . . . to save this worthy nation from an ultimate, impending downfall, and so that one may sooner be inclined to come to a Christian, amicable, and final agreement, until such a Christian, amicable, and final agreement of the religious and confessional matters is made, we will unhesitatingly, firmly, and unwaveringly uphold and loyally fulfill such peace as is written in all the articles above. . . . Should such an agreement not succeed by way of a general council, a national assembly, colloquiums, or imperial negotiations, then this state of peace (in all the aforementioned points and articles) shall nonetheless be established and remain in effect until an ultimate agreement on religious and confessional matters is established. Hereby shall be concluded and established, in the aforementioned form and in all other ways, an enduring, stable, and unconditional peace, for ever and ever.

7

EMPEROR FERDINAND II

The Edict of Restitution

1629

The Edict of Restitution was issued by Emperor Ferdinand II on March 6, 1629. At this point in the Thirty Years War, the Catholic imperial forces seemed triumphant after a decade of uninterrupted military victories, and the edict signaled the victors' plans for a postwar settlement. Catholic militants such as the Jesuit advisers of the emperor exerted a strong influence on the edict's formulation and propagation. For them, the restoration of former Catholic Church property was a means to restore Protestant souls to the old faith. Although the rhetoric of the Edict of Restitution was conservative—it harkened back to the Peace of Augsburg, claiming

From Ferdinand II, Holy Roman Emperor, *Der Röm. Käys. auch zu Hungarn und Böheimb Kön. Mayt. Ferdinandi II. Außspruch, Decision, und Käys. Edict, Uber Etliche Puncten den Religion Frieden, sonderlich die Restitution der Geistlichen Güter betreffen . . . (Proclamation, Decision, and Edict of the Roman Imperial, Also Royal Hungarian and Bohemian Majesty, Ferdinand II, regarding Several Points of the Religious Peace, Especially the Restitution of Ecclesiastical Estates . . .)* (Aschaffenburg: Quirinum Botzerum, 1629), 3–4, 22–23. Available as a digital facsimile at Herzog August Bibliothek Wolfenbüttel, http://diglib.hab.de/drucke/240-35-2-quod/start.htm.

only to defend and enforce the former settlement—contemporaries saw its legalized seizure of Protestant lands and outright intolerance of Calvinism as highly aggressive. Of course, Calvinists were outraged by the prohibition of their religion. Even moderate Lutherans who had expected (and tacitly accepted) the "restitution" of ecclesiastical lands feared that it would tip the balance of power in the empire too far in favor of the emperor. They also feared that the Edict of Restitution was only an indication of further aggressive edicts to come. Even most Catholic leaders, apart from the militant Jesuits, found the edict to be overreaching and unrealistic, and they anticipated that it would prolong the war by hardening Protestant resistance.[1] *Finally, the edict was implemented unevenly and unjustly. Defeated enemies of the emperor were especially vulnerable to losing property, regardless of their legal status, and the crass avarice of some on the Catholic imperial side was laid bare by their competing claims to "restituted" property.*

. . . And the kind of destructive conflict and disorder in the midst of which our beloved fatherland of the German Nation has been held for such a long time is beyond a doubt and will be known and recognized all too well by you and yours and everyone. The start and the wellspring of this mistrust and highly dangerous disunion was originally the vexing religious division and still is. Second to this, though, is that not only have various despoliations and other highly destructive attacks been committed, in violation of the religious peace [of Augsburg], which was especially established so that the estates of both religions would conduct themselves agreeably with each other . . . but also that some have worked against the religious peace itself, under all kinds of attempted pretexts and through highly destructive disputes regarding its content and those who would justify and defend it.

[. . .]

We are finally determined to bring to real effect both the religious and worldly peace. For this purpose we have sent our imperial commissioners into the empire and ordered them to demand back the archbishoprics, prelacies, monasteries, and other clerical endowments, hospitals, and foundations which were in the possession of the Catholics at the time of the Treaty of Passau [1552] or since that time, but which they have since been deprived of. The unlawful holders shall be replaced

[1] Peter H. Wilson, *Europe's Tragedy: A History of the Thirty Years War* (London: Allen Lane, 2009), 446–51.

with suitable and qualified people, selected according to the rules of the institutions and foundations. Each should be helped to reclaim what belongs to him and what he is authorized to possess according to the religious peace, without unnecessary digression or delay.

We also want to declare and make recognized again . . . that the aforementioned religious peace only applies to the ancient Catholic religion . . . and the Augsburg Confession, as unchanged from June 25, 1530. All other heterodox teachings and sects, regardless of what they are called, or whether they have already appeared or may still appear, are illegitimate and therefore excluded, forbidden, and not to be tolerated.

8

JOHANN DANIEL FRIESE

A Childhood Memory of the Edict of Restitution

1629

Johann Daniel Friese (1619–1677) was ten years old when the Edict of Restitution was published in the spring of 1629. Johann Daniel's father was Daniel Friese the Elder, the city secretary of Magdeburg and the highest-ranking civil servant in that important trading city on the Elbe River in northern Germany (see Map 2, pages 10–11). From the time he was a small child, Johann Daniel developed an acute political sensibility and memory of the events and dangers of the Thirty Years War, which he experienced up close. Decades later, he recorded his recollections as an adult, among them the destruction and devastation of his hometown, Magdeburg, by the troops of the Catholic League in May 1631 (Document 42). In this passage, he describes how, during a diplomatic journey from Magdeburg to General Wallenstein's headquarters in the nearby city of Halberstadt in June 1629, his father for the first time read a copy of the

From "Historischer Extract aus einem Manuscripto, welches Herr Daniel Frisius, Cancell. Secret. zu Altenburg von seinen Fatis hinter sich gelassen . . . Vom Magdeburger Unglück" ("Historical Extract from a Manuscript, Which Daniel Frisius, Chancellery Secretary in Altenburg, Left Behind Regarding His Fate . . . Relating to the Catastrophe in Magdeburg"), in Friedrich Friese, *Leichte historische Fragen* (*Light Historical Questions*) (Leipzig: Groschuff, 1703), 279–327, here 287.

Edict of Restitution, which had just been published, and then discussed it with his colleague, the mayor of Magdeburg. From the perspective of decades later, Friese's recollections interweave his experiences as an observant child with his later experiences as a civil servant who was present at the negotiations that led to the end of the Thirty Years War in 1648. From these two perspectives, the edict appears as a stepping-stone in a generation-long war, the end of which his adult contemporaries in 1629 could not hope to live to see.

In the year 1629, in June or so, my father was ordered to Halberstadt as an envoy to General Wallenstein, along with Mayor Thaut, regarding a sum of money that the emperor wanted from the city as a loan.

My father took me along, and because the imperial Edict [of Restitution] had just then been openly publicized, they sat in the coach and my father read it. After they saw what kind of havoc the edict would wreak, they talked a long time with each other and bemoaned the future war to be anticipated. Among other things, Mayor Thaut said, "We will not live to see the end of the war at all, but the little one [meaning me] may live to see it." With that he laid his hand on my head. So the man had really forecast the truth, because I ultimately not only experienced the conclusion of peace, praise God, but I was also at the peace negotiations in person.

9

MELCHIOR KHLESL

The Edict of Restitution as Seen by a Pragmatic Catholic Hard-Liner

ca. 1629

This critical view of the Edict of Restitution from the Catholic side was included in the Annales Ferdinandei [Annals of the Deeds of Emperor Ferdinand II], *a monumental contemporary work of history by Count Franz Christoph von Khevenhüller (1588–1650), an Austrian nobleman, diplomat, and confidant at the imperial court. Khevenhüller attributed the statement to Cardinal Melchior Khlesl (1552–1630), whom he knew personally. As bishop of Vienna and trusted adviser of Emperor Matthias (r. 1612–1619), Khlesl was a leading promoter of the Catholic Counter-Reformation in the Habsburg lands. However, even as a religious hard-liner, he appears to have focused on long-term objectives and to have been open to short-term pragmatic arrangements with Protestants, such as in the Bohemian crisis of 1618. As the succession of Emperor Ferdinand II (r. 1619–1637) loomed, Khlesl appeared too powerful to the new ruler and his advisers. He was forcibly exiled, first to the Tyrol and later to Rome. In 1627, Khlesl was allowed to return to Austria, where until his death in 1630 he continued to express his opinions regarding politics and religion, even when they were critical of imperial decisions. In the case of the Edict of Restitution, instead of forcibly carrying out its aims, Khlesl argued for a more moderate approach that appears quite tolerant.*

Then Cardinal Khlesl, bishop of Vienna and the Neustadt [Wiener Neustadt], arrived back in Austria from Rome, and he was restored to his original status, and everything that was taken from him during his imprisonment was reimbursed to him. . . . He regarded the Edict of Restitution as too harsh, saying: Through it one loses the love for the rulers

---

From Franz Christoph von Khevenhüller, *Annales Ferdinandei; or, Wahrhaffte Beschreibung Kaisers Ferdinandi des Andern Thaten . . .* (*True Description of the Deeds of Emperor Ferdinand II . . .*) (Leipzig: Weidmann, 1724), 10:1481–82. Available as a digital facsimile at Universitätsbibliothek Augsburg, http://gateway-bayern.de/BV003989321.

of the land, one loses the money, which will leave the country, and one also loses many souls. The love of subjects will be lost insofar as the edict will not only make many people emigrate, but it also will deport them, as if they were beggars and thieves. The money and the commerce will move away, in that the richest people will go, and they will take many of their goods with them. And one will not win souls, because the un-Catholic will not become Catholic, but rather they will leave the land with their children, and so their children's children will continue in their error forever. If one would allow the parents their religion in the land, without public exercise and schools, then the children would become Catholic, and so the entire posterity would remain Catholic forever, and the money would not be taken out of the land, the commerce would not go lost, and the rulers would not be so hated in all places, and when somebody did something unjust to someone, one would have the opportunity to punish him bodily and monetarily.

Religious Violence as an Expression of Confessional Identity

10

BARTHOLOMÄUS DIETWAR

Forced Conversion and Book Burning

1630–1631

The Edict of Restitution of 1629 (Document 7) not only aimed to return church properties to the control of Catholic authorities but also

From Bartholomäus Dietwar, *Chronik: Leben eines evangelischen Pfarrers im früheren markgräflichen Amte Kitzingen von 1592–1670, von ihm selbst erzählt; Zugleich ein Beitrag zur Geschichte des 30jährigen Krieges in Franken . . .* (*Chronicle: The Life of a Protestant Preacher in the Former Margrave District of Kitzingen, 1592–1670, Told by Himself; A Contribution to the History of the Thirty Years War in Franconia . . .*), ed. Gerd Högner (Kitzingen: published by editor, 2009), 48–49, 52.

forced Protestants in some areas to choose between two difficult alternatives: either convert to Catholicism or emigrate. This also applied to independent communities such as the town of Kitzingen, which had been an independent city but in 1629 was again subjected to the rule of the bishop of Würzburg.[1]

The Lutheran preacher in Kitzingen, Bartholomäus Dietwar (1592–1670), was a witness and victim of the ultimately unsuccessful attempts at forced conversion. In this excerpt from his chronicle, Dietwar describes the force used by Catholic priests and monks in attempting to convert the residents of his town and the surrounding area to the old faith. This included not only seizing and burning Protestant books but also enforcing Catholic practices such as making sure that people were not cooking and eating meat on fast days. In the end, approximately 1,100 of the 2,500 inhabitants of Kitzingen emigrated, including Dietwar.

[1630]

Also now again a new inquisition was held in Kitzingen, and it was decided that whoever did not want to become papist must leave the city in fourteen days. Now the disgrace has begun in Kitzingen, Hoheim, Repperndorf, and in all the areas where the bishop has installed priests. The people are forced by the Capucins [Franciscan monks] and priests with great tyranny to renounce the Gospel. They took all of their Protestant books from their houses and burned a great pile of them in the public marketplace in Kitzingen. On the fast days they entered the houses and searched the pots by the fires, and anyone found with meat was severely punished. . . .

[1631]

They again took the Protestants' books away.

[1] This was Bishop Johann Georg II Fuchs, Baron von Dornheim (1586–1633). A notorious persecutor of Protestants, he was also known as one of the most fanatical witch-hunters of the time.

11
HANS KRAFFT
The Seizure of the Cathedral of Erfurt by the Protestants
1632

The Protestant dyer Hans Krafft describes here the Protestants' occupation of the Cathedral of Erfurt on September 17, 1632, the first anniversary of the Battle of Breitenfeld.[1] *For the author, this was more than just another episode in his chronicle of events. Just as the victory of the Swedish army under King Gustav Adolph at Breitenfeld had represented the greatest victory of the Protestant side to date, the seizure of the cathedral represented for Krafft the greatest victory of Protestantism in his hometown. He proudly indicates his personal involvement in the action, which was characterized not only by the violence of the seizure but also by the pomp and ceremony of celebrating the achievement, which he describes not by using an ego-centered "I" but with the characteristically communal rhetoric of "we."*

In the year 1632 on the 17th of September, an anniversary festival of celebration was ordered for His Royal Majesty Gustav Adolph, because with God's help he won the battle near Leipzig [Battle of Breitenfeld] on the 17th of September 1631. So we celebrated in the morning in our parish church, and at nine o'clock the first main sermon was delivered in our beloved Church of St. Mary [the Erfurt Cathedral] by my brother-in-law, Master Valentin Wallenberger.[2] With two organs [and]

[1] The date given here and in the document is in the modern Gregorian calendar. The old-style Julian calendar, which was still used by Protestants at the time, dated the Battle of Breitenfeld (and its anniversary) ten days earlier.

[2] Valentin Wallenberger (1582–1639) was preacher at the Barfüsser Church in Erfurt from 1621 to 1639. He was one of the most vociferous Lutheran preachers in Erfurt during the Thirty Years War.

From Hans Krafft, *Chronik aus dem Dreißigjährigen Krieg* (*Chronicle from the Thirty Years War*), ed. Hans Medick, Norbert Winnige, and Andreas Bähr (electronic publication: Thüringer Universitäts- und Landesbibliothek Jena, 2008), 66r. Available as a digital facsimile at www.mdsz.thulb.uni-jena.de/krafft/quelle.php.

instruments like lutes, harps, drums, fifes, and violins, we played glorious, splendid, [and] exceedingly beautiful music. But it did not please the papists, and they didn't want to open the church towers. [We] had to break open three doors so that one could get to the bells. Three of them, the big bell along with the Spirit and the Wolf, were rung.[3] And they did not want to open the church, but . . . it didn't help them, they had to, [and] it was a bitter pill [for them]. In the evening, a salute was fired with big cannons that stand around the city, three times, and from the Cyriaksburg,[4] and with muskets, which were fired during the day.

[3] Krafft is referring to the names of individual bells.
[4] The main citadel fortification in Erfurt. Originally constructed in the late fifteenth century, it was expanded and improved by the Swedes during the Thirty Years War.

12

MAURUS FRIESENEGGER

Desacralization and Its Limits

1632

In these passages from his diary, the abbot of the Bavarian monastery of Heiligenberg (at Andechs, near Munich), Maurus Friesenegger (1590–1655), relates some of the consequences of the occupation and plundering of his monastery by Swedish troops in the summer of 1632. Friesenegger's version of events is not an eyewitness report of the occupation, because before the Swedes arrived, the abbot had fled and taken the precious relics and other items from his monastery's treasury to a nearby town. His description is instead based on the testimonies of other members of his monastery. What seems most remarkable about this report is that although the sacred space had been desecrated through its use as a stable for the occupying soldiers' horses, Friesenegger emphasizes the limited violence done to the religious objects in his monastery's church.

From Maurus Friesenegger, *Tagebuch aus dem 30jährigen Krieg: Nach einer Handschrift im Kloster Andechs* (*Diary from the Thirty Years War: From a Manuscript in the Andechs Cloister*), ed. Willibald Mathäser (Munich: Allitera Verlag, 2007), 17–18.

What had befallen Heiligenberg in the period of three weeks, and beyond, during the presence of the enemy . . . was found out afterward, after the retreat of the Swedes, and the return of some domestic servants and clergy. The church was full of stink and horse manure, on the altar were the remains of the horse feed, the offering boxes were all broken, and the grave of the [monastery's] founder was opened. The altars and the altarpieces on the same were all undamaged, except for the effigy of Saint Rasso, which was found damaged and covered in feces outside the church. The liturgical garments and vestments that were stolen were of no great value, because all the better ones had been taken out of the way [before the Swedish occupation].

What was miraculous, however, was what befell the Mother of God painting, which formerly stood on the high altar, but at the time had been moved to the lower choir altar in place of the miracle-working image, which had been taken to safety. Apparently with no amount of force could this painting be moved from its spot or thrown down from where it stood, which the blasphemers attempted with all their strength. Being awestruck by this and imagining that behind the painting a treasure could be hidden, they brought this news to the colonel's attention. When he was told what had already been done, he forbade laying another hand on the image, with the express comment that it was not the will of their king [Gustav Adolph] that they would make holy war against symbols. . . .

It was just as miraculous that the cloister buildings never caught fire. The enemy often and at several spots tried to set them on fire, to prevent any further pilgrimages and to destroy everything, as the Protestant heretics at Augsburg, Ulm, and Nuremberg had demanded. Even the godless ones were amazed after these efforts at destruction had failed, and afterward they told of the matter in many places, and also in Herrsching people asked what kind of place this was, that would not catch fire.[1]

[1] Herrsching is a town approximately 1¼ miles (2 km) north of the Heiligenberg monastery.

13

LIBORIUS WAGNER

A Catholic Martyr

1631

Because of the special circumstances of their deaths, martyrs obviously cannot leave behind ego-documents regarding their own martyrdoms, even when they have prepared for or summoned martyrdom. Their status as martyrs depends on the attestations of contemporaries and the pious memory of posterity. This was the case for the Jesuit priest Liborius Wagner, who was killed on December 9, 1631, near the village of Schonungen in the Bishopric of Würzburg (see Map 2, pages 10–11), during which time the bishopric was occupied by the Swedes.

The son of Protestant parents, Wagner was baptized in 1593 and raised as a Protestant. Most likely because of the lack of career opportunities in his hometown of Mühlhausen in Thuringia, he moved to Würzburg and was converted by Jesuits to Catholicism. He entered the Jesuit order, and as a priest he was sent to nearby Altenmünster in 1626 to re-Catholicize the population. At this time, the people there were overwhelmingly Protestant, although the local Catholic church and its possessions in Altenmünster were administered by the Catholic cloister at Neustadt. Wagner saw himself as a member of a militant church, and he understood the restitution of souls to Catholicism to be the most important objective of the ongoing war, which he viewed as a religious war. For him, this could mean dying for the salvation of the souls of others, just as Christ had. As Wagner wrote in a letter to a fellow priest in 1628, "What could be more valuable than a soul which was ransomed with the precious blood of our Savior, Jesus Christ?"[1]

Conflicts with the Protestant population and the local nobility led to Wagner's capture, torture, and murder at the hands of German members of the Swedish army. Immediately after his death, Wagner was portrayed as the victim of religious violence and celebrated as a martyr, as this excerpt from a Jesuit annual report for 1635 reveals:

[1] Johannes Strauss, "Liborius Wagner aus evangelischer Sicht" ("Liborius Wagner from the Protestant Perspective"), *Zeitschrift für bayerische Kirchengeschichte* (*Journal of Bavarian Church History*) 77 (2008): 179.

> *Liborius Wagner from Mühlhausen, a man known for his integrity, was handled in a barbaric way by a certain Truchsess of Pommersfelden, because he had previously defected from Luther to the [Catholic] Church and had influenced heretical villages in Franconia to go in the same direction. In winter and in very cold weather, he was bound half-naked to a horse. Led this way, his head was sprinkled with nitrite powder,[2] he was pricked with needles, and he was thrown into a bundle of thorns when he asked for a break from the bodily abuse. As he endured such injuries mixed with insults, his plight was noticeably alleviated at the request of a noblewoman, but ultimately he was given over to the wantonness of the soldiers.*
>
> *There is talk that this exemplary man was badly abused by the kitchen servants and baggage carriers, hung from a balcony, [and] finally pierced with bullets, and that he followed the not unknown example of the ancient martyrs.*[3]

As a local religious hero, Wagner was part of the "rediscovery of heroic saints" and the martyrdom cults in the Catholic world that emerged in the seventeenth century.[4] *His grave at the church in Heidingsfeld, close to the site of his death, quickly became a pilgrimage site and remains so today. Wagner was beatified in 1974 by Pope Paul VI. That year, Wolfgang Lenz painted this picture,* Liborius Wagner, Ascending into Heaven *(see page 60), which hangs in the pilgrimage church in Heidingsfeld and is sold there as a postcard. It shows Wagner, with a sword in his right hand and a quill pen in his left, hovering above the village of Heidingsfeld as he ascends to heaven. From there (note the irony), King Gustav Adolph of Sweden extends a martyr's crown to him.*

[2] An explosive.

[3] "Historia Domus" of the Bamburg Jesuits for the year 1632, quoted in Strauss, "Liborius Wagner," 164.

[4] Peter Burschel, *Sterben und Unsterblichkeit: Zur Kultur des Martyriums in der frühen Neuzeit* (*Dying and Immortality: On the Culture of Martyrdom in the Early Modern Period*) (Munich: R. Oldenbourg, 2004), 210, 247.

14

The Nürtingen "Blood Bible"

1634

Due to the violent circumstances of its owner's death, the Protestant pocket Bible that contains the blood-spattered page (see page 62) gained the status of a Protestant martyr's relic.[5] *After the Battle of Nördlingen on September 6, 1634, which was a serious defeat for the Protestant Swedish forces, plundering Spanish imperial troops advanced into Württemberg. Reverend Wölflin, a Protestant preacher from Owen in Württemberg, carried this Bible with him as he fled from the enemy troops to the nearby fortified town of Nürtingen. When the Spanish imperial forces subsequently took Nürtingen, Wölflin and many other Protestants sought refuge in the chapel of the palace, where he and many others were killed by Spanish soldiers on September 7, 1634. The Bible, which Wölflin was carrying as a shield at the time of his death, shows many marks of violence. Contemporaries viewed it as an especially auspicious sign of martyrdom that among the heavy damage to this Bible, this particular page was marked with blood stains. The page contains a verse from Paul's second letter to Timothy: "I have fought a good fight, I have finished my course, I have kept the faith: Henceforth there is laid up for me a crown of righteousness, which the Lord, the righteous judge, shall give me at that day: and not to me only, but unto all them also that love his appearing."*[6]

Wölflin remained a martyr in the cultural memory of the area. In the eighteenth century, the blood-spattered spot in the Nürtingen palace chapel where Wölflin was killed and the page from his Bible marked with his blood were still venerated as evidence of a Protestant martyr. The clergyman Friedrich Wilhelm Fromann included the following note in a handwritten list of the Württemberg preachers: "Circa 10 years ago [ca. 1742] I myself saw his [Wölflin's] blood sprayed on the wall of the chapel and the little pocket Bible that he had in his hand then, in which the verse 'I fought the good fight' was encircled with his blood."[7]

[5]Today the Bible is in the Bible Collection of the Württembergische Landesbibliothek in Stuttgart, accessible under call number: B deutsch 1627 03. The image is of page 229.

[6]Timothy 4:7–8 (Authorized [King James] Version).

[7]Landeskirchliches Archiv Stuttgart, A12, Diener- und Stellenbücher Nr. 8: Gestorbene Geistliche, 1616–1786, Eintrag 1634.09.07. We thank Andreas Butz for this reference.

kempffet/ich habe den lauff vol-
ndet/ ich habe glauben gehalte. Hin-
ort ist mir beygelegt die kron der
erechtigkeit/ welche mir der Herr
n jenem tage/ der gerechte richter/
eben wird/ nicht mir aber allein/
ondern auch allen/ die seine erschei-
ung lieb haben. Fleissige dich/ daß
u bald zu mir kommest. Denn De-
mas hat mich verlassen/ vnd diese
elt lieb gewonnen/ vnd ist gen Thes-
onich gezogen/ Crescens in Gala-
n/ Titus in Dalmatian. Lucas
allein bey mir. Marcum nim zu
/vnd bringe jn mit dir/ denn er
mir nützlich zum dienst. Tychi-
m habe ich gen Ephesum gesandt.
en mantel/ den ich zu Troada ließ
Carpo/ bringe mit/ wenn du kom-
est/ vnd die bücher/ sonderlich aber
s pergamen. Alexander der schmidt
at mir viel böses beweiset/ der Herr
ezahle jhm nach seinen wercken/ für
lchem hüte du dich auch/ denn er
t vnsern worten sehr widstanden.
n meiner ersten verantwortung
nd nieman bey mir/ sondern sie
erliess mich alle/ Es sey jnen nicht
re t. Der Herr aber stund
r bey/ vnd stercket mich/ daß
ch mich die predig beste tige
urde/ vnd alle heyden horete/ vnd
h bin erloset von deß lowens rache.
der Herr aber wird mich erlösen von
lem vbel/ vnd außhelffen zu seinem
mlischen reich/ welchem sey ehre von
vigkeit zu ewigkeit/ Amen. Grüsset
rilcan vnd Aquilan/ vnd dz hauß
nesiphori E stus bleib Corin-
o. Trophimum aber ich zu
il ranck. Thue flei vor
em w ter konest. Es grüsset dich
u lus/ vnd Pudens nd Linus
Claudia/ vnd alle der. Der
r JEsus Christu sey mit
nem geiste/ die gna sey mit
e y/ Am .
G schr n von Rom/ die ander
Epistel an imotheum/ da Paulus
um a ernme für dem keyser
ro ward dargestellet.

Die Epistel S. Pauli
an m.

CAP. I. Fürbild eines rechten Bischoffs.

Paulus ein knecht Gottes/ aber ein Apostel Jesu Christi/ nach dem glauben der außerwehleten Gottes/ vnd der erkentniß der warheit zur gottseligkeit/ In der hoffnung deß ewigen lebens/ welches verheissen hat/ der nit leuget/ Gott/ vor den zeiten der welt/ hat aber offenbaret zu seiner zeit sein wort durch die predigt/ die mir vertrawet ist/ nach dem befehl Gottes vnsers heilandes. Tito meinem rechtschaffenen sohn/ nach vnser beyder glauben. Gnade/ barmhertzigkeit/ friede von Gott dem vatter/ vnd dem Herrn Jesu Christo/ vnserm heiland. Derhalben ließ ich dich in Creta/ dz du soltest vollend anrichten/ da ichs gelassen habe/ vnd besetzen die stette hin vnd her mit eltesten/ wie ich dir befohlen habe. Wo einer ist vntadelich/ eines weib der glaubige kinder habe tiget/ dz sie schweiger vn sam sind ... nnen tad ... rete G ...

... gor ... en/ recht/ heilig ... wort/ dz gewiß ist/ vnd lehre ... dz er mechtig sey zu ermahnen durch die heilsame lehre/ vnd zu straffen die widersprecher. Denn es sind viel freche vnd vnnütze schwetzer vnd verführer/ sonderlich die auß der beschneidung/ welchen man muß dz maul stopffen/ die da gantze heuser verkehren/ vnd lehren dz nicht taug/ vmb schendliches gewins willen. Es hat einer auß gesagt/ jrer eigen prophet: die C... sind jmmer lügner/ böse thier/ vnd faule beuche. Diß zeugniß ist war. Vmb der sache willen straffe sie scharff/ auff daß sie gesund seyen im glauben/ vnd nicht achten auff die jüdischen fabeln vnd menschen gebot/ welche sich von der warheit ... den. Den reinen ists alles rein vnreinen aber vnd den vngl... ist nichts rein/ sondern verv... beyde jr sinn vnd gewissen. Si...

K vij

3

Soldiers and Civilians: Confrontations and Relations

The relationship between soldiers and civilians in the Thirty Years War has often been described as being characterized solely by military violence and the imperatives of a war economy—the necessity of financing and supplying great armies or smaller military units. From this perspective, civilians were turned into essentially helpless victims from whom resources were extorted. The ego-documents presented in this chapter prove, however, that a much broader spectrum of civilian-military relationships existed. Civilians acted of their own volition in a variety of ways, ranging from countering violence with violence, as peasants did throughout the war, to "softer" strategies of pacifying the enemy, a tactic used especially successfully by nuns and their religious institutions.[1]

This acknowledgment of a broad spectrum of relationships between soldiers and civilians is not meant to relativize or minimize the dominant role of brutality and military violence. On the contrary, it brings to the fore forms of gendered violence—for instance, the rape of defenseless women, which was a common practice in the Thirty Years War—acts of such brutality that they cannot be subsumed under the economic imperatives of military force.

This chapter also looks at civilian households and their plight during the war. Quartered soldiers, in their desire to rule and dominate, employed certain forms of violence and extortion that often left civilian heads of household powerless and humiliated. The soldiers robbed them not only of their possessions and money but also of their honor and the honor of their wives and children. In addition, the chapter sheds light on the difficulty of maintaining emotional connections with loved ones when separated from them by the exigencies of war. A unique body of letters, written mostly by women, affords a snapshot-like glimpse of

[1] A forthcoming work by Sigrun Haude will shed new light on these feminine strategies of pacifying potentially violent gendered situations during the war.

this problem and the attempt to overcome it by communicating through letters.

Friction and Conflict

15

FRIEDRICH FLADE

The Military Occupation of Olmütz

1642–1643

Friedrich Flade's diary describes the surrender and occupation of the city of Olmütz in Bohemia (see Map 2, pages 10–11) in 1642–1643. Flade, the city secretary and notary, was an eyewitness to and even a participant in the events recorded. A leading figure on the soldiers' side was Goeran Payckul (1605–1657), the son of a German miller living in the Baltics, who served with the Finnish infantry in the Swedish army from 1630 to 1635. Later, from 1642 to 1645, he was commandant in Olmütz.

The account begins with the negotiated surrender of the city and the departure of the imperial troops. An important part of the accord between the representatives of the newly arriving Swedish troops and the city was an agreement over the "contribution" to be paid, which resulted from a highly confrontational negotiation. The contribution was to be paid in various installments, both official and unofficial ("under the table"). Flade explains the material and financial exploitation of the city's residents, emphasizing the symbolically humiliating aspects of the Swedish military's arbitrary rule, which affected all levels of civilian society, elites as well as lower classes. Payckul's arrogant behavior especially upset Flade, as evidenced by the fact that only when describing

From Friedrich Flade, *Tagebuch des feindlichen Einfalls der Schweden in das Markgrafenthum Mähren während ihres Aufenthalts in der Stadt Olmütz, 1642–1650. Geführt von dem Ölmützer Stadtschreiber und Notar Friedrich Flade (Journal of the Invasion of the Swedes in the County of Mähren during Their Occupation of the City of Olmütz, 1642–1650. Recorded by the Olmütz City Secretary and Notary, Friedrich Flade)*, ed. Bela Dudik (Vienna, 1884), 12–15, 17, 107–9.

the commandant's actions in 1643 does he lapse into writing in the first person.

1642

Now when Colonel Miniati[1] and the new troops commanded by Krackow[2] departed at the appointed hour, at twelve o'clock noon on June 15 [1642] the [Swedish] Major General Wittenberg[3] and Colonel Derflinger[4] arrived and wanted the city council to appear before them at once, so that it could receive and carry out the instructions, which they carried in the name of His Excellency, the Swedish field marshal.[5] The order was that the city should (and must) at once surrender 150,000 talers as ransom. Because the councilors said they were not in a position to do this, the commanders finally agreed, after the councilors had begged and argued ceaselessly with them day and night, that the city would pay 30,000 talers officially, and in addition 4,000 talers under the table, and that they must hand over the money immediately, apart from the remaining 4,000 talers. Field Marshal Torstensson, together with the money and the rest of the soldiers, departed for Silesia on the 16th of June and left behind as a garrison three regiments, those of [Colonel] Horn[6] and of [Colonel] Hammerstein,[7] both of horse, and then a regiment of infantry, commanded by Colonel König, who was also made commandant of the city. . . .

On the day of St. John the Baptist [June 24] Colonel König was ordered away, and in his place as commandant came Colonel Goeran Payckul, who immediately demanded to be appropriately accommodated as a colonel and commandant. It followed that in addition to room and board (which Jakob Rzynka and Mrs. Ludmilla Kamperger provided), we had to agree to give him 100 talers weekly, to be paid by the councilors out of the town's purse. At the same time he demanded that

[1] Antonio Miniati (died 1644), a colonel, councilor of war, quartermaster, and imperial war commissioner.

[2] Colonel Joachim Ernst von Krockow (Krackow) (1601–1646).

[3] Arwid Wittenberg von Debern und Neuberg (1606–1657). He had served with the Swedes since 1622.

[4] Georg von Derflinger (1606–1695), later Prussian field marshal.

[5] Lennart von Torstensson zu Ortala und von Virestad (1603–1651). One of the most capable Swedish commanders, he was famous for the speed of his campaigns. He had worked his way up through the ranks and in 1641 was made commander in chief of the Swedish forces.

[6] Colonel Gustav Horn, Freiherr von Marienburg (1614–1666), a colonel since 1640.

[7] Friedrich Christoph von Hammerstein (1608–1685).

diggers, carpenters, and masons be made available, and when he came into the town he had the Ostra [a district of Olmütz] and then subsequently the entire suburb set on fire and burned down.

The 1st of July, Horn's regiment of horse, after they had plundered several lords' houses and their quarters, went from here to Silesia. However, Lieutenant Colonel Wancke[8] with the Guards regiment of dragoons [heavily armed cavalry] arrived instead, and they moved into the town on the 2nd and 3rd of July, after quarters were arranged. The soldiers and especially the officers robbed the lords' houses in violation of the terms of the Accord, and they took away what there was to be found; in total this amounted to substantial treasure. When the council asked that this should stop and appealed on the basis of the terms of the Accord, the first commandant, Colonel König, said it was his order, and he would take responsibility for it. . . .

The 5th of this month [July], on the earnest orders of the commandant, Colonel Payckul, the honorable council had to begin coordinating the ration of bread and beer for 1,578 people, amounting to 48 measures[9] of flour and 14 kegs[10] of beer daily, just for the musketeers and dragoons. Besides that the commandant wished that each common soldier be given 1 shilling for meat every day. Because the city was denied any income, we still owed His Excellency 4,000 talers, and [the commandant said that we] should also pay another 1,500 talers to the new recruits. Due to this, the commandant was asked for an exemption [from this burden] because of the notorious and obvious impossibility of paying. . . .

On this day [July 18] in the evening the commandant communicated the following points, which he demanded be fulfilled instantaneously, but after having been appealed to with the greatest possible desperation, he gave the following Monday as a deadline.

1. We should not fail to deliver the 4,000 talers, which had been allotted and promised to His Excellency, between now and Wednesday or Thursday.
2. Next week the councilors as well as the clergy should give each soldier a taler for his improved sustenance.
3. Twice weekly each soldier should be given half a measure[11] of wine.

[8] Jacob Wancke, once a miller's servant, later a Swedish colonel.
[9] One measure of flour equaled approximately 3½ gallons (13 liters).
[10] One keg equaled approximately 102 gallons (393 liters).
[11] One measure of wine equaled approximately 1.6 quarts (1.5 liters).

1643

[The Commandant's Behavior]

After the commandant on the evening of the 24th of November 1643 had been gambling and in the course of the night had become totally drunk, he first went to the guard posts and then to the stone mill. He woke up the miller, who had to dance barefoot in front of his door with his wife for an entire hour, during which he was mishandled badly and beaten, and the miller's servant, too, was beaten senseless by the commandant. Thereafter he ordered that the cannons on all the bastions and the muskets of all the musketeers be fired. He finally made it back to his quarters at four o'clock, and he had the seamstress and her daughter, who live in [imperial court judge] Herr Berken Graf's house, brought to him to dance. For this occasion the musketeers and the officers of Meyer's regiment were ordered to come there, and they had to fire salutes various times from the three small cannons in front of his door. The musketeers had to shoot with their muskets, too. After he had spent until seven o'clock [in the morning] with dancing, drinking, and shooting, he requested and demanded six times that the imperial judge be brought to him. But because he didn't want to come and said he was indisposed, the commandant demanded that Master Köppel and the notary Friedrich Flade [the author of this diary] come in his place. He sat at the place in front of the door of the dwelling of Colonel Miniati and first received them with harsh words about the clothes they wore and asked if they did not know to whom they were coming.

Then he announced that today he would like to speak with the honorable imperial judge and that there would perhaps never be such a merry opportunity to speak with him again. He now explained in a drunken manner that he would thereafter act as an honorable knight, as much as was in his power, either protecting the imperial judge and leaving him alone or imprisoning him; yes, he was going to be very good to him, but if the judge would not speak with him right now, when the commandant wanted to confer and deal with him (which would be good for both of them), then the commandant would never again grant him an audience later. When we delegates did our best to excuse the judge because of his indisposition and then offered to relay his message to the judge anyway, then he was satisfied. He had us sit on a sleigh in front of him for an hour while he had another bucket[12] of wine, and whenever he ordered the officers and soldiers in attendance to fire a salvo, then we were ordered to stand up properly.

[12] One bucket equaled approximately 20 gallons (76 liters).

Meanwhile Lieutenant Colonel Winther had earnestly encouraged us to dance, which was very popular with the commandant, who ordered us to do so. However, when we modestly excused ourselves because we were sober and planned to go to church, he demonstrated his dislike for Master Köppel in the open street with many soldiers and citizens [present], and he fell into the greatest fury and ordered the three cannons be turned and used to shoot us down. Then he took us both, by grabbing our clothes with one hand, in front of the cannons, and he pushed me forward, though I am a notary, and said, "This man should be shot first." This horrified the commanders and officers who were standing around, but nonetheless none of them could say anything, until finally Lieutenant Colonel Winther spoke to him and averted the mishap.

However, we then had to dance with the . . . whores and the seamstresses, mother and daughter. The kind of derision and obscenity and taunting and shameful talk and questions that we had to tolerate should not be mentioned for the sake of chastity and honor.

In the meantime I will only note as a memorial that this comedy ended at nine o'clock . . . at which point he raped an approximately fourteen-year-old girl from the house of his host, the noble Lord and Prince von Dietrichstein.

16

MARTIN BÖTZINGER

Torture: The Swedish Drink and Water Boarding

1640

This report by the Thuringian pastor Martin Bötzinger (1599–1673), recorded several years after the events it describes, was part of a short autobiography, or curriculum vitae, of the pastor. It was probably meant more for his colleagues than for a succeeding generation of family members. In it, Bötzinger describes, among other things, his own experience of

From Martin Bötzinger, "Vitae Curriculo," in *Beyträge zur Erläuterung der Hochfürstlich Sachsen-Hildburghäusischen Kirchen- Schul- und Landes-Historie*, Teil 1, *Greitz* (*Contributions to the Explanation of the History of the Princely Saxon-Hildburghausen Church, School, and Land*, part 1, *Greitz*), ed. Johann Werner Krauß (Greitz: Abraham Gottlieb Ludewig, 1750), 349–68, here 353–56.

capture, torture, and flight during the occupation of the city of Heldburg in Thuringia by Catholic imperial troops in the spring of 1640. At the time, Bötzinger had sought refuge inside the walls of Heldburg because the situation in his nearby rural parish, located in Poppenhausen, had become too dangerous. The city walls provided little protection, however, against an onrush of plundering soldiers in search of food and supplies. Bötzinger and his household became a direct target of the looting, and he was taken prisoner by the soldiers. When he refused to provide any information of value about other civilians, he was subjected to various kinds of torture. These ranged from strikes on the head with a dagger, to kicks in the belly, to the application of the so-called Swedish drink.[1] *After repeated application of the last practice did not lead to the desired result, Bötzinger was bound and systematically dunked in the river to give him the sense that he was drowning.*[2] *Bötzinger endured all these tortures and later returned to Poppenhausen. He continued to serve as a minister there and in other parishes for three more decades.*

The imperial and Swedish armies set up camp in Saalfeld between Easter and Pentecost anno 1640, and Franconia and Thuringia were destroyed from near and far. Imperial troops fell upon Heldburg in force on the sixth Sunday after Easter, at four o'clock in the morning, when most citizens were still lying in bed. My whole street and my courtyard were quickly filled with horses and cavalrymen, as if they had been shown my house on purpose. My wife and I were seized five times in one hour. When I got loose of one, then another grabbed me. I simply led them through the chambers and the cellar and let them look for themselves for what they wanted.

Finally they all left me, and they left me alone at home, but the terror, fear, and anxiety were so great that I did not think about my money,

[1] The Swedish drink (in German, *Schwedentrunk*), as it came to be called during the Thirty Years War, had been used under different names long before the war and was used by all sides during and after the war. It was inflicted by forcibly pouring liquid—in the worst case, liquid manure—into the mouth of the victim until his stomach reached such a distended state that the consequent pain would force him to provide the information his captors sought. In sixteenth-century France, but also later in other contexts, forced ingestion of large quantities of liquid was a form of judicial torture used to procure "confessions" or other information. We thank Michèle Violet for this information.

[2] Bötzinger's dunking was a precursor of the modern torture technique of water boarding, in which the person's head is wrapped in cloth, he is placed on a board on his back, the head of the board is lowered, and water is poured over the cloth. Water boarding simulates the sensation of drowning by filling the victim's breathing passages with water.

which I might have saved ten times over if I had been daring enough to take off with it. But all the houses and streets were full of cavalrymen, and it could have happened that if I had taken my money, then I would have wound up simply carrying it to one of them.

But I was so fearful I did not think of money. I had men and women, convoyed out by [imperial general] Gil des Haes's cavalry, who had been quartered with us. I got back to my wife and children, and we hid in the next woods, near Hellingen. Everybody, young and old, clergy and layman, hid there day and night. Most people had nothing to eat but black juniper berries. Then several citizens dared to go into the city, and they came back and brought something to eat and whatever was dear to them. I thought that if I could get to my house and pick up the couple of pennies I had, then I could get myself and my children out of here.

I dared it, and I snuck into the city. . . . Inside [the mill gate] were lurking one or two soldiers, and I was caught unawares, like a mouse by a cat. I was bound with new ropes, so that I could neither walk nor use my hands, and I was to either give them money or tell them about rich people. I had to feed the horses in the manor courtyard, water the horses, and do other lowly work for the thieves. Because I then thought that I was free, I ran off, but not knowing that there was a group of soldiers standing in front of the courtyard gate, I ran right into their arms. They beat me to the ground with their daggers and bandoliers [cartridge belts], bound me tightly with the ropes, and led me from house to house. I was to tell them whose house this one or that one was. So I was finally led into my own house, and I saw on the floor the copper pot in which my 300 talers in cash had been. I thought to myself, if I had only known that the money was gone, then I would've stayed outside town.

Because I did not want to betray anybody else, one of them put on me one of my own hats, which lay in my house on the floor, and then struck me with a cutlass so that blood ran out of my ears, but there was no hole in the hat because it was made of felt. Even worse, the same one, out of wantonness, put his cutlass to my belly and wanted to test if I [as a clergyman] was airtight. He pushed really hard, but God didn't want for him to get any more blood out of me.

Twice in one hour, namely in the tailor Wittib's courtyard in the manure and again in the forest ranger's barn, they gave me the Swedish cocktail, filled with manure drippings. My teeth were almost all loose after this, because as they put a big stick in my mouth I resisted as best as I could while tied up.

Finally they led me away in ropes and said that they were going to hang me. They brought me out through the mill gate to the bridge.

One took the rope in his hands, with which both my feet were bound together, and the other took the rope round my left arm, and they shoved me in the water. They held the ropes, so that they could pull me up and let me drop down into the water again. And because I lashed out and tried to find something to hold on to, I caught the wooden stakes that were placed in the stream to collect debris, but they gave way, and I couldn't hold on there. However, through an act of God a hole was made, and I could slip under the bridge. As much as I wanted to hold on, they hit me with the same stakes, so that they broke like slate. By then they were not only tired of this work but also thought that I was finished and would drown in the water, so they let go of the ropes, and I slipped under the bridge like a frog. I searched in my pants pocket and found a little folding knife, which they had not found, though they had searched me often enough. I used it to cut the ropes on my feet, and I jumped from one story up, down to where the mill wheels lay. The water was up over half my body, and the scoundrels threw pieces of tile and firewood at me to finish me off. I wanted to climb out of the water and get to the miller's back door, but I couldn't, either because my clothes were full of water and held me back, or because God didn't want to allow that I should die there. Like a drunken man sways back and forth, so did I, and I came to the other side at the back of the brewing yard. Because they now saw that I was going to escape by the city ditch, they all ran into the city and collected more of their accomplices. They were watching the fermenting houses to see if I would come out of [one of] them. But when I noticed this, I lay waiting in the water. I hid my head behind a willow bush, and I rested in the water for four or five hours, until it was nighttime and it was quiet in the city. Then I crawled out, half-dead, and because of the beatings I could barely draw breath. . . .

I had to stay there into the night, and then I went over the water pipes, always downstream, and climbed over a willow branch, so that I came in on the other side by Poppenhausen. When I came down the road from Poppenhausen, there lay here and there lots of white linens,[3] which the soldiers had thrown away or lost. I couldn't bend down to pick them up, and I finally came to Poppenhausen. I found no one who lived there, except Clasen Hön, whose wife had given birth six weeks before. He had to cut the clothes off me because I was so swollen, and he laid the clothes out so that they would dry. He had to loan me a shirt, and he saw my skin, which was very colorful from the beatings, and my back and arms, which were black with bruises.

[3] White linens were considered precious household goods.

The next day my nice parishioner asked me to leave, because he feared that they were hunting me and that he would have trouble because of me. So with his help I put my wet clothes back on, and I went in the direction of Lindenau, always through the thickest brush. I stopped just outside of the Lindenau gardens, where I could see the village. I saw that some people were going into a house, and I went to them, and they did not want to let me in because they were too afraid. Only when they saw through the window that their pastor was coming could I come in, and I stayed with them for several days.

17

VOLKMAR HAPPE

Violence between Peasants and Soldiers

1627 and 1637

The following excerpts are taken from the Chronicon Thuringiae (Thuringian Chronicle)*, an ego-document of some two thousand pages written by Volkmar Happe, an administrative official and court councilor, during the Thirty Years War. Living in the central German region of Thuringia from the 1620s to the 1640s, Happe painstakingly recorded thousands of war-related events, both small and large, with the accuracy of an administrative official. His chronicle thus serves as a gigantic recording of the war's violence in the central German region of Thuringia from the 1620s to the 1640s. In these passages, Happe describes the grinding cycle of violence between soldiers and peasants, a cycle in which victims seemed to be selected at random.*

The 25th of May [1627], a soldier from the quarters in Holzsussra attacked a peasant on the road and wanted money from him; however, the peasant overpowered him and took the horseman's own pistol from

From Volkmar Happe, *Chronicon Thuringiae* (*Thuringian Chronicle*), ed. Hans Medick, Norbert Winnige, and Andreas Bähr (electronic publication: Thüringer Universitäts- und Landesbibliothek Jena, 2008), 1:75v, 76v–77r, 82v; 2:114r–16r. Available as a digital facsimile at www.mdsz.thulb.uni-jena.de/happe/quelle.php.

his saddle and shot him dead with it. The same day, in Mittelsömmern, some peasants beat to death a soldier's wife and boy. . . .

The 29th of May [1627] was Whitmonday, and some frivolous knaves, who were horsemen, wanted to take some lambs from the shepherd of Wiedermuth. The peasants learned of it, and some of them came forth with the mayor [of Wiedermuth] and pleaded for peace. At this one of the frivolous knaves pulled out a pistol and shot the mayor, Valentin Engellmann, an old and gray, pious and honest man. He was shot through and through, so that he quickly fell down and died. That night, some soldiers plundered the village of Hagen and badly injured many poor people. The 30th of May some peasants shot three soldiers near Mehrstedt. Over this other soldiers were so enraged that they plundered the village. The same day the peasants shot another soldier, one of the nobility. . . . On the 31st of May a peasant, who was to fetch beer for the soldiers from the town of Duderstadt, was shot at Zaunröden. . . .

[On the 19th of June], in Schönewerda some horsemen wanted to take sustenance or money by force, but the peasants drove them away and shot to death eight horsemen. The same day in Bottendorf by Ziegelroda some horsemen also tried to take sustenance by force. However, when the peasants resisted, the horsemen shot one through the arm. Thereupon the peasants fired back at them and shot to death twenty-three horsemen, plundered and undressed the same, and threw the naked bodies in the water.

[. . .]

The 13th of May [1637] our district scribe Tobias Schuchart rode with three horsemen from Frankenhausen to Sondershausen. As they approached the Bendeleben woods, the Harz sharpshooters[1] fired at them. The lieutenant was shot through the hat but was otherwise unharmed, and our scribe was grazed by a bullet on the knee. They both escaped, as did an adjutant who was not harmed or hit at all. However, the third rider, who was the equerry[2] of Lieutenant Colonel Johann de Nove, was hit by three bullets, and the horse under him was also shot. Afterward they dragged him off into the woods, beat him completely to death, and left him laying stark naked, so that he did not even have on a shirt. That evening he was brought to Sondershausen, very badly cut to pieces and stark naked. The killed man is supposedly from Büttstedt.

[1] These sharpshooters (in German, *Harzschützen*) were semi-organized bands of armed peasants who, from their retreats in the nearby Harz Mountains, came down onto the Thuringian plain to launch raids against the soldiers, but at times they also attacked civilians.

[2] The servant in charge of the horses.

18

PETER HAGENDORF

Peasant Violence against Soldiers and Retribution for It

1641

In his diary, Peter Hagendorf, a mercenary in the Thirty Years War, describes in sober terms his violent struggle for survival throughout the war.[1] *This struggle consisted not only of meting out violence to others in military actions and using open or indirect force to obtain food or other goods. It also involved dealing with the violence practiced by others, be they soldiers or, as in the case described here, civilians.*

In this passage, Hagendorf describes being attacked and robbed by a small group of peasants. Four months later, he managed to identify and arrest one of the perpetrators. It is noteworthy that in demanding justice, Hagendorf did not seek revenge through the usual punishment of hanging, as provided for by martial law. Instead, he was much more focused on extorting a tidy reparation payment for the attack.

From Bonames to Limburg through the Westerwald, a rough land. To Montabaur, here a meeting was held with the army. The 12th of June [1641] to Dierdorf. A terrible land. Here we got army bread, and [even] the dogs didn't want to eat it.

Here I got a bit drunk during the evening, and in the morning I was straggling a stone's throw behind the regiment because I had a headache. There were three peasants hidden in the brush, and they attacked me there and took my coat, pack, everything. Through God's

[1] When Jan Peters first published the diary in 1993, he did not know the name of its author. Since then, historian Marco von Mueller has investigated the soldier's wide-ranging movements throughout the war and first identified him as Peter Hagendorf. Jan Peters in further research produced additional evidence on Hagendorf's life, which in 2012 led to a new edition of the diary.

From Peter Hagendorf, *Tagebuch eines Söldners aus dem Dreißigjährigen Krieg* (*Diary of a Mercenary from the Thirty Years War*), ed. Jan Peters, 2nd rev. ed. (Göttingen: V & R Unipress, 2012), 127, 128.

grace they jumped away from me at once, as if somebody was chasing them, although nobody was back there. So I came back to the regiment beaten-up, without my coat, without my pack, and they just laughed at me. . . .

[Hagendorf moved around the Rhineland with his regiment for several months, until the beginning of November, when he returned to the army's headquarters in the area where the robbery had happened.]

I went to the headquarters, to look around, to see if I couldn't find any of the three who had taken my things. . . . I came across one of them, whom I immediately took to the military police and then to jail, with the declaration that he must return my things, or he must hang. And so Field Marshal Wahl,[2] who heard about this right away, offered to me, in front of the commander of the military police, the auditor general,[3] the quartermaster general,[4] and the entire watch, to have the peasant hung if he did not satisfy me. So the authorities in his village gave me 12 talers. In addition the commander of the military police received 1 taler, the auditor 1 taler, the quartermaster 1 taler, [and] the jailer a 20-kreuzer coin. So I was happy again.

[2] Joachim Christian, Count of Wahl, commander of the military police since 1631. At the time of this incident, he was field marshal of the Catholic Bavarian troops.

[3] The head of the military court of a regiment, responsible for investigating and prosecuting all violations of martial law.

[4] The head of the civil administration of the army, responsible for quartering and the mail.

19

AUGUSTIN GÜNTZER

Quartering Soldiers: A Household under Stress

1633–1635

Augustin Güntzer, a devout Calvinist, was a tinsmith in the imperial city of Colmar in Alsace. This firsthand account reveals the trials and tribulations of quartering and feeding foreign soldiers in one's home. Instead of receiving protection in return for quartering the soldiers, the widowed tinsmith and his two daughters were at the soldiers' mercy, to the point that they felt compelled to leave their own home. Complaints to the soldiers' superiors were in vain, and in the end Güntzer had to strike a bizarre bargain.

In this year [1633] I was onerously burdened with the quartering of soldiers. Therefore I had to argue with them often, because they wanted to have better food than I and my children have. Every time the worst soldiers of all were quartered in my house, and so I was tormented by them to the utmost. . . . Sometimes I had to secretly hide in my house, so that they did not know I was there. In the night they took my housewares and took wine from the cellar. I was heavily burdened with watch duties, sometimes every third night. When I then went home in the morning to see what had happened there overnight, often I found the tablecloth on the table, the mugs and glasses full of urine, the tablecloth cut with a knife, and other housewares defiled and destroyed. Then my two young daughters complained with crying eyes that the way that they were handled by the soldiers, they could not stay in the house. I went to the quartermaster for help, and I received as an answer that I had better get along well with the soldiers, so that the soldiers wouldn't have reason to complain about me.

So my cross became heavier and heavier. And I thought that I had deserved better, but when I thought about my sins, and if God would

From Augustin Güntzer, *Kleines Biechlen von meinem gantzen leben: Die Autobiographie eines Elsässer Kannengießers aus dem 17. Jahrhundert* (*A Little Booklet about My Whole Life: The Autobiography of an Alsatian Tinsmith from the Seventeenth Century*), ed. Fabian Brändle and Dominik Sieber (Cologne: Böhlau Verlag, 2002), 237–39.

punish me for my sins, then it should not be any easier for the servant than for the Lord. I thought of Christ, my savior, who was my consolation and who suffered though innocent. I, however, have earned it more than a thousand times over with my various sins against God. I trust in God, and he will help me in my moment of need.

In this year 1635 two foreign (*welsch*)[1] man-animals[2] were lodged with me, and I was tormented by them to the utmost. On top of all the torments that they did to me, within three days they stole eight barrels of wine from my cellar in the night and sold some of it.[3] The other part of it they swilled in my house, and they invited other soldiers to be their guests for this. They lied to me that they had bought the wine, though it was my own best wine. As they drank, they got loaded and furious, and they chased me and the children out of the house.

I appealed on the 4th of June to the city authorities, to save me from such misery and to send me a contingent of our own German soldiers so that I could get back in my home. As an answer I was told that they could not help me. I replied to them: "Then my citizenship rights in the city are voided, and I will revoke my vow to the city this week."

With that I went to the commandant major, and I asked him to come with me to my house to calm the soldiers down. He came along with me, and we found a tableful of soldiers, celebrating at their pleasure. My hens lay in the platters, and they were eating contentedly. The major hit them on the head with his staff, but the soldiers only became worse.

When my lords now saw that I was earnestly going to move away with my two children, they sent for me the next day. They offered to me that if I would join the other sixty citizens in a newly formed militia, then they would get the soldiers out of my house. I did not want to go, but I reconsidered the matter, that my two children and the house and the things in it would thereby be safe, and therefore I promised to go along.

Then I had to swear an oath with the other sixty citizens to serve for three months, so that when the imperial troops invaded the countryside around Colmar to take away fish, fruit, and vegetables by force, they could be driven away. In the meantime the militia encountered roughly eighty imperial soldiers. Because the militia was much too small to

[1] Here Güntzer uses the derogatory term *welsch* (which refers to speakers of languages with Latin rather than Germanic roots) to describe the French soldiers who had occupied his town since October 1634, when Colmar had "accepted" the protection of the French army.

[2] In German, *Menschgetierer.* These men were actually musketeers.

[3] It was usual practice in that area to store large quantities of wine as an investment.

resist the enemy incursion, the citizenry armed another company of one hundred horsemen. The other citizens marched out of the city with fieldpieces, supply wagons, and flags flying to stop the enemy, so that the fruit would not all be picked and ruined by them. However, the militia was misused, and therefore I excused myself and had again to suffer the quartering of soldiers, which was worse than before.

20

CHRISTOPH BRANDIS

Gains and Losses: Quartering and Occupation

1636

In these passages from his diary, Christoph Brandis, the mayor of Rüthen in Westphalia, describes the violence and abuse that occupying Protestant Hessian soldiers heaped on the Catholic civilians of his hometown, including Brandis himself. He cites as an exception Nicholas Seiffert, the soldier quartered in his own home, who responded to his report of plunder by finding him other food and drink. Brandis remains silent, however, regarding where and how his guest acquired these supplies. They could easily have been forced "contributions" from another household in town.

The 15th of March [1636]. My Nicholas Seiffert, born in Ziegenhain [Hesse], is a really decent man. At noontime today, just as we wanted to eat a little at twelve o'clock, a soldier came and took away all the food from the table and also took our entire supply of bread, four loaves. When I told him that it was for my quartering [soldier], he gave me as

---

From Christoph Brandis, "Kriegstagebuch des Rüthener Bürgermeisters Christoph Brandis (ca. 1578–1658) über die hessische Einquartierung 1636" ("War Diary of the Mayor of Rüthen Christoph Brandis [ca. 1578–1658] regarding the Quartering of Hessian Troops in 1636"), in *Sterbzeiten: der Dreißigjährige Krieg im Herzogtum Westfalen; Eine Dokumentation* (*Time to Die: The Thirty Years War in the Duchy of Westphalia; A Documentation*), ed. Horst Conrad and Gunnar Teske, Westfälische Quellen und Archivpublikationen (Westphalian Sources and Archival Publications) 23 (Münster: Landschaftsverband Westfalen-Lippe, Archivamt für Westfalen, 2000), 309, 310.

an answer a smack with a thick cudgel and said, "You damned scoundrel, your Antichrist can pray that you get something else." His Papal Holiness is wont to refer to all adherents of the new teaching [Protestants] as the Antichrist. This had just happened when the aforementioned Seiffert came home. I explained everything to him, adding that I could offer him nothing more to eat and that he would have to wait [to eat] with me until evening, when I would see if I could get something. He was satisfied with that, but he went out and after an hour came back with meat, bread, and a mug of wine and shared everything with me. He said it was his manner: If the host had nothing, then he would host the host. . . .

The 27th of May, Colonel Leuttenberger came and was quartered in the same house in which Dickmann already was quartered. On the 29th of this month Leuttenberger cut off the hand of a local carpenter, because he had not seemed quick enough in doffing his hat. Some inhabitants would say that he shot off his mouth a little crudely at the colonel. This could well be, although I cannot really confirm this. This Leuttenberger proved to be not so bad, because on the very same day he defended and saved a barn at the gate, which some of the enlisted men wanted to set on fire, as they said, to make fireworks.

The 9th of July, finally Dickmann and Leuttenberger departed with their men. The city is very happy, since they extorted 8,976 Reichstalers and 24 groschen from us and took from us terribly for four months. If I had wanted to write down all the atrocities committed, then I would have had to write an entire book. But I must say that they were nowhere near as bad as the Hessian general Melander.[1] As is written in detail above, I was satisfied with my Seiffert to the end, and there never was a harsh word between us. Only once, when I did not want to eat meat with him on a Saturday, though I know well that in the exigencies of wartime one is allowed to do so, he blasphemed terribly against this rule of the holy church. He was otherwise a decent man.

[1] Peter Melander, Graf von Holzappel (1585–1648), was one of the greatest war profiteers of the Thirty Years War. Lieutenant general for the Protestant state of Hesse-Kassel from 1633 to 1640, he changed sides in 1642 and became an imperial field marshal.

Rape and Violence against Women

21

CHRISTOPH BRANDIS

A Case of Rape

1636

The quartering of soldiers in civilian households frequently led to conflicts and confrontations, and not only regarding the requisitioning of household resources to supply the military. Almost always conflicts were also about dominance in the household—the dominance of the male head of household was contested by the soldiers. The most brutal and humiliating form of military rule by force in the home was the rape of female family members, which in this passage from Christoph Brandis's diary (see Document 20) is coupled with the extorted delivery of food.

The 7th of April [1636] a shameful deed was done. A [Protestant Hessian] soldier named Mathes was quartered in D.'s house.[1] This Mathes had already done D. a lot of harm by breaking windows, doors, and furniture, even by inflicting serious beatings, but the worst, the crowning blow in this assemblage of cruelties, was yet to come. On the morning of the 7th, as the aforementioned Mathes was still lying in the loft, he called

[1] Because this man's family name still existed in Rüthen in 1789, the year of the first printed edition of this text, the editor explained in a note that he thought it was better to leave it out, even more than 150 years after the event. However, the full name seems to have been used in the original text.

From "Kriegstagebuch des Rüthener Bürgermeisters Christoph Brandis (ca. 1578–1658) über die hessische Einquartierung 1636" ("War Diary of the Mayor of Rüthen Christoph Brandis [ca. 1578–1658] regarding the Quartering of Hessian Troops in 1636"), in *Sterbzeiten: der Dreißigjährige Krieg im Herzogtum Westfalen; Eine Dokumentation* (*Time to Die: The Thirty Years War in the Duchy of Westphalia; A Documentation*), ed. Horst Conrad and Gunnar Teske, Westfälische Quellen und Archivpublikationen (Westphalian Sources and Archival Publications) 23 (Münster: Landschaftsverband Westfalen-Lippe, Archivamt für Westfalen, 2000), 309–10.

down that somebody better bring him a pitcher of milk, or he would tear the whole place apart. D. sent his daughter, a brave seventeen-year-old girl, to the neighbor's house to retrieve some milk. Because it took the girl a little while and Mathes was making more and more noise, when she finally came back, her father told her to bring it up to the soldier. She was obedient to her father, but she hardly got upstairs when Mathes tried to have his way with her. She defended herself as well as she could, and she called for help, but the soldier hit her with a closed fist in the mouth. Meanwhile the father had heard what was going on, and he and his wife hurried upstairs, but Mathes had locked the door. The poor parents could only watch, through a hole which Mathes had already previously hacked in the door, as their own child was raped, without being able to help her. Because she had presumably defended herself too strenuously, the wretch totally tore open her right breast, so that later a whole piece fell out. The girl was inhumanely mutilated, and after fourteen days of unremitting pain she died. Today the father went with me to the captain to complain about the aforementioned Mathes, but he defiantly answered that if she's dead now, then he couldn't help anymore. He didn't punish Mathes at all, but instead let him run around free like the others. The father is inconsolable, and everyone mourns the girl, may she rest in peace.

22

CHRISTIAN LEHMANN

Hounding Civilians

1640

Christian Lehmann was pastor in the Saxon city of Scheibenberg. He wrote his chronicle in the 1660s, and it was printed by his son in 1699. In the following passage, Lehmann provides an eyewitness account of events that took place in 1640 in and around Scheibenberg, which lay in the upper Erzgebirge mountains in Saxony. Lehmann describes how the Swedish troops of General Baner's army hunted and committed acts of violence against civilians. In the last phase of the war, these troops were starving. The troops were no longer able to provide for themselves with regular "contributions" from the towns and villages, because most of the inhabitants had fled and taken refuge in the mountains and their forests. Therefore, there remained no other option but to search and "hunt" for the civilians who had fled with their provisions.

The enemy on horse and on foot hounded the people terribly through the woods and came closer and closer. . . . The 13th of March [1640] three hundred musketeers came from the villages. . . . They caused a great fear among the refugees. They plunged farther into the woods, until they found the camps and huts of the people and cattle. They seized people, horses, cattle, money, and victuals, whatever they found, and they incited the other hungry soldiers on horse and on foot to do the same, so that daily some one hundred came and plundered through these woods two miles[1] long. . . . The 21st, 22nd, and 23rd of March the rampaging and the hunting was the worst. In those days there were four thousand soldiers who overran all the places in the woods. They

[1] The author was presumably measuring in old German miles, each of which equals approximately 4.6 modern English miles.

From Christian Lehmann, *Das sächsische Erzgebirge im Kriegesleid: erzgebirgische Kriegschronik; nach dem Originale der "Deutschen Kriegschronik" Magister Christian Lehmanns (The Saxon Erzgebirge Suffering in the War: Erzgebirge War Chronicle; From the Original Text of the "German War Chronicle" by Master Christian Lehmann)*, ed. Leo Bönhoff (Annaberg: Sächischer Erzgebirgsverein, 1911), 130–33.

surrounded them and hunted through, and took away many hundreds of head of cattle and many thousands of talers' worth of household and precious goods. . . . One figures now that several thousand people were taken from these woods. Now when hungry foraging parties came and found nothing and couldn't load themselves up with anything, then they vented their rage on the people. They caught them, beat them, and forced them to show where their people and their livestock were. They stripped males and females stark naked, they ravished decent women in the woods, and they bound maidens with straps to abuse them and led them to their quarters and so disgracefully mishandled them that they died afterward. One saw shame and dishonor, but also love and decency. The sick men were thrown out of bed and the healthy were undressed, so that they had to cover their private parts with brush or old sacks. Some men held on to their wives, mothers to their daughters, and allowed themselves to be beaten bloody and senseless with pistols before they let go of each other to be taken away. Some chaste women defended themselves from their violators, and they nobly escaped from them. Then again, some of the half-naked people had to load up their own livestock or clothes or sacks with grain, and then carry them to the soldiers' quarters or to Schwarzenberg,[2] which had a *salvaguardia* [paid guard].

[. . .]

They took many females along with them to war; others they took only to the nearest city, and kept them only until they ransomed them. There is no way to describe the fear, anxiety, and distress in the woods. They hung a schoolmaster from a tree by his feet, though the women begged them not to, because he knew of no booty to show them. A pastor [Lehmann's marginal note: "caught me myself"],[3] with his wife, off of whom they wanted to cut the skirt, and his maid, off of whom they did cut the skirt, and two small sick children; they left them with nothing but their lives and they convoyed them to Annaberg[4] for 2 ducats. The other fleeing people were so hounded and were so terrorized and beaten that the pregnant women miscarried; in the riot two newborns were suffocated, and the prematurely born babies died without baptism. Others became ill from hunger, cold, and fright and were taken and hidden in wells, in pits, or in holes and covered with moss and wood

[2] Schwarzenberg is approximately 7 miles (11.3 km) west-southwest of Scheibenberg.

[3] Lehmann's marginal note refers to this episode as one that he himself and his family had to endure.

[4] Annaberg is approximately 6 miles (9.7 km) east-northeast of Scheibenberg.

chips. Sometimes they crawled into hollow logs, and they even crawled into bear caves and drove out the bears. Then it looked as if all the evil spirits in the soldiers and bears had united to pursue the poor refugees into the woods. In the uproar it happened that a great ferocious bear was driven out of his lair and ran around between the refugees and the soldiers looking for a place to escape. Because everywhere he met with people, either chasing or hiding, and he could not find anyplace to retire, his fear turned to fury. In a rage he ran not far from the Flossteich lake and at Klein Mittweida he struck, bit, and tore to pieces a crippled girl of twelve years, Miriam, the daughter of Hans Günther from Mittweida. Friends had carried her to the woods in a basket to escape from the desecrators and had had to stop there. It followed that as he fled with his mouth dripping blood, he knocked down another maiden from Elterlein, Salome, Andres Jäger the butcher's daughter, but because the horsemen were right behind him, he let her go unharmed. The refugees took some of their animals all the way to Gottesgabe past Breitenbrunn [in Bohemia] to the Golden Heights and Glücksburg, but the enemy rode crisscross through the whole woods following their tracks. They overtook some of the livestock, and the people ran away, but they were caught in Gottesgabe and in other places and were coerced to drive their own and Bohemian animals through the woods and to ransom their children with cold cash. Because when the soldiers saw a fine child, they thought it was an aristocrat's or a lord's child and they wanted by all means to rob the parents. Thereby there was hunger and sorrow, so that people in four to five days did not have a bit of bread, and they fed their children bran and water porridge and satisfied their own hunger with sauerkraut without lard and salt. Married couples were separated from each other, and parents from their children, and friends and neighbors from one another, so that some did not know for six days where the others had really gone, and they met up strangely. The women came from the plateau or the Golden Heights; the men came from Schwarzenberg, Zwönitz, and Geyer;[5] and the children came from the Sehma River, from Annaberg, or Marienberg,[6] so they met up again. The 24th of March was a relief.

[5] Zwönitz is approximately 9 miles (14.5 km) northwest of Scheibenberg, and Geyer is approximately 8 miles (13 km) north of Scheibenberg.

[6] The Sehma River flows approximately 5 miles (8 km) east of Scheibenberg, and Marienberg is approximately 18 miles (29 km) northeast of Scheibenberg.

23

PETER HAGENDORF

A Soldier's Various Ways of Dealing with Women

1634 and 1641

The diary of Peter Hagendorf (see Document 18) allows a glimpse of the everyday life of a soldier in the Thirty Years War. Hagendorf traveled widely with various armies and in various campaigns, often with his wife and children in tow. His diary offers several perspectives on the treatment of women. Indeed, he himself dealt with some women as spoils and goods, just as he respectfully cared for others such as his wife.

[Spring 1634]

Here [at Friedberg in Bavaria] Duke Bernhard[1] joined us with his army. We moved to Freising, over the Isar [River], to Landshut, which we shelled and took by storm.

We stayed here for eight days and plundered the city. I received as spoils a pretty maiden and 12 talers' worth of gold, clothing, and linens. As we were leaving, I sent her back to Landshut. . . .

[October 1634]

Here in Durlach there was good wine. There was a church festival, and everything was spoils. Here I got shirts again, and my servant took as plunder a horse, a bay. I am well-off again.

From Durlach to Pforzheim. Here I also led away a young girl. But I let her go again, because she had to bring me linens, which I often regret, because I had no woman at this point. . . . In this year, on the 23rd of January, 1635, I married the honorable Anna Maria Buchlerin,

[1] Duke Bernhard of Saxe-Weimar (1604–1639) was one of the most prominent military entrepreneurs and leaders in the Thirty Years War. He served as a general in the Swedish army and later as a general in the French army.

From Peter Hagendorf, *Tagebuch eines Söldners aus dem Dreißigjährigen Krieg* (*Diary of a Mercenary from the Thirty Years War*), ed. Jan Peters, 2nd rev. ed. (Göttingen: V & R Unipress, 2012), 109, 110, 111, 113, 125.

the daughter of Martin Buchler. Dear God keep us healthy for a long time. I had the wedding in Pforzheim, and it cost 45 guldens. The father contributed 10 guldens. . . .

The 11th of November [1635] my wife had a child. It was immediately baptized. His name was Jürg Martin; he lived twenty-four hours. God grant him a joyous resurrection. . . .

[Spring 1641]

From Straubing to Paring. In Paring my wife became ill, and she had such pain in her legs that I could not take her away. I had to leave her in Paring, with the judge there, who was a good acquaintance of mine. Little by little I followed after the colonel to Ingolstadt. There I was quartered in a tavern.

The wife together with the child remained behind, together with my horse. After fourteen days I went back to get them. She still could not walk any better than before, so I led her on the horse. I moved like Joseph traveling to Egypt.[2] The 16th of April I left her there; the 30th I picked her up again. She could not go any farther than I carried her.

The 19th of May in the year 1641 my daughter [Barbara] died in Ingolstadt. No. 3.[3] Dear God grant her a joyous resurrection. . . .

The 24th I had to sell my horse. It brought 24 guldens. I needed money here. The 26th I appealed to the mayor about my wife, and so he took her in. That required money, because she has become like a cripple. She walked with two crutches for seven weeks. But in seven weeks the hangman's wife made her fit again with baths.

[2] Hagendorf is referring here to an episode from the New Testament of the Bible. After Jesus's birth, his parents, Joseph and Mary, fled with him from Israel to Egypt to avoid King Herod's henchmen, who had been sent to bring Jesus to Herod.

[3] This was his third child to die during the war.

24

MARIA ANNA JUNIUS

Fear of Rape, Management of Relations, and Sweet Pacifications

1632

This noteworthy but in no way singular account of Maria Anna Junius, a Dominican nun in the cloister at St. Mary's Church in Bamberg, expresses how frightened women were of male violence against them. In 1632, the Protestant Swedish army under Duke Bernhard von Weimar[1] *occupied Bamberg. In this excerpt, Junius describes how the nuns escaped this extremely confrontational situation unharmed.*

The shooting began at 6:00 p.m. and lasted until early, around 1:00 a.m., then some burghers went to the city hall and shot over at the enemy, so that none of the enemy dared come out of the houses. But then the enemy quickly shot them down, which we all heard. And when we looked into the city, we saw nothing but fire, so that our cloister was illuminated from it. Then we couldn't think anything, except that the entire Kaulberg[2] was burning away. As they told us, they were very angry that the burghers had broken the truce, and they would spare no human being, but rather slay everyone and burn the city. Oh, what terror and deadly fear we had then. Oh, what strange thoughts struggled within us, because we didn't know if we should leave or stay there, and in this and every hour the moment of death seemed to be upon us, which we

[1] See note 1 in Document 23.
[2] Part of the cathedral district of Bamberg, where St. Mary's Church is situated.

From Maria Anna Junius, "Die Aufzeichnungen der Bamberger Nonne Maria Anna Junius: *Bamberg im Schweden-Kriege*; Nach einem Manuscripte (Mittheilungen über die Jahre 1622–1634)" ("The Chronicle of the Nun Maria Anna Junius in Bamberg: *Bamberg in the Swedish War*; From a Manuscript [Entries about the Years 1622–1634]")," ed. Friedrich Karl Hümmer, *Bericht des Historischen Vereins für die Pflege der Geschichte des ehemaligen Fürstbistums Bamberg* (*Report of the Historical Association for the Commemoration of the History of the Former Prince-Bishopric of Bamberg*) 52 (1890): 32–37; 53 (1891): 182–84.

didn't fear so much as something else.[3] But we gave ourselves up to the will of God and relied entirely on the help and mercy of our most beloved bridegroom, Jesus, and very bravely and faithfully stayed in our cloister. . . .

[In the middle of the night] our cabinetmaker, who had also been at the city hall, came to us at 1:00 a.m., and he told us, too, that there was no human soul left at the city hall. They had all fled, and the shooting that continued was the enemy's. "If you want a protective guard, [you should] send somebody into the city soon, because before daylight the enemy will advance over the bridge." We didn't know what to do for fear and terror. Immediately I and another sister went to the mother superior. We asked her for God's sake to quickly write a request for a guard troop now, because by daylight the enemy would be upon us. Immediately she wrote to the colonel and asked for a guard troop, but we couldn't get anyone who would take the note into the city, so we were in great need and worried, and again we did not know what to do. We were in the greatest need, though, and it was already 4:00 a.m., so our gardener's apprentice came to us and said he would risk his life and body for ours and carry the letter in, which we were happy about with our whole hearts. We thought nothing other than: "Our beloved groom, Jesus, send us miserable sisters an angel from heaven to comfort us." So we sent off the message.

When the gardener's apprentice arrived [at the Swedish headquarters], Colonel [Georg Wulf von] Wildenstein, who had taken quarters in the tavern house on the market, was still lying asleep. But after our boy had to wait quite long, he asked the cook for God's sake to wake up the colonel; otherwise his virgins were going to die miserably before daylight. She reported it to the colonel, and as soon as he heard this, he asked immediately, "Is anybody there to whom I am related?" Then immediately a nobleman, who must have been descended from a fox [because he was clever] and was cousin to our prince [Bernhard of Saxe-Weimar], went to him. He said to the colonel, "Cousin, here I am." Then the colonel sent him with five musketeers to be our guard troop.

Oh, God, we were in such deadly fear and terror during this time, because we assumed that the apprentice gardener had been killed. Therefore we were ready for death at any moment, because we constantly thought that the enemy was coming and would kill us. We had

[3] Junius alludes here to the nuns' fear of rape.

willingly given ourselves up to that and were willing to live or die according to God's merciful will, as it pleased His Godly Majesty. But then, when it was already going on 7:00 [a.m.], there were several sisters on the lookout, and they saw several soldiers coming to our cloister and thought they were the enemy. They ran up here quickly and screamed, "Oh, oh, you dear sisters, the enemy's coming and headed for our cloister. Oh, let's go together into the chamber and when they come, beg for mercy or die with each other, as God wants."

While we were in such a great panic, a sister came and spoke: "Be calm, you dear sisters. The boy who carried our message down there is coming with the soldiers; this will be our guard troop." When we heard that, we were a little at ease. We were in the windows, and the soldiers saw us weeping so heartfully. They said to us that we should be at ease: "Nothing will happen to you." Also the nobleman said to us quite friendlily that his honorable cousin sent his greetings to all the virgins and also ordered him with the musketeers to keep guard here. We should not be afraid of anything; nothing would happen to us. Then we thanked God the Most High for them and brought them something to eat and drink, because of our great joy that we could stay in our cloister. Oh, who was happier than us, because it was no different than if we had been dead and then brought back to life. And if we had not gotten the guard troop so soon, we would have been plundered three times before noon, because our guard troop dealt with such a shoving and hitting at our door. Therefore we were in great fear and need day and night.

[. . .]

The morning of Saturday the 8th Duke Bernhard's *Hofmeister* [court administrator] came to us and requested from us a cow. To this we said that we wanted to immediately write to the prince himself that we were very poor sisters and to send along some preserves. He was shocked then and said that we should not hold it against him that he came out to us [to requisition a cow], because the members of the town council had referred him to us, and with that he took his leave again. As we had supper that same night someone came to us and cried that the prince, Duke Bernhard himself, was coming. We went quickly, and as soon as the gate was opened Duke Bernhard happily came to us with a laugh and gave one sister after another his hand and asked how we lived. After the prince came Colonel Gratz [Johann Philipp Cratz von Scharfenstein] and after him very many prominent colonels and nobles, which was more than twenty people. Then the prince asked to see our church. Immediately I went in and prepared a couple of bowls of preserves.

Meanwhile the prince wanted to leave again, but the sisters asked if His Princely Grace wanted to go into the convent chamber. There the prince sat on the pew before the crucifix and spoke quite friendlily with the sisters. Then someone cried that the prince had stood up and was about to go, and I ran quickly with the two bowls of precious preserves. As I came out, the prince was going directly for the gate. I got there first and kneeled and said to him, "I ask, Your Princely Grace, would you like to take something from the bowl beforehand?" Then the prince laughed and reached into the bowl and took a lemon tart and ate from it. And I spoke again: "Would your princely grace also take a big handful?" And he said, "It is enough, thank you." And he went right away. Likewise I gave Colonel Gratz a tart and a handful, after which I gave each person something.

After the enemy all rode away, immediately a lieutenant colonel came who said that His Princely Grace ordered him that he should provide us with a wagon. He came in our garden and said to his vanguard that they should be careful and do no harm to the beehives. When we said that we did not want His Grace to place a wagon in our garden because this would be unseemly, and that Duke Bernhard had promised us all possible aid, mercy, and protection, he said that if it was not to the liking of the virgins, then he would not ask to do it.

The Hardships of Separation

These letters, discovered by the archivist Fritz Wolff, were sent from the war zone in central Germany in the upper Hessian Werra region. They were preserved because they were intercepted and subsequently archived. These exceptional ego-documents allow a rare insight into the relationships between women at home and men—friends, lovers, and husbands—who were away serving as soldiers in the war. They show the difficulties, worries, and emotional intensity of communication between friends, family members, and lovers who were separated in these unstable times.

25

MARGARET, THE MOSBACHERS' MAID

Letter to Her "Dearest Brother"

ca. 1625

Address on the outside of [undated] letter:

To be delivered to the hand of my most dearest brother Joseph the Spaniard[1]

With all the best wishes, first, my dearest brother Joseph.

[1] Based on the contents of this emotionally charged letter, it seems possible that the relationship between the writer and the recipient was not that of brother and sister but rather of lovers. Presumably, she addressed the recipient as her brother to prevent recriminations from other possible readers of the letter. Margaret was probably the servant of a local peasant and a Protestant. Joseph, as his nickname "the Spaniard" implies, was serving in the Catholic imperial army.

From Fritz Wolff, "Feldpostbriefe aus dem Dreißigjährigen Kriege: Selbstzeugnisse der kleinen Leute" ("Military Mail from the Thirty Years War: Ego-Documents from Common Folk"), in *Hundert Jahre Historische Kommission für Hessen, 1897–1997* (*One Hundred Years of the Historical Commission of Hesse, 1897–1997*), ed. Walter Heinemeyer, Veröffentlichungen der Historischen Kommission für Hessen (Publications of the Historical Commission of Hesse) 61 (Marburg: N. G. Elwert Verlag, 1997), 481–512, appendix 2, 509–10.

If you are still unharmed and healthy, then I am most glad, and I wish you many hundreds of thousands of times good night, and I ask that you don't forget me, because we often spoke with each other. I cannot and will not forget you because of the great love, anguish, and pain, and I commend you to the protection and safety of the Lord. May God shield you from all of your enemies. This time I am not sending more [news] than God's blessings.

MARGARET THE MOSBACHERS' MAID.

26

ANNA IMMICK OF ALLENDORF

Letter to the "Most Honorable" Soldier Balthasar Wahs

1625

Address on the outside of letter:

The most honorable, manful [*sic*] soldier Balthasar Wahs, via the hands of the shoemaker.

With wishes for [a] good day.

You, Balthasar Wahs, will remember well that you promised a great deal to me, Anna Immick of Allendorf, but you have held to little. I really thought that you would be thoughtful of me and that you would not do such a thing to me. Do you remember what you told me and the hatmaker and Andreas Suchfort? Now I am asking you, for God's sake, to be thoughtful of me, poor woman, and not let me be slandered and ridiculed by my friends. I trust entirely that you will conduct yourself suitably. But I am in great sorrow and ask you a thousand times, for God's sake, that you might send me comfort and hope and all the best.

From Fritz Wolff, "Feldpostbriefe aus dem Dreißigjährigen Kriege: Selbstzeugnisse der kleinen Leute" ("Military Mail from the Thirty Years War: Ego-Documents from Common Folk"), in *Hundert Jahre Historische Kommission für Hessen, 1897–1997* (*One Hundred Years of the Historical Commission of Hesse, 1897–1997*), ed. Walter Heinemeyer, Veröffentlichungen der Historischen Kommission für Hessen (Publications of the Historical Commission of Hesse) 61 (Marburg: N. G. Elwert Verlag, 1997), 481–512, appendix 2, 510.

And as much as for you is possible, for you to come here again, so that I can escape this great sorrow and that I will not be separated from my children and chased away, which, as you already know well, the mayor is already talking about. And I wish you all the best.

DONE, THE 17TH DAY OF JULY, ANNO 1625

27

BARBARA CAUTZNER FROM WITZENHAUSEN

Letter to Her "Dear Husband"

ca. 1625

Address on the outside of [undated] letter:

To be delivered to my dear husband Hans Cautzner

My entirely willing obedience first and always to you, most dearest husband.

Your letter I received and had read to me. But the schoolmistress had opened the letter before I received it. You can certainly remember that you said to me that you would come back to me again, as soon as you could take your leave. So don't stay away too long and don't leave me sitting here like an owl among the birds.[1] Our son Hans Martin has had the pox. All your good friends send their greetings. From Junckmann[2] I have received no letter. Regarding us, we are still entirely unharmed and healthy. God bless.

WITZENHAUSEN, YOUR HOUSEWIFE.

[1] A contemporary idiom based on an image of the owl as an immovable, elderly loner among the society of fluttering birds. Cautzner uses it here to convey the idea that people in her small hometown regarded her as the odd one out in her husbandless state.

[2] An acquaintance of her husband from whom he was apparently expecting a letter.

From Fritz Wolff, "Feldpostbriefe aus dem Dreißigjährigen Kriege: Selbstzeugnisse der kleinen Leute" ("Military Mail from the Thirty Years War: Ego-Documents from Common Folk"), in *Hundert Jahre Historische Kommission für Hessen, 1897–1997* (*One Hundred Years of the Historical Commission of Hesse, 1897–1997*), ed. Walter Heinemeyer, Veröffentlichungen der Historischen Kommission für Hessen (Publications of the Historical Commission of Hesse) 61 (Marburg: N. G. Elwert Verlag, 1997), 481–512, appendix 2, 512.

28

MICHAEL KRAFFT

Letter to His "Precious"

1625

Address on the outside of letter:

This letter is sent to the honorable and virtuous maid Anna N., Resident in Fambach.

Allendorf in the Gulcherlandt[1] [*sic*], written anno 1625

First my friendly greeting and all my love and all the best, dear Precious. I couldn't fail to write to you and to let you know that I am still unharmed and healthy. To hear the same from you would be a real joy. Dear Precious, I ask that you pick up five hundred hoof nails from my landlord in Schmalkalden and send them to me with the courier carrying this letter when he comes back to us again in three weeks. Also ask my landlord about the elk skin, whether it is ready [tanned]. Could you please pay for it and keep it there. Somebody told me, with certainty, that Fambach has been plundered. If this is right, then I am truly sorry. I ask you, dear Precious, to write to me again at the earliest opportunity, whether this is true or not. My greetings to your mother and also everybody else and one thousand times to you.

Your obedient and goodwilled
MICHELL [MICHAEL] GRAFFT [KRAFFT]

[1] *Gulcherland* was a contemporary term for the Duchy of Jülich. Allendorf referred to the village of Altendorf near the small town of Radevormwald, near Cologne.

From Fritz Wolff, "Feldpostbriefe aus dem Dreißigjährigen Kriege: Selbstzeugnisse der kleinen Leute" ("Military Mail from the Thirty Years War: Ego-Documents from Common Folk"), in *Hundert Jahre Historische Kommission für Hessen, 1897–1997* (*One Hundred Years of the Historical Commission of Hesse, 1897–1997*), ed. Walter Heinemeyer, Veröffentlichungen der Historischen Kommission für Hessen (Publications of the Historical Commission of Hesse) 61 (Marburg: N. G. Elwert Verlag, 1997), 481–512, appendix 2, 509.

4

"War Nourishes War": Contributions, Robbery, and Plunder

"If for the soldier the war was in the last analysis his livelihood, the civilian was ultimately the paymaster."[1] With this sentence, historian Geoff Mortimer captures a dynamic that lasted throughout the Thirty Years War and transformed the domain of everyday civilian life. The larger the mercenary armies became during the course of the war, the less capable either side was of marshaling and funding them through normal methods, such as taxes. The financial and organizational resources of the early modern state proved to be far too limited to meet the requirements of a war this long and intense.[2] Thus the warring parties and their militaries were in continuous need of money, and they had to fall back on new financial instruments and ways of recruiting. Increasingly, they delegated the responsibility to recruit troops and raise money to contractors and subcontractors. These military entrepreneurs, or enterprisers, raised money using their own credit to recruit troops. They received in compensation for their service not only the privilege of command but also the privilege of collecting taxes in the areas they occupied, in order to finance the costs of their armies.[3] "War nourishes war"—a phrase attributed to the most powerful commander on the imperial side, Albrecht von Wallenstein, Duke of Friedland—aptly characterizes the practice of local and regional taxation and appropriation by the armies of the Thirty Years War. They forced the populations in occupied

[1] Geoff Mortimer, *Eyewitness Accounts of the Thirty Years War, 1618–48* (Basingstoke, U.K.: Palgrave, 2002), 45.

[2] See especially Ronald G. Asch, "State Finance and the Structure of Warfare," in *The Thirty Years War: The Holy Roman Empire and Europe, 1618–1648* (New York: St. Martin's Press, 1997), 150–84; and Thomas A. Brady, "The Thirty Years War," in *German Histories in the Age of Reformations, 1400–1650* (Cambridge, U.K.: Cambridge University Press, 2009), 375–404.

[3] Regarding military enterprisers, see Fritz Redlich, *The German Military Enterpriser and His Work Force: A Study in European Economic and Social History*, 2 vols. (Wiesbaden: F. Steiner, 1964–1965).

territories to pay the costs of their lodging and their military campaigns, without differentiating between friend and enemy.

This chapter focuses on the unprecedented financial burdens that the war placed on civilians caught up in the seemingly endless conflict. It begins with the subject of so-called contributions, the taxlike payments (in cash, but also in kind) imposed to defray military costs. Military leaders negotiated these contributions with local or regional civilian authorities. Individual households were then assessed a portion of the total payment. However, these payments were only part of the financial burden that civilians shouldered. The cost of quartering individual soldiers was also apportioned to civilian households, and frequently the expense of housing and supplying soldiers led to contention and, ultimately, violence. Remarkable, too, were the extra contributions that were regularly required from Jewish communities. Jews found themselves discriminated against not only by the military but also by their neighbors in the towns or settlements where they lived. Christian authorities did not offer them protection against discrimination. On the contrary, as Document 32 makes clear, they often collaborated with occupying armies to allow the additional exploitation of the Jews.

Whether they were indirectly or openly extorted, contributions and quartering were only part of a broad spectrum of practices that shifted the costs of making war to civilians. At the other end of this spectrum of forceful taxation and appropriation were more irregular forms of violence, practiced especially by smaller units that operated outside the control of their military superiors. Though illegal, these actions were nonetheless widely practiced and often condoned by the military leaders or even justified as legitimate. They included the taking of persons as hostages for ransom, the extortion of plunder from civilians in a newly occupied town or rural district, and open acts of looting and robbery. In extreme cases, especially when soldiers suffered under chronic shortages of food and supplies, as during the final stage of the war, acts of violence and plundering erupted even between military units of the same army.

29

JOHANN GEORG MAUL

The Burden of Contributions on a City and on a Household

1637

These entries from the diary of Johann Georg Maul, a lawyer and state official living in the Saxon city of Naumburg, make clear the burden of contributions borne by one household. Naumburg was occupied by Swedish troops under Field Marshal Johann Baner during the last phase of the Thirty Years War.[1] *During this later period of the war, money and goods were scarce, and the competition for resources between the military and civilian populations was intense—thus the critical tone that Maul uses in his diary to characterize the behavior of the soldier's family quartered in his home.*

Maul's diary was formatted like a household account book. He painstakingly listed in the following entry for the period from January 1637 to February 7 all the expenses that his bourgeois household had to pay in connection with the military occupation of his city. These included not only the specific expenditures associated with the quartering of a soldier's family in his house but also the more general burden of the contribution, which he had to pay in cash as his household's portion of the entire city's contribution.

Anno 1637

At the beginning of this year the Swedish general Baner was here again [in this region]. He again assigned our good city 24,000 florins for the

[1] Johann Baner (1596–1641) became a Swedish officer in 1614 and worked his way up through the ranks until he was ultimately promoted to field marshal in 1633.

From Gottfried Staffel, Justinianus Wolff, and Justinus Heinrich Wolff, *Notabilia: Naumburger Denkwürdigkeiten aus dem 17. Jahrhundert 1608–1623, 1680–1683, 1695–1702, ergänzt um Johann Georg Mauls Diarium 1631–1645* (*Notabilia: Memorable Events from Naumburg from the Seventeenth Century, 1608–1623, 1680–1683, 1695–1702, Complemented with Johann Georg Maul's Diary, 1631–1645*), ed. Siegfried Wagner and Karl-Heinz Wünsch (Naumburg: Uder Verlag, 2005), 118.

arson prevention assessment[2] and turned over the occupation and the collection of the money to Colonel Zabeltitz.[3] I received as quartering in my house his regimental judge, Johann Magitius, with his wife, two children, one maid, one servant, and a boy. This was a godless devil's pack. The man was Calvinist, the woman Catholic. They led such an epicurean lifestyle that it is impossible to describe it. They invited similar godless people as guests. They ate, drank, and whored day and night, so that the food alone cost me 9 florins, according to my food register's account. Additionally I was forced to give away a golden chain, which I had given to my wife and she had sewn into her dress. I had to cut it out and give it to them. Also, because the wife of the regimental judge gave birth to twins, I had to arrange for the baptism festivity, which cost me 18 florins and 12 groschen. In addition as extra expenses:

45 f - g[4] wine from Johann Hasenscharten, for 4 groschen
21 f - g for 3 kegs of beer[5]
- f 20 g for 5 jugs of vinegar[6]
- f 12 g for 2 pounds of olive oil
12 f - g for 4 cords of wood
3 f - g for one cartload of hay
22 f 12 g for 2½ bushels of oats[7]
1 f 18 g for 1½ ss [unknown measure] straw
- f 12 g for ¼ [unknown measure] wheat flour
2 f - g for 2 hats of sugar[8]
1 f - g for 2 soles [fish]
4 f - g for 4 hams
2 f 12 g for 10 pieces of smoked meat
- f 12 g for 3 smoked sausages
1 f 12 g for meat to take along
All in all 146 f 2 g for the 10th quartering.

[2] In German, *Brandschatzung*. Residents paid this assessment to prevent arson and plunder.

[3] Baron Friedrich von Zabeltitz, a Swedish general.

[4] In this document, "f" is the abbreviation for florin (gulden), "g" for groschen, and "d" for pfennig.

[5] One keg equaled 420 jugs, or approximately 104 gallons (392 liters).

[6] One jug equaled approximately 1 quart (0.9 liter).

[7] One bushel equaled approximately 184¼ gallons (695 liters).

[8] A hat of sugar was a large piece of crystallized sugar formed into a cone in the production process.

Additional Costs

114 f - g - d for the contribution as my household's part of the 24,000 florins for the whole city. Above and beyond that, the honorable council demanded in an assessment an additional 56 f 7 g 6 d contribution for my two leased houses, so 34 [f] 16½ g for the house in the Marien alley and 20 f 12 g for Martin Seyfarth's house, which I had to pay in silver pieces.

30

THOMAS SCHMIDT

Contribution Arrangement for the City of Wernigerode

1626

Thomas Schmidt served as councilman, mayor, and cantor in the city of Wernigerode in the Harz region. He maintained a diary in which he carefully noted the burdens of forced contributions to foreign troops during the frequent occupations of his hometown. The following excerpt concerns the agreement between city officials and the commander of the imperial troops made on August 3–4, 1626, an agreement in which Schmidt, then mayor, was personally involved. Especially noteworthy is the stark difference between the ample supplies for the commander and the scanty provisions for his soldiers.

The 3rd [of August 1626] Mayor Smith and the chancellor were taken by musketeers to the palace and brought to the imperial colonel. He [the imperial colonel] demanded that each and every soldier be provided with a sheet, a sack filled with straw, one pillow, and a rug as a cover; this was granted to him.

From [Thomas Schmidt], "Bruchstücke aus der Geschichte des Vaterlandes: Schicksale Wernigerode's während des dreissigjährigen Krieges" ("Fragments from the History of the Fatherland: The Fate of Wernigerode during the Thirty Years War"), ed. Christian Heinrich Delius, *Wernigerödisches gemeinnütziges Wochen=Blatt: Zum Besten des Waysenhauses* (*Wernigerode Public Weekly Paper: For the Benefit of the Orphanage*), April 24, 1809, 65–66. Many thanks for this reference to Uwe Lagatz (Wernigerode).

The 4th [of August 1626] an honorable councilman, the Six Men,[1] and a committee[2] were called to the palace. They agreed to what the colonel wanted and desired to have provided weekly, and daily, for the maintenance of his person and his table. These were:

Daily two jugs of wine[3]	weekly 14 tlr. [talers]
One keg of beer, from Zerbst or Torgau[4]	8 "
For 6 riding horses, 3 bushels of oats, or 12 groschen[5]	21 "
For 8 wagon horses, 3 bushels of oats	21 "
2 cartloads of straw (hay comes extra from elsewhere)	4 "
2 bushels of wheat[6]	2 "
2 rams, which have to be fat	3 "
Per week, one whole cow	15 "
Also, what could be gotten regarding fish, geese, doves, hens, and eggs	10 "
Also, the necessary spices	5 "
Also, salt, butter, and cheese	2 "
	Total 105 tlr.

There were also 130 soldiers. They had to be provided daily, each and every one, 2 pounds of meat, which amounted to 260 pounds altogether per day, which was 1,820 pounds altogether per week. Also 1¼ pounds of bread, daily, so 1,085 pounds per week. Also, a keg of beer daily, but this would prove not to be sufficient, anyway. Also, half a bushel of salt. Also, candles, onions, turnips, and so on as needed.

[1] This body was created from the members of the city council as a check on the power of the patricians in the city government.

[2] The committee was composed of directly elected representatives of the citizens.

[3] One jug equaled approximately 1 quart (0.9 liter).

[4] One keg equaled about 420 jugs, or 104 gallons (392 liters). The beer from Zerbst and Torgau, areas of Saxony, was known for its high quality, and it was more expensive than local beer.

[5] One bushel equaled approximately 9.4 gallons (36 liters). A bushel of oats weighed about 122 pounds (55 kilograms).

[6] A bushel of wheat weighed about 77 pounds (35 kilograms).

31

JOHANN GEORG PFORR

Paying Contributions and Expressing Animosity toward Jews

1636 and 1638

These passages from Johann Georg Pforr's chronicle of his hometown, Schmalkalden in Thuringia, are significant for two reasons. First, they describe the enforcement of an extraordinary contribution to the foreign Hessian ruler (the landgrave of Hesse-Darmstadt) who occupied Schmalkalden at the time.[1] *Second, they explicitly describe the extra financial burdens placed on the Jews there. Pforr, a Lutheran, was a member of the town council and hence among the elite of Schmalkalden's officeholders. He addresses the animosity toward Jews among council members and citizens alike, both of whom blamed the Jews for the town's financial woes and therefore wanted to expel them. Pforr also mentions that the landgrave of Hesse-Darmstadt did not respond positively to the town authorities' plea to expel the Jews. On the contrary, the ruler and his officials unequivocally warned the inhabitants of Schmalkalden not to attack the Jews. He cited the example of the citizens of Frankfurt, who some years before had revolted against their government in the Fettmilch Uprising (1612–1616) and at its culmination, in 1614, had plundered the Jewish ghetto and temporarily expelled the Jewish population.*

[Year 1636]

The 15th of September [1636] the officials here issued to the entire citizenry a very pointed order from His Princely Highness Count Georg.[2] The substance was that the city and district of Schmalkalden should

[1] Since 1589, Schmalkalden and the surrounding county of Henneberg had been part of the landgraviate Hesse-Kassel, but from 1636 to 1638 Henneberg was temporarily occupied by troops and officials from a rival dynasty, the landgraves of Hesse-Darmstadt, who were allies of the emperor.

[2] Count George II of Hesse-Darmstadt (r. 1626–1661), a Catholic imperial ally.

From Johann Georg Pforr, *Beschreibung etzlicher denckwürdigen Geschichden: Eine Chronik von Schmalkalden, 1400–1680* (*Description of Some Memorable Stories: A Chronicle from Schmalkalden, 1400–1680*), ed. Renate T. Wagner (Jena: Stitzius Verlag, 2008), 139, 147.

pay to his Princely Highness 10,000 talers within two months without any argument, and that if anyone protested, complained, or said it was impossible, he should be prosecuted and severely punished. Because nobody was allowed to gripe about it, in the city 4 talers were assessed for every hundred in property [i.e., 4 percent of the assessed tax value], which the Jews also paid, as well as having to pay another 5 talers for the Jewish head tax.

[. . .]

At this time the mayor and council and the citizenry humbly petitioned Count Georg to expel the Jews from here, because of their great usury and extortion. However, they received a negative answer, because the prince cannot do without them, with the reprimand that this petition may have been instigated by the clergy, and they should therefore be careful that here no [anti-Jewish] riot breaks out like in Frankfurt.

[Year 1638]

And after many foreign Jews took refuge here with the local resident Jews for several years without the required letters of permission, they were fined 500 gold florins. The money, according to common rumor, was kept by the aforementioned envoys, sent by the Count of Hesse-Darmstadt.

32

A Complaint from Three Jewish Heads of Household

1624

Three Jewish heads of households acting as representatives for the Jews of the town of Dülmen submitted this petition to their superior, the archbishop and elector of Cologne. The petition makes clear that Jewish households were in excessive and disproportional ways exposed to the quartering of soldiers in their homes and to the payment of financial

Leopold Schütte, ed., *Der Dreißigjährige Krieg und der Alltag in Westfalen: Quellen aus dem Staatsarchiv Münster* (*The Thirty Years War and the Everyday in Westphalia: Sources from the Münster City Archive*) (Münster: Nordrhein-Westfälisches Staatsarchiv, 1998), 166–67.

contributions above and beyond those of Christian households. Further, it criticizes the lack of protection the Jews of Dülmen received from town authorities in confronting demands by the military. It also touches on the religious sphere by criticizing the military's lack of respect for the Sabbath and the absence of any help from town authorities in this regard.

It began last year, on February 12, 1623, when the soldiers from Anhalt, namely Colonel Bock with his company of cavalry and Ferdinand Roqui with his company of infantry, entered Dülmen. All three of us, the undersigned Jews, first appealed to the high bailiff as well as the mayor and city councilors of Dülmen that we not be burdened with quartering soldiers. We wanted very much to pay contributions to the council, and we offered to be wholly obedient in this respect. Despite this, three cavalrymen were quartered with Isaac, two cavalrymen with Moses, and two musketeers with Samuel; furthermore, each in addition to the quartering had to pay a [monetary] contribution to Colonels Bock and Roqui. And although we have often appealed as a group and as individuals to the city authorities with crying eyes and asked that our complaints of the excessively large quartering be addressed, every time we have received a dismissive reply, and we were once again referred to the aforementioned colonels, with whom we should seek some accord. Therefore all of us had to get along with them, but we were also pressured to do favors for the quartermaster and the supply officers.

And just when we thought that with such agreed-upon contracts we would be left in peace, then four weeks long before his final decampment Colonel Bock sent three horses to the house of Isaac on our Sabbath day, about which I immediately complained to the gracious authorities and asked for help but received none. Rather I was again referred to the colonel with the reply that he, Isaac, was responsible for quartering the colonel, and so he must deal with him: The mayor and the council could do nothing for him. So he, Isaac, had to deal with the colonel in the presence of the electoral bailiff of Dülmen. After his decampment, when Licutenant Colonel Eckstätt returned to Dülmen on horse, all three of us Jews and besides us also Jobst, Johann, and Bernt von Marle were ordered to quarter the colonel, and therefore we again appealed to the gracious authorities to withdraw this additional quartering, with the argument that we had neither hay, nor oats, nor other appropriate supplies, but that otherwise we really wanted to pay contributions. We received this answer, that the mayor and the council could not help us regarding such orders, much less ameliorate them, because the colonel wanted us Jews all for himself, and even wanted more of us. Therefore we had to deal with the colonel and gave him a great deal, because we thought that he would remain with his company for a long time in Dülmen, although he moved away in the fifth week thereafter. But because after his departure Lieutenant Bönninghausen remained with his infantry, we had to deal with him the same way, and so from the beginning of the occupation on we have been onerously quartered upon and greatly burdened, so that we therefore reasonably should not have been further molested.

Nevertheless it happened that after the eldest mayor Kortendiek and various other town councilors passed away in the meantime, the current council ordered us to be subjected to and burdened with new contributions, and therefore they had goods seized from us, under the pretext that our outlays and previous contributions were not sufficient. Indeed we unfortunately could not do anything different, even if we always would have much preferred to pay contributions directly to the council than to the aforementioned colonels. But even when we offered as much, as mentioned above, we were not allowed to, as the billets [receipts from the quartering] prove, which we could present if necessary and of which quite a number of councilors will surely have good knowledge.

As additional proof that after quartering three different commands we were in no way spared, it is undeniable that especially on last Sunday, which was the 15th of June, not more than seventy soldiers were quartered in the city, which was fewer than before, but all three of us and every one of us Jews got a soldier to quarter, although the city, as is known, is several hundred citizens and houses. This was all ordered by the high bailiff and the treasurer on Friday, the 22nd of June. Additionally it was ordered that under penalty of punishment the demanded contribution, which would amount to nearly 700 talers, must be delivered in cash to the honorable council within four days, and it was forbidden, under penalty of punishment, to appeal to Your Highness or the councilors regarding this, which seemed very strange to us, the more so because we could not get any support from the authorities regarding the aforementioned heavy contributions. So we hope that Your Highness will graciously listen to us poor defenseless Jews and our case and grant us a helping hand according to the enclosed written order of 30 May.[1]

[1] This probably refers to a letter of protection issued earlier by the archbishop and elector of Cologne on behalf of the Jews of Dülmen. Such letters were issued in return for considerable payments by those they claimed to protect, but they were often not enforced.

Postscript by the editors:

One year later, on June 29, 1625, after a renewed supplication by the Jews of Dülmen, the archbishop and elector of Cologne issued an order that special taxes were not to be demanded from the Jews there.

33

PETER HAGENDORF

A Soldier's Fortunes: Everyday Life and Surviving the War

1627–1630

The unique diary of the soldier Peter Hagendorf (see Document 18) affords us a look into the everyday life of a common soldier in the Thirty Years War. Often accompanied by his wife and those few of his children who survived the war, Hagendorf constantly struggled to eke out a living in precarious situations in which abundance could quickly be followed by hunger and destitution. These everyday concerns about food, shelter, and illness were punctuated relatively rarely by participation in battles or other violent mass actions. In this excerpt, Hagendorf describes his movements during the war not as moving from battle to battle but rather as moving from quarter to quarter.

On the third of April in this year 1627 I enlisted as a lance corporal with Pappenheim's regiment in Ulm, because I was totally destitute. From there we moved to the review ground, in the duchy of Baden. There we lay in quarters, eating and drinking, and it was good.

Eight days after Pentecost, on the holiday of the Holy Trinity, I married the honorable Anna Stadlerin from Traunstein in Bavaria.

On the feast day of St. John we struck our colors and marched to Rheinbischofsheim. Here we embarked with the entire regiment in ships and

---

From Peter Hagendorf, *Tagebuch eines Söldners aus dem Dreißigjährigen Krieg* (*Diary of a Mercenary from the Thirty Years War*), ed. Jan Peters, 2nd rev. ed. (Göttingen: V & R Unipress, 2012), 102–4.

sailed to Oppenheim, where we disembarked. But under way one ship ran aground and broke apart, and some were drowned.

From Oppenheim to Frankfurt, through the Wetterau and Westphalia to Wolfenbüttel in the county of Braunschweig. We laid siege there and built entrenchments and dammed the river to flood the city, so that finally they had to give up. My wife was sick during the entire siege, the eighteen weeks that we were there. On Christmas Eve 1627 they [the enemy] pulled out, but mostly they enlisted again [in our regiment].[1]

A support of two hundred men or so came from the Altmark to transport the sick and wounded. I sent my wife with them, too. Then we moved to the Altmark. Our headquarters was at Gardelegen. Our captain, Hans Heinrich Kelman, was encamped with his company at Salzwedel.

Here I got sick and the wife got healthy again. I was laid out for three weeks. Four weeks after my illness we were ordered to Stade, near Hamburg. So I was ordered along.

Then my wife was laid low, but the child was not yet ready to be born and died quickly. God grant him a happy resurrection.

+ 1. Was a young son.[2]

We were encamped in front of Stade. On Good Friday we had enough bread and meat, and on Holy Easter we could not get a mouthful of bread. As they [the enemy troops] now pulled out in 1628, we went in and were again in our quarters for the summer.

Afterward we went with our company to Stendal, where we also had good quarters. In 1629 First Lieutenant Gonzaga, Prince of Mantua, took 2,000 men from the regiment (because the regiment had grown 3,500 men strong) and went to Pomerania and encamped us at Stralsund. But they would have shown us the way[3] if we had stayed one more day. The baggage had to be left in quarters.

[1] Hagendorf is referring here to the siege of the strongly fortified city of Wolfenbüttel during the second half of 1627 and to the final capitulation of the Danish troops, who had garrisoned the city. Some of these troops immediately enlisted in Hagendorf's regiment, that is, with their former enemy.

[2] All through his diary, Hagendorf carefully notes the births and deaths of his nine children from two marriages. Of these nine children, only two survived. Remarkably, he numbers only the children who died, not those who survived, and he started this numbering anew for each marriage.

[3] Hagendorf is using a figurative expression here, implying that he and his fellow soldiers would have been thrown out by force, if they had tried to stay in the town much longer.

This time, while I was away, my wife was again blessed with a young daughter. She was baptized during my absence, Anna Maria. She also died while I was away. + 2. God grant her a happy resurrection.

From Stralsund we went in two ships up the river, which is called the Swine, to the area of the Kaschuben [Wends]. It is a wild land but effective in raising all sorts of cattle.

Here we did not want to eat any more beef, rather it had to be goose, duck, or chicken. Where we camped overnight, the host had to give everybody a half taler, but he gave gladly, because we were satisfied with him and left his cattle in peace.

So we were sent back and forth with 2,000 men, every day a new quarters, seven weeks long. At Neustettin we stayed for two days. Here the officers supplied themselves well with cows, horses, and sheep, because there was plenty of everything.

From there we went to Spandau, which was a narrow pass that did not let more than one company through at a time. As we were again in the Mark and reached our quarters there, shortly thereafter in 1629, along with the entire regiment, [we] broke camp and moved into the Wetterau.

Wiesbaden, near Frankfurt, was the headquarters of Count Pappenheim. Our captain, with the company, was encamped on the Vogelsberg.[4] The captain himself camped in the town of Lauterbach, the company in the countryside. Here we again had good quarters, for twenty weeks.

Here my wife was again honored with a young daughter, who was baptized Elisabeth.

After twenty weeks we broke camp and moved to Westphalia. Our quarters were in Lippstadt; we stayed there for the winter. In this country there are large, strong people, men and women, and a fruitful land and much livestock. In the countryside there's almost exclusively unit farms: They have their own fields, woods, and meadows, everything near the house.

In Lippstadt there's good "old beer"[5] and also bad people. I saw them burn seven [people]. Among them was even a beautiful maiden of eighteen years, but she was burned.[6]

[4] A mountain region in Northern Hesse.

[5] Hagendorf is referring to fermented dark beer, which remains today a specialty in Westphalia and the Rhineland.

[6] He refers here to the burning of people who were accused of being witches.

In this country they bake square loaves of bread that are as big as a grinding stone. The bread has to stay in the oven twenty-four hours. They call it pumpernickel. It's good and tasty bread, totally black.

In the year 1630 we broke camp and moved to Paderborn. Lippstadt is located on a navigable river, called the Lippe. Went from Paderborn to Niedermarsberg, which is located on a high mountain. To Goslar in the Harz [Mountains] and to Magdeburg.

34

VOLKMAR HAPPE

"Wolf Devours Wolf"

1639

In this excerpt from Volkmar Happe's chronicle (see Document 17), the court councilor at Sondershausen describes one band of soldiers from the Swedish army preying on another band of their supposed comrades. The passage provides insight into the unclear local and regional lines of conflict typical during the Swedish-French phase, the last stage of the Thirty Years War. However, it also shows a certain scope of action for the civil authorities in these situations, an opportunity of which Happe was aware and which he used to protect the interests of the local population.

The 12th of July [1639] some Swedish horsemen from Erfurt, who now and again were stationed as *salvaguardia* [paid guards] in the county of Schwarzburg, banded together and stole a horse from the pastor of Holzengel, another horse from the pastor of Trebra, and a third horse from a peasant there, too. As they came with their stolen goods through the village of Kirchengel by the brickworks, they were stopped by twenty or

From Volkmar Happe, *Chronicon Thuringiae (Thuringian Chronicle)*, ed. Hans Medick, Norbert Winnige, and Andreas Bähr (electronic publication: Thüringer Universitäts- und Landesbibliothek Jena, 2008), 2:274r–75v. Available as a digital facsimile at www.mdsz.thulb.uni-jena.de/happe/quelle.php.

so horsemen from Königsmarck's regiment.[1] They attacked the horsemen from Erfurt, and they took not only the stolen horses but also the soldiers' own horses, and they left them [the soldiers] to go on foot. So one wolf devoured the other. The Erfurt horsemen came here to Sondershausen on foot, and the pastors from Holzengel and Trebra pursued them and accused them here at the chancellery. Because we had them all arrested and found them guilty of the theft, they promised to get the stolen horses back or to pay for them. In the meantime news arrived that Königsmarck's horsemen had taken an entire herd of sheep from Heringen and that they were headed to Jena. I knew that this way was impassable. So the Erfurt horsemen, in their turn, set out with some of our citizens to chase after the horses and the livestock. That night they found them near Rockensußra[2] and attacked them, and they took everything and brought some of them [the Königsmarck horsemen] back here as prisoners.

[1] Hans Christoffer von Königsmarck (1600–1653) worked his way up the ranks to become a Swedish colonel. He was ultimately promoted to field marshal and elevated to count.

[2] A village approximately 35 miles (56 km) northwest of Erfurt.

5
Scourges of War: Plague, Starvation, and Cannibalism

Of all the soldiers and civilians who died during the Thirty Years War, only a small portion were killed through direct military violence. A greater portion died from contagious diseases, primarily in epidemics of the plague but also of typhus and other diseases, or from hunger or malnutrition. Historian Peter Wilson analyzed countless individual research studies and concluded that for soldiers in the war, "disease proved more potent than muskets, swords and cannon. . . . It is likely that three men died of disease for every one killed in action, suggesting that up to 1.8 million soldiers died during the war."[1]

What about the civilian population? Here, too, demographic analysis offers a means of determining an approximation of the incidence of death in the war. For the entire Holy Roman Empire, a loss of five million civilians, or 20 percent of the population in 1618, is estimated. Of course, the population decrease would have been less than this average in regions that were spared the direct impact of the war, such as northern Germany, but far higher in regions that were hit hard by the war, such as Brandenburg, Thuringia, Saxony, Württemberg, Bavaria, and the Palatinate. Even in the areas with the greatest losses, disease and hunger always resulted in more deaths than did actual military violence. Disease and hunger often followed in the wake of armies, whether they were occupying an area or just passing through. This was especially devastating along marching and campaigning routes, because here the soldiers often fell upon defenseless villages and smaller towns, more so than the larger cities.

The people who wrote the documents collected in this chapter did not argue along the lines of calculated averages or demographic statistics. The intensity of their accounts is explained by their direct observations

[1]Peter H. Wilson, "The Human and Material Cost," in *Europe's Tragedy: A History of the Thirty Years War* (London: Allen Lane, 2009), 790–91.

of the events described. From the fatalistic reflections of the village pastor Johann Daniel Minck regarding the plague (Document 35), to the calm and distanced travel journal of the English diplomat William Crowne describing the widespread devastation, disease, and hunger in Germany (Document 36), to the report of the Bavarian abbot Maurus Friesenegger about a famine that drove soldiers and peasants to battle in his cloister (Document 37), all portray how people suffered appallingly from the scourges of war and how they coped.

The most desperate way of coping with famine was consuming the corpses of friends and family, as described in the report of the horrified priest Michael Lebhardt (Document 38). This account makes it clear that cannibalism was a real, albeit extreme, means of survival and a serious transgression of norms that contemporaries were forced—at least in exceptional cases—to confront.

35

JOHANN DANIEL MINCK

The Plague as the Scourge of God

1635

During the seventeenth century, epidemic diseases such as the plague were understood as the scourge of God, second only to war. The actual causes of the plague (bacteria) were unknown, and it was instead attributed to "miasma," or poisonous gas, which came out of the atmosphere. Even today in Central Europe, the term "foul air" is associated with anxiety and terror. Of all the plague epidemics of the Thirty Years War, which were primarily caused and spread by military campaigns and troop movements, those of the 1630s were the most deadly. Large sections of the civilian population died from these epidemics.

From *Südhessische Chroniken aus der Zeit des Dreißigjährigen Krieges* (*Southern Hessian Chronicles from the Thirty Years War*), ed. Rudolf Kunz and Willy Lizalek, *Sonderband der Geschichtsblätter des Kreises Bergstrasse* (*History Pages of the District of Bergstrasse, Special Volume*) 6 (Heppenheim: Verlag Laurissa, 1983), 254–55.

The chronicle of Johann Daniel Minck (1611–1644), the Protestant preacher in Bieberau in central Hesse, contains his firsthand impressions of the effects of the plague. Minck describes the mass death, the destabilization of everyday life, and the disruption of normal practices, especially the impossibility of burying the dead in the usual manner. At the same time, his chronicle allows a look at the preacher's belief system: like many of his contemporaries, he saw the plague as God's just punishment of sinful humanity.

Meanwhile, in addition to the soldiers as scourge of war, God sent the plague after us. It already started at the beginning of the 1,635th year as a general weakness, from which many died. In the spring of the same year, as the heat began to build up, the poison increased massively and the disease changed to a poisonous pestilence, from which the people quickly fell in such masses that one could not bury them. Thus was fulfilled Leviticus 26:25. ["And I will bring the sword upon you to avenge the breaking of the covenant. When you withdraw into your cities, I will send a plague among you, and you will be given into enemy hands."]

Because, as mentioned above, Lichtenberg was so full of people [in flight] that many had to sleep outside, many headed for home, because they wanted to die under their own roofs. However, there they were not safe from the robbers, who threw the sick out of their beds, searched them, and even tortured the sick, thinking that they could find some money or bread.

Many died in the open countryside, so that nobody knew anything about them, and therefore very many lay unburied for a very long time, so that they were totally decomposed and full of worms. Often the sick lay by the dead in one bed. I myself heard a sick girl at the school in Umstadt pitifully screaming and yelling and bewailing about the worms which crawled onto her from her dead mother. Therefore I arranged with the magistrate to have the mother buried. After this happened, people—who they were, I do not know—left dead bodies in front of the door to my schoolhouse. If I wanted to have them removed, I had to have them buried.

It was the same situation in the entire district of Lichtenberg, not to mention other areas of the land; therefore special grave diggers were requested by the authorities. Among them was Hans Weiss from Bieberau, still alive. They had to go to the villages now and again to look for and bury the dead. They found some [bodies] that were so decomposed that they had to drag them to the hole with hoes. Some had been torn up by dogs and were unrecognizable, in accordance with the wise saying of Jeremiah 15:3. ["I will send four kinds of destroyers against them, declares the Lord, the sword to kill and the dogs to drag away and the birds of the air and the beasts of the earth to devour and destroy."]

[. . .]

They made great holes, threw eight, ten, or twelve and fifteen in a hole, without a single coffin, without any ringing or singing.[1] Relatively few were brought to the proper graveyard; rather, because of the great danger in Hausen and Lichtenberg, they were simply buried in masses on the hills, in fields, pastures, vineyards, and gardens, especially toward the bulwark next to the donkey path, including two preachers who had fled from Erbach.[2] And even Görg Uloth, tax collector of Lichtenberg, could not bring his dear old mother to Bieberau to the graveyard, and instead had her buried in the flower bed next to his winepress.

And there came down from the air so much poison that everybody thought that no one would survive it; therefore such pestilence was no longer feared by anyone, because everyone gave up hope of living.

[1] "Ringing and singing" (*Klang und Gesang*) is a German phrase used here to refer to the ringing of church bells and the singing of church music as fundamental elements of an honorable burial.

[2] Hausen is part of Anspach, approximately 31 miles (50 km) north of Darmstadt. Erbach is approximately 18½ miles (30 km) southeast of Darmstadt.

36

WILLIAM CROWNE

War, Plague, Devastation, and Danger: Traveling in Germany during the Thirty Years War

1636

William Crowne was part of the entourage of Thomas Howard, the Earl of Arundel, who in 1636 was sent as a special envoy by King Charles I of England to Emperor Ferdinand II in Vienna. The earl's task was to negotiate the restitution of the family of the deposed and deceased Winter King, Frederick V of Bohemia and elector of the Palatinate (1596–1632), and his wife, Elizabeth Stuart (Charles's sister), to the succession in the Palatine. In connection with this negotiation, he was also charged with seeking an end to the ongoing war in the Holy Roman Empire. Crowne and the rest of the earl's sizable entourage journeyed over eight months all the way from the Netherlands across Central Europe and back. Along with lengthy descriptions of their ultimately unsuccessful diplomatic efforts, Crowne's travel journal includes details about the hazards of travel during the Thirty Years War. Crowne witnessed and described the widespread and appalling effects of plague, famine, and plundering, and he made repeated mention of the dangers posed by the armies on both sides—even the danger that his party would be mistaken for marauding troops.

Early next day we weighed anchor and sailed up the Rhine . . . to Wesel, a town on the left side of the Rhine, opposite which we cast anchor and stayed all night, for at this time more than thirty people a day were dying of the plague.

Originally appeared in Crowne, Wiliam [sic]. *A True Relation of All the Remarkable Places and Passages Observed in the Travels of the Right Honourable Thomas Lord Howard, Earle of Arundell and Surrey, Primer Earle, and Earle Marshall of England, Ambassadour Extraordinary to His Sacred Majesty Ferdinando the Second, Emperour of Germanie, anno Domini 1636.* London: Printed [by F. Kingston] for Henry Seile and are to be sold in Fleet-street at the signe of the Tygres-head betweene the bridge and the conduit, 1637. Reprinted in William Crowne, "The Diary," in *Connoisseur and Diplomat: The Earl of Arundel's Embassy to Germany in 1636 as recounted in William Crowne's Diary, the Earl's Letters and other contemporary sources with a catalogue of the topographical drawings made on the journey by Wenceslaus Hollar,* ed. Francis C. Springell (London: Maggs Bros., 1963), 55–62, 80, 86–89, 91–92.

Nevertheless, next morning we took eighteen wagons, displaying our English colours on three of them, and . . . came to Duisburg to dinner. . . .

At this place none of the travellers in our carriage could enter for, as His Excellency [Thomas Howard, Earl of Arundel] neared the gate, one of the watch discharged his musket right in front of the horse's breast and though his comrades were commanded to let us go forward, the gates of the town were by this time barred against us and we were kept outside the walls until such time as the townspeople were satisfied that we, with our carriages and large company, were not enemies.

After dinner we passed through an extensive wood in much danger of rogues who did not, however, attack us because of our large numbers. Yet, fearing attack, we sent to the next town for a convoy of musketeers who eventually met us, but not until we were clear of the wood.

From this point we entered into Bergischland and went by Kaiserswerth to Düsseldorf guarded by the Duke's[1] personal guard, a well-armed company of night [knights] and here was staying the Duke of Neuburg, at this very time walking with his Duchess. On our approach he quickly returned to the town and, thinking we were some enemy, gave orders that the gates were to be closed. Once he knew that it was His Excellency, however, he was overjoyed and sent his coaches with the invitation to His Excellency to come and have supper with him and to stay at his house as long as he remained in Düsseldorf. . . .

. . . We weighed anchor early and, passing Engers on the left, entered the district of Trierische Land and so Koblenz, a town adjoining the Rhine on the right, where the French had been recently driven out by the Emperor's forces into the Castle of Ehrenbreitstein, situated on a very high eminence opposite and overlooking the town. These forces were skirmishing when we arrived, consequently we cast anchor half a mile short of the town and sent a trumpeter to request a safe passage for us.

Passage was willingly granted, both sides interrupting the fight. The [imperial] general in the town, making preparation to entertain His Excellency, caused the gate to be opened in readiness for His Excellency's entrance, but the [French] forces in the castle [of Ehrenbreitstein] immediately fired a cannon to the great danger of the town defenders, who now took cover until His Excellency actually appeared at the gate. . . .

[1]Duke Wolfgang Wilhelm of Pfalz-Neuburg (1578–1653), who had succeeded at this time to the duchy of Jülich-Cleves and resided at Düsseldorf.

From here, on the left side we passed Kaub, which is the first town in the "Pfaltz."[2] So difficult are conditions here that poor people are found dead with grass in their mouths. . . .

Next we passed the fine town of Bingen on the right side and Ehrenfels Castle on the left, to Rüdesheim, a town on the left side of the Rhine into which I entered and saw poor people praying in a little old house where dead bones lay. Here His Excellency gave some relief to these poor wretches who were so starved that they struggled with one another for the food which he gave them. . . .

Then we came to Mainz, a great city built on the right side of the Rhine. Here we cast anchor and stayed aboard for there was no comfort to be had in the city, which had been badly damaged during its capture by the King of Sweden. It was in a pleasant corner house near the river that the King of Bohemia died[3] and here, likewise, the poor people were almost dying of starvation, those who had been able, before, to relieve the suffering of others now humbly begging for food and clothing for themselves. So violently did these poor people struggle when provisions were sent from our ship that some of them fell into the Rhine and were in danger of being drowned. . . .

From Cologne to Frankfurt all the towns, villages, and castles are battered, pillaged, and burnt and [during] every one of our halts we remained on board, every man taking his turn on guard duty. . . .

On Sunday, May 7, leaving the Main [River] on our left hand, we set off with our wagons, through the city and over two bridges which are always guarded by soldiers. And because of the dangers to travellers we took with us a convoy [escort] of [sixty] musketeers and passed by Offenbach and Seligenstadt, between our route and the Main, and through a great forest where we considered ourselves to be in considerable danger for we could hear the rapid discharge of the great guns at Hanau, less than three miles away, which the Swedes formerly captured and which was, at this time, besieged by the Emperor's forces.

. . . After passing through a wood, [we] came to a wretched little village called Neunkirchen [in Franconia], which we found quite uninhabited yet with one house on fire. Here, since it was late, we were obliged to stay all night, for the nearest town was four miles away; but we spent that night walking up and down with carbines [rifles] in our hands, and listening fearfully to the sound of shots in the woods around us. We did,

[2]Name for the Lower Palatinate—that is, the territory of the elector of the Palatinate.

[3]Crowne refers here to the deposed Winter King, who died at Mainz on November 29, 1632.

however, make use of some of the burning fragments of the house that was on fire for we used them to roast the meat that was prepared for His Excellency's supper.

Early next morning, His Excellency went to inspect the church and found that it had been plundered and that the pictures and the altar had been desecrated. In the churchyard we saw a dead body, scraped out of the grave, while outside the churchyard we found another dead body. Moreover, we entered many houses but found that all were empty. We hurried on from this unhappy place and learnt later that the villagers had fled on account of the plague and had set that particular house on fire in order to prevent travellers from catching the infection. . . .

Here [at Neustadt on the Aisch River], seeing wretched children sitting at their doors almost dying of hunger, His Excellency ordered that food and money should be given to their parents. Next we came to Emskirchen, a miserable village where we dined on food of our own for there was no food to be had there; and after dinner we passed a succession of pillaged and devastated villages and so entered Nüremberger-Land. . . .

Early next morning we set off, passing churches razed to the ground, and fearing attacks from Croats who lurked in the woods through which we passed, until we reached the wretched little village of Hemau which has been pillaged twenty-eight times in the space of two years and has been sacked twice in a single day. . . .

This day [August 29, 1636], after a widespread search, the corpses of His Excellency's Gentleman of Horse and his Trumpeter, together with the corpse of their guide, the Postmaster, were found. They had been barbarously murdered five days before, as they were returning to Regensburg, and their bodies were found tied to separate trees about pistol shot range from the highway, at a point within four miles of Nuremberg. It appeared that each must have witnessed the death agonies of his companions. The head of the Gentleman of the Horse had been shattered by a pistol shot, the Trumpeter's head had been cut off and the guide's head had been split open. . . .

After a stay of three days at Nuremberg, we left on the morning of Monday, November 14, with an escort of a hundred musketeers who accompanied us for five Dutch miles until we reached [Neustadt].

We ended our day's march travelling through woods by torchlight, then slept the remainder of that night on straw on the floor. The devastated town was inhabited by only five burghers, though in the days of peace there had been 250 or more. . . .

Leaving early next morning through hilly, wooded country, we passed through Külsheim and various other unfortunate villages, all of which had been burnt down and devastated. In the woods alongside our route we kept seeing bands of Croats who were pillaging and robbing the whole countryside; fortunately they made no attack on our company. On this day's journey, after travelling four Dutch miles, we rejoined our outward route at Neunkirchen, the village which I described earlier as being so burnt and devastated that only four or five poor people now live there. . . .

On the following morning, His Excellency went to Hanau to visit. . . . For a year and a half, Hanau endured all the hardship of a siege by the Emperor's forces, including a terrible plague from which 22,000 people died in the space of seven weeks, until it was finally relieved by the Land-Grave of Hesse, whose men slew a large number of Imperial troops and put the rest to flight. This was the fight which we heard taking place on our outward journey. . . .

Next morning we sailed down to Mainz where His Excellency went ashore to see if it were in a better state than it had been on our outward visit. Alas, it was in the same sorry state as before, with various poor wretches lying on dunghills, almost starved to death and scarcely able to crawl to receive alms from His Excellency. After returning to have dinner on our boat, we distributed the remnants of our meal to many poor, hunger-stricken people, then we sailed down the Rhine to Rüdesheim, five Dutch miles away, where we cast anchor and stayed for the night. . . .

. . . Farther down, we came to Bacharach where some of our company went ashore till a boat was sent to summon them back forthwith. To their surprise, our friends were pursued by five musketeers who kept firing shots at them but, by good fortune, failed to hit anyone. The pursuers kept up the chase until our companions reached His Excellency's boat, whereupon they pursued no further. . . .

During the night we remained in considerable danger for on either side of us were bands whose habit it was to rob and pillage all passers-by. Just before we cast anchor, we saw one such party of upwards of fifty men moving along the shore, and about ten o'clock of that very dark night, the watch raised the alarm that a party of men was coming against us. Immediately we rushed for our weapon[s], but were relieved to discover that only one boat was approaching and that those who manned it were calling out that they were friends from the Duke of Neuenburg. But for their shouts of explanation, we would have shot at them; as it was, they told us that some of their number wished to travel to England with our company. . . .

Below Nijmegen we passed, at regular intervals of half a league, a succession of redoubts [fortifications], each one manned by guards whose duty it was to patrol the river. From the fourth of these, four or five cannons were fired at us and only narrowly missed our boat—and this in spite of our having informed them that we carried an English ambassador. After this incident we cast anchor and lay in the middle of the Rhine but we were unable to discover with certainty who these people were who had fired at us.

37

MAURUS FRIESENEGGER

Hungry Peasants, Starving Soldiers

1633–1634

This excerpt from the diary of Maurus Friesenegger, abbot of Heiligenberg (see Document 12), describes with rare intensity the extreme famine in and around his monastery in the winter of 1633–1634. The imperial army was stationed across southern Germany, and a regiment of imperial troops had moved into winter quarters near Heiligenberg. At the same time, to escape from these very troops, a large part of the peasant population from the surrounding countryside had fled with their grain supplies and livestock to the apparent safety of the walled monastery. The grounds of the monastery itself became the stage for a bitter struggle over food. The desperately hungry soldiers and civilians literally fought over the last cow, the last pig, and the last of the grain supply. In this conflict, the legal and sacrosanct protection of the monastery's walls could not withstand the scourges of war.

After we had once more waited impatiently for the 23rd of December [1633] to arrive, when the Spaniards were expected to move on, we

From Maurus Friesenegger, *Tagebuch aus dem 30jährigen Krieg: Nach einer Handschrift im Kloster Andechs* (*Diary from the Thirty Years War: From a Manuscript in the Andechs Cloister*), ed. Willibald Mathäser (Munich: Allitera Verlag, 2007), 49–59, 60–72. The excerpts from the year 1633 here quoted with slight changes were first translated by Gerhard Benecke, ed., *Germany in the Thirty Years War* (New York: St. Martins Press, 1979), 66–67. The excerpts from the year 1634 were translated by John Mangum.

received orders that they would stay longer, since no winter quarters had been made ready for them. Heavens! Soldiers and peasants were now to be seen half-naked and pale with misery, emaciated with hunger, and walking about with bare feet in the great cold. What would happen in the long term? The soldiers were eating dogs, cats, and any stolen meat. For days on end the peasants had not even a crust of bread. Many searched our monastery garden for greens, winter lettuce, roots, and herbs, which they then ate raw or stewed. The army sent to Munich for provisions, and in the monastery we slaughtered the cattle and baked bread for as many people as possible. Bakers from as far afield as Diessen[1] as well as others also supplied us with bread. But what help was that against so many? There were 1,500 soldiers in the village, and inside the monastery the people from several other places, too. Since the suppliers of provisions were often robbed with violence of their money on the way and of their goods on their return journey, they soon gave up. So hunger increased to the utmost among the soldiers, and even the officers began to feel it, as hard cash no longer bought anything.

On 28 December those who were starving broke into the Church of Our Dear Lady in the village and climbed under the roof, removing the seed corn stored there for next spring. Thus disappeared the last hope of the peasants, besides the other things which they found.

On 30 December the troops of the foreign and Italian regiments mustered, and it proved to be quite a spectacle. There were half-filled companies of blackened and jaundiced faces, starved bodies, half-clothed or bedecked in rags and stolen women's clothing. It was the face of hunger and famine. Next to them the officers appeared well fed and elegantly dressed. Many soldiers were ill, and many also died of starvation and cold, to the extent that their regimental priest had to hear the confession of thirty of them who were fatally ill in one day alone. And all this made us all fear death—which is the end of all evils, fears, and hopes—or rather hope for it. . . .

[January 1634]

Our misery during these days was truly indescribable. More than a thousand people found themselves in the monastery; all of the rooms were completely filled, one person's body very close to the other. It was winter, and there was no oven, no bed, and often, for three or four days, no crumb of bread; nevertheless, the soldiers, who were just as

[1] Diessen is approximately 12 miles (19 km) west of Andechs, site of the monastery.

hungry, always begged us for bread. From their village the Erlingers[2] heard nothing but alarms, pounding, and hammering as their houses were torn down to provide firewood [for the military]. . . .

After this, first the remaining officers and then the rank and file began a new action and [said] . . . they would not rest until all of the victuals that the peasants had deposited in the monastery had been carried off, for what belonged to the peasants also belonged to the soldiers they said, and their hunger was the most extreme. They had already waited for several days for supplies from Munich and received none. And on top of this, during the most recent night, two died, who, before dying of starvation, had bitten into their arms and gnawed on their fingers. And the prior [abbot's deputy] gave them twelve sacks of the peasants' and the monastery's grain that they at once took to the mill in Diessen, and the next day, 1,600 loaves of bread—so strong was the military—were baked.

No sooner had this action come to an end than another tumult broke out. A mass of hungry soldiers showed up at our steward's house and forced all of the doors of the stalls open in order to take whatever they wanted. And what they especially wanted were the pigs, but they ran away from the soldiers into the open. We quickly called on the officers quartered with us at the monastery for assistance, who rushed to the steward's house with the colonel to set themselves against these native robbers. If, in these times, we had been able to laugh, then this certainly would have been a funny scene to see, with the rank and file chasing the pigs across the field, and the officers chasing the rank and file across the field, all of the scoundrels with their rags flying in the air and the officers with flying hair. In the end, two of these criminals, of whom there had been ninety, were captured (our commanders were not only too tough on our peasants but also on their own men), bound to a pillory driven into the ground in the courtyard of the steward's house, and sentenced to be shot to death, and we had to plead for their pardon, perhaps to place them under obligation to us. . . .

. . . When the peasants also finally saw that it really looked like everything would be taken from them and they would be left to starve to death, they slaughtered the few cattle they had left and sought to silence their own hunger rather than that of the soldiers. It looked as though what [imperial] general Altringer had once said would come true, that the only cow to be found in Bavaria after this war would be embroidered with silver.

[2]The inhabitants of the nearby village of Erling, who had fled to the monastery.

38

MICHAEL LEBHARDT

Report on Cannibalism in Agawang

WITH

KASPAR ZEILLER

Response to Lebhardt

1635

Most mentions of cannibalism in the Thirty Years War can be traced back to hearsay rather than eyewitness observation. Usually, contemporaries referred to cannibalism metaphorically to describe the extreme hunger and misery prevalent during some periods of the war. In some confessional texts, religious opponents were accused of cannibalism in an attempt to discredit them based on this barbaric behavior.

The community of Agawang, near Augsburg in southern Germany (see Map 2, pages 10–11), gained the sad notoriety of producing one of the few firsthand reports of people resorting to cannibalism in order to alleviate their hunger. The report was from Father Michael Lebhardt, a priest from the neighboring parish of Kutzenhausen, to his superior, Dr. Kaspar Zeiller, the general provost[1] in Augsburg. We have no record of how the shocked priest responded to his superior's request to show compassion for the flesh eaters.

[1] As general provost, Zeiller was immediately below the bishop in the church hierarchy. It was not unusual that someone in his position was a doctor of theology.

"Zwey merkwürdige Aktenstücke über die zur Zeit des Schwedenkriegs im Winter des Jahrs 1634/35 zu Agawang geherrschte grässliche Hungersnoth" ("Two Noteworthy Documents from the Time of the Swedish War in the Winter of 1634–1635, Regarding the Terrible Hunger in Agawang"), ed. Franz von Baader, *Jahres-Bericht des Historischen Kreis-Vereins im Regierungsbezirke von Schwaben und Neuburg* (*Annual Report of the District Historical Association for the Administrative Region of Swabia and Neuburg*) 35, 1869/70 (Augsburg: Hartmannsche Buchdruckerei, 1872), 71–72.

Before Christmas, in a house in Agawang, which belonged to Leonard Weber, four people starved to death, and then five more, one after another. When I learned that they were still lying unburied after such a long time, because nobody was doing anything for anybody anymore, and indeed nobody would do what he was told or asked to do, and Christian charity among people was extinguished, especially in places like Agawang, where there was no priest anymore and things were really going miserably, I went to Agawang last January. I offered the Mass there, and after I finished the church service I gave orders to the subbailiff, the schoolmaster, and the chief magistrate in the name of Your Honor and Grace as diocesan provost, that they should immediately, while I was present, dig a grave, collect the bodies, and lay them to rest to prevent further sacrilege. They were agreeable, and they started the grave. They said that there were only the four people in the aforementioned house to be buried, because the others were in a house in the parish where the widow Else Miller and Christina Regler lived, and they had been eaten up. I was quite horrified to hear this, and with the schoolmaster I hurried to the house to make inquiries about the matter. I was about to go in the door when two women came out carrying a basin full of human entrails. I asked them, aghast, what they were doing. They only answered me that things were miserable. To which I immediately replied, it is of course the greatest of all miseries that such godless people are so impudent and insolent that they allowed themselves to eat these dead bodies, which had died so long ago. They said, "It was the great unbearable famine that did it."

Because I saw that they still to a certain extent could walk, and that they perhaps could have gained their subsistence by bringing hay to the city [of Augsburg], as others had done, I beat them vigorously with a stick and earnestly commanded them to carry to the churchyard the four remaining bodies, together with even the smallest pieces of bone in a little sack. After this task I had them come to the bailiff's house, and I inquired how many people they ate and whether they had all eaten them. They said unanimously that they had eaten in one sitting two women, named Barbara Mayer and Maria Weldeshofer, who died fourteen days before, along with two men. One of them was Gregor Thüringer, on the fifth day after his death. The other was Jacob Kreiner, who lay five whole weeks unburied in his house. They had eaten them on two occasions. I asked about how it tasted and how it was. They answered, "It didn't taste bad, and the best of it was the brain, the heart, and the kidneys." While admitting this they bitterly cried and raised their hands and promised never to do such a thing again for the rest of their lives. With these aforementioned people there were two others in the neighborhood, the widows Appolonia and Anna Thüringer, who joined them and were also involved. One of them, namely Appolonia, did not shy away from devouring her own husband, Gregor Thüringer.

I could not fail to tell Your Reverence and Grace about this.

Actum Kutzenhausen, February 3rd 1635
Your Reverence's and Grace's
Most subordinately and obediently [signed],
Michael Lebhardt, Plebanus [Pastor]

Dr. Kaspar Zeiller, *Response to Father Lebhardt*, February 1635

What you reported on Feb. 3, regarding the parish of Agawang and the ghastly deeds that recently happened there, I read with the greatest astonishment. Because God has inflicted such a horrible famine for our manifold sins, we must submit this case to His inscrutable judgment. I would only remind you that you should be compassionate toward the same poor people suffering from this extreme famine and that you should spare them any beatings.

6

Battle and Massacre: Experiences of Mass Violence and Death

A central paradox of the Thirty Years War is that although large armies were established to fight the war, relatively few full-scale battles actually took place.[1] Military leaders were reluctant to risk losing their costly and unwieldy war machines in battle. The longer the war lasted, the more it became a war of attrition, a long drawn-out struggle to control territory and resources and to withhold them from the enemy. Siege warfare, which typically pitted enemy armies against fortified towns or cities and their garrisons, was a more common military activity than open battles. These sieges often ended with a negotiated surrender, so that the besieged garrison was granted mercy, and the citizens of the town were guaranteed that it would not be sacked, assuming that they were prepared to pay contributions and quartering costs to their conquerors.

Nonetheless, huge and decisive battles occurred during the war, and by no means did all sieges of towns end with their peaceful surrender. Major battles included White Mountain in November 1620, Breitenfeld in September 1631, Lützen in November 1632, and Nördlingen in September 1634 (see Map 2, pages 10–11). Several fortified cities, such as Münden in 1626 and Magdeburg in 1631, were notoriously stormed and the greater part of their inhabitants massacred. These spectacular instances of mass violence and death were widely reported in the contemporary media, and they are still regarded as the most significant events of the Thirty Years War in both popular memory and historical scholarship.

Two of these key events, the sacking of Magdeburg and the Battle of Lützen, are described by eyewitnesses in this chapter. Also treated from an up-close perspective are two smaller events, the attacks on Münden and Sondershausen, which are more typical of the relatively small-scale

[1] For further discussion of this issue, see Geoff Mortimer, *Eyewitness Accounts of the Thirty Years War, 1618–48* (Basingstoke, U.K.: Palgrave 2002), 38ff.

armed conflicts during the war and the corresponding loss of life and property.

The storming and destruction of the Protestant city of Magdeburg on May 20, 1631, following a siege that began in the autumn of 1630, has been called a "defining event" of the Thirty Years War not only because of the large number of civilians who were killed, either by fire or by violent action, but also because of the widespread depiction of this event as an extreme case of confessional violence.[2] It has been said that it was the success of the anti-Catholic propaganda in the wake of the destruction more than Protestant military resistance that prevented the Catholic imperial side from making further or permanent inroads in northern Germany.[3]

In the view of historians, the Battle of Lützen was less important in determining the course of the war than was the decisive Swedish Protestant victory at the Battle of Breitenfeld in 1631, which turned the tide of the war, or the Spanish imperial victory at the Battle of Nördlingen in 1634, which ended the period of Swedish dominance in the war. However, in the view of both Catholic and Protestant participants, Lützen had universal historical significance. To the Catholic imperial commander Albrecht von Wallenstein, writing the very next day, it seemed as if the battle had been fought with "such a fury as no one has ever seen or heard . . . [and] with the greatest resolution in the world." To Protestant contemporaries, it was an exemplary victory made possible by the sacrifice of the Swedish king Gustav Adolph. Indeed, it was his heroic death in battle and its publicity in the contemporary media (as documented in chapter 7), not the killing of thousands of participants on both sides, that ensured the Battle of Lützen's enduring place in cultural memory.

[2] Peter H. Wilson, *Europe's Tragedy: A History of the Thirty Years War* (London: Allen Lane, 2009), 470.

[3] The late Ernst Schubert, historian at the University of Göttingen, conversation with Hans Medick in 2005.

39

ASMUS TEUFEL

The Siege and Capture of Münden

1626

In June 1626, General Johann Tserclaes, Count von Tilly's imperial forces invaded the duchy of Brunswick-Wolfenbüttel, a Danish ally, and laid siege to the city of Münden (see Map 2, pages 10–11). A garrison of 800 mercenaries under Danish command was stationed in Münden, which had about 2,500 inhabitants. Tilly offered to negotiate a surrender—in accordance with the rules of war—but the Danish commander, Eusebius von Lawich, who had previously deserted from the imperial side, refused.[1] *At dusk of June 9 between 8 and 9 o'clock, Tilly's troops started to storm the city with ladders and through breaches in the walls. Their violent action continued all through the night of June 10 until pardon was granted to survivors the following morning. More than 2,000 persons—inhabitants, but also refugees from the countryside and soldiers of the garrison—were killed in the massacre. A resident of Münden named Asmus Teufel recorded his memories in a report to a local pastor several years later. Teufel, a master linen weaver in the city, was especially close to the events he described. He not only served as a sexton at the local Church of St. Blasien, but he also took an active part in Münden's defense as a constable and a commander of the city's militia.*

At your request I will write, at least as much as I can remember, about the terrible, indescribable bloodbath in this city. Much has gone forgotten

[1] If Lawich had surrendered, he would have risked being summarily executed by his former masters.

From Asmus Teufel, manuscript, Stadtarchiv Hannoversch-Münden, A 2/2001 Nr. 688 – M 1/Sch 2/21. The editors thank Thomas Kossert, University of Göttingen, for making available to them this important text and having contributed the headnote.

because of my often difficult situation, and therefore it is not possible to describe everything.

The commandant in the city at the time had betrayed the emperor. He feared for his life because he had led away so many imperial soldiers and was a rebel. Because they [Tilly's forces] sent heralds from outside and asked if the city wanted to surrender with terms or not, the clergy and the most prominent members of the city council pitifully and pleadingly appealed to the commandant to consider that way out and what might otherwise happen in the end. But this did not help. And when he saw who had the upper hand, he had his servant stab him to death, over by the ruined church, after which his servant stabbed himself.[2] The commandant lay in our church without a coffin in a grave. I saw him still lying there fifteen weeks after his death. They should have just buried him at the gallows hill!

In the days of the siege there was an unceasing firing of large cannons from several places where they had batteries, and they killed many. On Tuesday [there were] 748 shots, including 200 exploding shells, horrible fireballs, which I recorded with my own hand. Then came the assault and the slaughter with halberds [spearlike pole weapons with axlike blades], and neither young nor old, not even the child in its mother's womb, was spared. The truly blind, crippled, and dumb were cut down, even eight preachers who had fled to the city from the villages. One of them was from Hemeln,[3] Johannes Deppe, who was cut down in front of my window. In sum every kind of person they encountered had to die.

And although some people wanted to save their lives with money, and gave up hundreds, even thousands, [of florins], the bloody murderers took the money from them, but then others came, who received nothing, and they cut them down. It's easy to imagine how they [the attackers] dealt with the womenfolk, many of whom they took back to their camp with them.

You can imagine what a wailing and screaming there was up at the castle, where they threw living and dead from the roof and out of the windows, even mothers with their children, so that in the trench behind the moat there was later more than enough evidence. They also cut people

[2] It may be that in retrospect Teufel confused the identities of two persons—the commander, Eusebius von Lawich, and his aide, the Danish lieutenant Clout. According to other contemporary sources, it seems to have been the latter who was killed in the way that Teufel describes.

[3] A village about 7 miles (11 km) from Münden, down the Weser River.

down, so that their blood flowed down the steps [of the castle], and at present there is still blood to see on the walls and on the tapestries.

And because at the time I lived in the tower on the bridge, from where the residents did a good job of watching the near gates [of the town], we thought that we were safe there. But while the gates were closed tightly, the enemy came at us from the city onto the bridge, and shot some people down. Only too late we now saw that it was the enemy. There was a giant fire mortar on the bridge, with three baskets filled to the brim with nails, old pieces of iron pots, and pieces of old iron stoves. Because we had originally planned to fire them at the breastworks of the castle, we now turned around toward the city, and I set fire to the mortar with my bare hands, as can still be seen on my body, and where the pieces flew can also still be seen [in the marks on the buildings]. What of the enemy were still alive had to stay where they lay. Our militia band of thirty-six went up the tower. We had many, many stones, and with them we bricked up the stairwell, and I had a rope ladder from a ship down in the river, which I now attached to the tower, and fourteen or so climbed down and finally escaped to Göttingen,[4] and for which we endured ten weeks of hunger, worry, and tribulations in this town, which has been forgotten here.

The others, who stayed up in the tower, were, with firm agreement and promise, granted their lives and given quarter by the blood-murderer Tilly. They loaded the dead on wagons and had to drive them onto the bridge at Hedemünden[5] and dump them into the water. And because the bodies were not carried away by the little amount of water in the river, they washed up in great numbers on the sandbar and hung up on the banks and lay there, so that they had to be eaten and torn apart by dogs, ravens, and fish.

. . . And though one hoped that the great misery and slaughter would now have an end, on the third day thereafter it started again anew. Tilly ordered that his powder also be stored in the tower where the city stored its powder. And presumably some was thereby spilled. Maybe the guards who stood there ignited it with their torches, and it ran under the door inside and blew up. The church next to the tower and many houses were flattened, and many [were] damaged, so that the remainders of doors and walls lay in big piles here and there. The murderers thought that the residents had dug a mine and maliciously detonated it, and the slaughter started again anew.

[4] One of the next fortified towns, about 18 miles (30 km) from Münden.
[5] A small town about 6 miles (10 km) from Münden on the Werra River.

What we endured then for such a long time, and had to suffer from them [the enemy], is unfortunately more than well enough known to God and us. And if anybody had experienced this catastrophe and would complain of his suffering, where would he find the tongue, feather, or paper to describe it?

That, then, was still not enough. Instead, after the bloodbath the city some time later was besieged again by the Hessians. And even without a further slaughter, we then had to suffer quite terribly the unheard-of arrogance, all the more so than from enemies, because they were our nearest neighbors. It is really true that people from Kassel,[6] whose relatives live here, came with sacks to plunder, and when I asked them what they were going to do with the sacks, they said, "We thought that it would go again, like last time, how Pappenheim, Kaiser's Schwarzen, Blanckerschen, Pfannkuchen, Wittmund did it."[7]

Without detailing the many losses of this city, I say again, they cannot be described. I wanted to write more about it—this really wound up too short—and I don't know [anything else] other than that more written information is available in the sacristy of the church. Perhaps Henricus would know of it. But I don't know. The Herr Magister [the pastor] can surely ask him.

[6] A large Protestant seat of government and a fortified city about 14 miles (23 km) from Münden.

[7] Refers to the names of Catholic League and imperial regiments led by Gottfried Heinrich von Pappenheim and Adam Philipp von Cronberg [Regiment of Kaisers Schwarzen, i.e., Imperial Black Regiment] and Otto Ludwig von Blankart. Pfannkuchen and Wittmund are likely the names of Danish regiments.

40

VOLKMAR HAPPE

An Attack on the City of Sondershausen

1640

In this excerpt from his chronicle (see Document 17), Volkmar Happe, who by this time was a high court official in Sondershausen, describes a raid on the city by Swedish troops. Sondershausen in Thuringia was a small residential city not well protected by walls. Its only fortification was the castle, the seat of government of the Count of Schwarzburg-Sondershausen. The kind of fighting that Happe describes from up close was typical of the small-scale, protracted warfare that especially characterized the Thirty Years War in its later years, all the more so because Sondershausen was ostensibly Protestant, as were the raiding Swedish troops. Especially interesting here is Happe's perspective as a victim of the destruction.

On the 30th [of May] between twelve noon and one o'clock more than a thousand Swedish horsemen arrived in front of the city of Sondershausen. Our guards pleaded with them not to use violence, but they [the horsemen] fired at them [the guards], chased them away from the gate, opened the gate by force, and in doing so gruesomely injured and even killed some poor women, children, and men. Thereupon we defended ourselves in the castle. However, they set the outlying part of the city near the main church on fire, and then the center of the city by the Stockheuser gate, too. Thereby over a hundred houses were burned down, including my own. Everything in my house was lamentably burned. Thereupon our troops moved down from the castle into the city and engaged them in heavy fighting. Six horsemen of the plunderers were taken prisoner, as well as nine horses, and they were chased from the city. On our side, thank God, no one was killed or injured, though

---

From Volkmar Happe, *Chronicon Thuringiae* (*Thuringian Chronicle*), ed. Hans Medick, Norbert Winnige, and Andreas Bähr (electronic publication: Thüringer Universitäts- und Landesbibliothek Jena, 2008), 2:317r–19r. Available as a digital facsimile at www.mdsz.thulb.uni-jena.de/happe/quelle.php.

the Swedes took losses: More than forty horsemen are said to have lain dead. The godless people also violated many females. This skirmish lasted until five o'clock in the evening, and then they finally withdrew, after we gave them back the horses. The prisoners are mostly from Witzleben's regiment.[1] Among others, I also had the additional misfortune that without my knowing, my daughter Anna Sabina and many females, out of sheer terror, fled from the castle toward the woods, and in the fields they fell into the hands of the horsemen. They undressed her and all the other females and let them run away in their underclothes, and thank God I got her back in the castle unharmed. Now two parts of the city of Sondershausen lie in ashes, and only the third part is still standing, as long as God allows. This robbing, murdering, and burning horde was commanded by two captains, one named Senckel, the other named Paul.

[1] Georg Melchior von Witzleben was the commander of a Swedish regiment.

The Storming and Destruction of Magdeburg

The siege of the Protestant city of Magdeburg (see Map 2, pages 10–11) by troops of the Catholic League headed by General Tilly and Field Marshal von Pappenheim attracted widespread public attention from its beginning in the autumn of 1630. After all, Magdeburg had had a special reputation for its resilience as the military stronghold, or "fortress city,"[1] of the Protestant Reformation since it heroically defended itself against Catholic imperial forces during the War of the Schmalkaldic League in the mid-sixteenth century.

As in the earlier siege, Magdeburg again rejected repeated offers to negotiate a surrender. When it was taken by storm on May 20, 1631, large parts of the city were destroyed by the attackers and especially by the fire that broke out during the assault. Approximately twenty thousand inhabitants and defenders of Magdeburg died. This was considered by contemporaries, not only in the German lands but also across Europe, to be the single greatest catastrophe of the Thirty Years War. It was widely reported and contentiously discussed in more than two hundred

[1] In this capacity Magdeburg was seen as a companion of Wittenberg, the "scholarly city" of the Protestant Reformation.

pamphlets, more than forty broadsheets, and countless newspaper articles published in 1631 alone. In addition, several contemporary personal accounts of the attack have been preserved and published.[2] Three of these testimonies from different perspectives are reproduced here.

[2] For an analysis of the media reaction and the perceptions of contemporaries inside and outside Magdeburg, see Hans Medick, "Historical Event and Contemporary Experience: The Capture and Destruction of Magdeburg in 1631," *History Workshop Journal* 52 (2001): 23–48.

41

PETER HAGENDORF

The Siege, Assault, and Destruction of Magdeburg

1631

This passage from the diary of Peter Hagendorf (see Document 18) gives the perspective of a soldier who actively participated in the siege of and assault on Magdeburg and witnessed the city's destruction. Especially remarkable in this document is the soldier's sober description of the siege operations and the casualties suffered by the attackers, as well as the blunt language he uses to describe the final assault, including the severe wounds that he suffered himself. This can be contrasted with his rather emotional description of how the sight of the burning city caused him to be "heartfully sorry."[1] *Also noteworthy is Hagendorf's description of his wife as a substitute for himself in the business of looting and plundering. In this way, he provides an insider's view into the predatory activities that contributed to the carefully balanced, highly flexible household economy of a professional soldier's family in the Thirty Years War.*

[1] Only recently (in 2011), the historian who edited Hagendorf's diary, Jan Peters, discovered that Hagendorf was born in the town of Zerbst, about 25 miles (40 km) southeast of Magdeburg. The proximity of this town explains why Hagendorf thought of Magdeburg as "his fatherland." See the afterword to the new edition of the diary, Hagendorf, *Tagebuch eines Söldners aus dem Dreißigjährigen Krieg*, 202.

From Peter Hagendorf, *Tagebuch eines Söldners aus dem Dreißigjährigen Krieg* (*Diary of a Mercenary from the Thirty Years War*), ed. Jan Peters, 2nd rev. ed. (Göttingen: V & R Unipress, 2012), 104–5.

To Goslar in the Harz [Mountains] and to Magdeburg. We encamped in the villages and blockaded the city, the entire winter out of action in the villages, until the spring of 1631. There we took a few outposts in the woods around Magdeburg. There our captain, with many others, was shot dead at an outpost. On this day we took seven outposts. Afterward we were moved up close and built up everything with bulwarks and trenches, but it cost a lot of men.

On March 22 Johan Galgort was introduced to us as our new captain. April 28 he was shot in a trench again. May 6 Tilge Neuberg was introduced again. He had our company ten days, after which he resigned.

May 20 we attempted, stormed, and triumphed. There I came into the city charging with my own hands without any injury. But in the city, at the Neustädter Tor [gate to the new parts of the city], I was shot twice through the body; that was my booty.

This happened May 20, 1631, nine o'clock in the morning.

Afterward I was brought to the camp [and] bandaged, because I was shot once through the front of the belly and again through both shoulders, so that the bullet was still in my shirt. The field surgeon had my hands bound behind me so that he could apply the bandage. I was brought to my tent half-dead.

I was heartfully sorry that the city burned so terribly, because it was a beautiful city and because it was my fatherland.

As I was now bandaged, my wife went into the city, although it was burning everywhere, to get me a pillow and towels to bandage me and for me to lie upon. So then I also had the sick child lying by me. Then the cry came into the camp that the houses were all falling down, so that many soldiers and women, who were pilfering, had to stay inside. So I was more worried about my wife because of the sick child than because of my own injuries. But God protected her. She came out of the city after an hour and a half with an old woman. She [the woman] led her out; she was a sailor's wife and was helping her carry linens. So she had also brought me a large jug of four liters of wine and also two silver belts and dresses that I later sold for 12 talers in Halberstadt. In the evening my comrades came to me, and they had all brought me something out of respect, a taler or a half taler.

May 24 Johan Philipp Schütz was introduced [as our new captain]. I and all the other wounded were taken to Halberstadt. We were quartered in villages there. From our regiment three hundred were quartered in a village, and all were healed.

42

JOHANN DANIEL FRIESE

Magdeburg: The Massacre Viewed from Within

1631

Johann Daniel Friese (see Document 8), the son of the city secretary in Magdeburg, experienced the catastrophe in his hometown as a twelve-year-old. His memoir, which he wrote as an adult, is especially noteworthy because he emphasizes his perspective and role as a child.

Then he [the soldier] came at father with a pick-axe. Mother ran up to them straightaway, screaming, and we children stood around the soldier, begging and crying that he should please let father live. Christian, my fourth brother, then a small child who could barely walk and stammer a few words, spoke in the greatest fear to the soldier: "Oh, please let father live, I'll gladly give you the three pennies I get on Sundays." . . . This, coming from an unformed and in those days simple child, touched the soldier's heart, perhaps by God's merciful providence, so that he immediately changed and turned to us in a friendly rather than a cruel manner. He looked at us children, as we stood around him, and said: "What fine little lads you are" . . . and then he said to our father: "If you want to get out with your children, leave immediately, for the Croats will be here in an hour, and you and your children will scarcely survive." Then the soldier thought it over and said: "Yes, but I haven't taken any booty,

---

From "Historischer Extract aus einem Manuscripto, welches Herr Daniel Frisius, Cancell. Secret. zu Altenburg von seinen Fatis hinter sich gelassen . . . Vom Magdeburger Unglück" ("Historical Extract from a Manuscript, Which Daniel Frisius, Chancellery Secretary in Altenburg, Left Behind Regarding His Fate . . . Relating to the Catastrophe in Magdeburg"), in Friedrich Friese, *Leichte historische Fragen* (*Light Historical Questions*) (Leipzig: Groschuff, 1703), 311–12, 316–17. Translation of the first part of this text by Pamela Selwyn, quoted in Hans Medick, "Historical Event and Contemporary Experience: The Capture and Destruction of Magdeburg in 1631," *History Workshop Journal* 52 (2001): 40–41.

I really would like to lead you out, but first I need to take some booty," and he wanted to leave. Then we really fell at his feet, and pleaded that he should take us with him, and we would gladly give him 200 tales if he would take us to Gommern, which was two miles from Magdeburg in Electoral-Brandenburg. But he said: he had to take booty first, and we should just stay there. He wanted to search a couple more houses, until he had booty, and then he would come back and get us, and he swore solemnly up and down, he would come back. . . .

[After some time, the soldier returned to lead the Friese family out of the city to safety.]

As we went through a couple of alleys, we saw various dead laying atop each other, and often in the great crowd we had to step over the corpses. Amongst others we saw a peasant jump down out of a gable, who was scalded by hot water, and he was smoking mightily. He lay in the alley writhing and crying piteously. Farther along in the alley lay a maid, who had been carrying meat in a basket. She had been shot, and a dog was standing nearby, eating the meat. . . . We saw very many dead in the alleys and a number of women lying totally naked, with their heads in a large beer barrel, which was standing full of water in the street. They had been pushed in and drowned, but half their bodies and their legs were hanging out, which was a wretched spectacle.

43

CHRISTIAN II OF ANHALT-BERNBURG

The Catastrophe of Magdeburg: A Local View

1631

This passage is taken from the diary of Duke Christian II of Anhalt-Bernburg (1599–1656). Twenty-four volumes in manuscript, this diary is one of the most extraordinary autobiographical accounts of the Thirty Years War. At the time of the event, the duke, a Calvinist, was residing in his castle at Bernburg, a few miles outside Magdeburg. He was not a direct eyewitness of the destruction of the city, but as a resident in its vicinity, he was immediately confronted with the consequences of the event. Throughout his diary, Duke Christian interweaves perceptions and evaluations, including political conclusions about what has transpired. Here he confides—in French, as if he wanted to hide this information from potential readers and possibly even himself—that he wrote a congratulatory note to Tilly. This sentence is an indication of both the anxiety and the political constraints Christian felt. Commending the Catholic imperial commander was surely not an easy task for an active Protestant.

(Wednesday), 11th May [1631][1]

News that yesterday morning at 8 o'clock Magdeburg was captured, plundered, set ablaze, men, women and children struck down, administrator taken prisoner, Field Marshal Falkenberg remained. This is no

[1] Anhalt-Bernburg used the Julian calendar. By the modern Gregorian calendar, this entry was written on May 21, 1631.

From "Aus dem Tagebuch des Fürsten Christian des Jüngeren von Anhalt-Bernburg: Aufzeichnungen, die Zerstörung Magdeburgs, die Unterredung des Fürsten Christian mit dem Administrator Christian Wilhelm von Brandenburg und den Entsatz Magdeburgs durch Pappenheim betreffend" ("From the Diary of Prince Christian the Younger of Anhalt-Bernburg: Records Regarding the Destruction of Magdeburg, the Conversation of Prince Christian with the Administrator Christian Wilhelm of Brandenburg, and the Relief of Magdeburg by Pappenheim"), *Geschichtsblätter für Stadt und Land Magdeburg* (*History Pages for the City and Province of Magdeburg*), ed. Max Dittmar, special issue, 29 (1894): 98–99, 101. Translation by Pamela Selwyn, quoted in Hans Medick, "Historical Event and Contemporary Experience: The Capture and Destruction of Magdeburg in 1631," *History Workshop Journal* 52 (2001): 28–29.

doubt the great and mighty fire that we saw burning yesterday. Now the imperial forces have attained their intention, and can bend the entire Upper and Lower Saxon Kreis[2] to their will and make such changes on behalf of religion (if God does not intervene) as they wish. This is a mighty victory and, both for his imperial majesty and the Catholic cause and more especially for General Tilly, is to the greater glory of his reputation and name.

After hearing the sermon the provost came to me and reported more of the circumstances in Magdeburg. News that the king of Sweden is supposed to be in Zerbst. *J'ay escrit derechef de mapropre main apart au gl. Tilly le remerciant fort des sa intercession et luy congratulant sa victoire de Magdebourg, desirant une bonne paix en Allemaigne etc.* [I wrote once again in my own hand to General Tilly thanking him warmly for his intercession and congratulating him upon his victory at Magdeburg, desiring a good peace in Germany, etc.]

Prisoners brought here from Magdeburg report that the slaughter continued this morning and the city is completely burnt down, that no building remains but the cathedral. . . . If this mighty and beautiful city has been destroyed in such a short time and reduced to ashes, it is much to be pitied and its downfall to be lamented. . . .

It recalls to me the destruction of the city of Jerusalem, and no such tragedy has befallen such a city in the German empire and lands, and no such excellent city fallen so rapidly and been so suddenly and ultimately ruined (which reminds me of the fall of Babylon . . .) since the time when Bardewyk,[3] out of whose rubble Lüneburg was built, was taken by Henry the Lion against Bernhard I of Anhalt, elector of Saxony, and finally destroyed.

[2] *Kreis* designates an adminstrative district of the Holy Roman Empire.

[3] Reference to the rich medieval trading city of Bardowick in northern Germany near Lüneburg, which was destroyed in 1189 by Duke Henry the Lion in a conflict with his rival Bernhard I, the elector of Saxony.

The Battle of Lützen

The Battle of Lützen took place on November 16, 1632, near the small town of Lützen. A Protestant Swedish army commanded by King Gustav Adolph, and later during the day by Duke Bernhard of Saxony-Weimar,[1] was pitted against the Catholic imperial forces led by Albrecht von Wallenstein, Duke of Friedland. Although the battle ended in a Swedish victory, it resulted in not only the retreat of Wallenstein to Leipzig but also the death of Gustav Adolph.

On the Swedish side were approximately 19,000 men (12,800 musketeers and pikemen, 6,200 cavalrymen) and a Saxon auxiliary contingent of approximately 6,000 men. On the imperial side was Wallenstein's army of approximately 17,000 men (10,000 musketeers and pikemen, 7,000 cavalrymen), which was reinforced during the battle by Pappenheim's troops, who numbered approximately 5,000 men. The losses in dead and wounded were high on both sides. Two days after the battle, the Swedish side counted approximately 5,000 of their own dead and wounded, and approximately 3,500 imperial troops were buried in and around Lützen.

[1] Duke Bernhard von Saxony-Weimar (1604–1639) served in the Danish, Swedish, and French armies. After Gustav Adolph's death, he became temporary commander of the Swedish forces.

44

ALBRECHT VON WALLENSTEIN

Request for Reinforcements before the Battle of Lützen

1632

This short message from Wallenstein to his field marshal, Count Gottfried Heinrich von Pappenheim,[1] *was written in Wallenstein's own hand and signed with his majestic signature in a situation of extreme urgency, one day before the Battle of Lützen* (*see Map 2, pages 10–11*)*. Wallenstein requests that his field marshal, who at the time was with his troops in the nearby city of Halle, come to his assistance as quickly as possible. Pappenheim followed suit, but he reached the battlefield with his troops only after the fighting between the two armies was already under way. He joined the battle with full force and paid for it with his life. The letter from Wallenstein, which Pappenheim carried with him into battle, was found, soaked in blood, inside Pappenheim's jacket* (*page 141*)*. Today the bloodstained document is exhibited as a precious relic of Habsburg-Austrian military history in the Museum of Military History in Vienna.*

The enemy is marching in this direction. The Lord leave everything standing and lying and make your way here with all men and cannons so that he can be here with us early tomorrow morning.

I however remain herewith

THY LORD'S WILLING SERVANT,
AhzM

[Wallenstein's signature, in shorthand for: Albrecht, Herzog von Mecklenburg (Albrecht, Duke of Mecklenburg)]

Lützen, 15 Nov. 1632

[1] Count Gottfried Heinrich von Pappenheim (1594–1632) had risen through the military ranks during the war. He became a Bavarian field marshal and then an imperial field marshal.

Brief und Hilfsgesuch Albrecht von Wallensteins an Feldmarschall Pappenheim (Letter and Request for Reinforcements by Albrecht von Wallenstein to Field Marshal Pappenheim), November 1632. Vienna: Heeresgeschichtliches Museum (Museum of Military History), Inventory Number NI 1773.

1632 125

Der feindt marchirt hereinwarths der herr lasse alles stehen undt liegen undt incaminiere sich herzu mitt allem volck undt stücken auf das er morgen frü bey unß sich befinde ich aber verbleibe hiemitt

Des herrn dienstwilliger

Lützen den 15 Novemb:
Ao 1632.

Er ist schon an dem paß wo gestern der weg gewesen ist.

P.S. He [the enemy] is already at the pass where yesterday there was the bad road.

[The backside of the letter carries an additional note of urgency in Latin, written in Wallenstein's hand:

Cito, Cito, Citissime, Cito (Quick, Quick, Very Quick, Quick)]

45

ALBRECHT VON WALLENSTEIN

A Battle like No One Has Ever Seen or Heard

1632

Wallenstein wrote and mailed this letter to his field marshal, Count Johann von Aldringen,[1] *on November 17, 1632, the day after the Battle of Lützen. Written from the perspective of a military commander, the letter expresses respect for the enemy commander, King Gustav Adolph of Sweden. Despite Wallenstein's restrained tone, it is clear that the generalissimo was impressed by the fury of this battle, like "no one has ever seen or heard." He admits that his troops retreated on his orders, and he cites as the reason the "desperation" (read "panic") of the rank and file. In opposition to the humiliation of this defeat, which he does not recognize as such, he presents at least a symbolic victory: His troops captured*

[1] Count Johann von Aldringen (1588–1634) rose through the military and social ranks as a protégé of Wallenstein but then helped to coordinate the ouster and assassination of Wallenstein in 1634. He was killed in battle later the same year.

"Extract Ihrer Fürstl. Gn. Herrn Generalissimi Schreiben, an ein Fürnehme Persohn, den 17. November 1632" ("Extract of His Princely Grace the Generalissimo's Letter to a Prominent Person, the 17th of November 1632"), in *Extract Underschiedtlicher Schreiben Deß Jüngst gehaltene Ernstlichen Treffens, zwischen Ihrer Fürstl. Gn. Herrn Generalissimo, Hertzogen zu Mechelburg,* [printing mistake for Lützen] *Fridlandt unnd Sagan, etc., unnd dem König auß Schweden. Geschehen bey Lupen, zwo Meyl von Leipzig, den 16. November* (*Extracts of Various Writings from the Recently Held Serious Engagement between His Princely Grace the Generalissimo, Duke of Mecklenburg, Friedland, and Sagan, etc., and the King of Sweden. Happened by Lützen, Two Miles from Leipzig, the 16th of November*) (Erfurt, 1632).

considerably more Swedish trophies than the Swedes took from them. The generalissimo's lack of reliable information also is noteworthy. The day after the battle in which Gustav Adolph was killed, Wallenstein still writes, somewhat uncertainly, "They say that the king is also dead."

After the king [Gustav Adolph] decided the day before yesterday to advance on me, and the same day stopped in the field only a short half mile from me, and stayed in battle order the entire night, then I also led my troops to battle, sent for [imperial field marshal] Count von Pappenheim to [come with his troops from nearby] Halle, and stayed in battle order the whole night. The king presented himself soon after daybreak, and Count von Pappenheim also arrived with the cavalry. Then the battle started at ten o'clock with such a fury as no one has ever seen or heard. From ten o'clock until into the dark of night there was one engagement after another, [fought] with the greatest resolution in the world. Entire regiments of the enemy, as they stood in the battle, were laid low, and on our side several thousand also fell, most of the officers were dead or wounded, and Count von Pappenheim was killed in the first engagement. They say that the king is also dead. But around nightfall our men were desperate, so that the officers, the horsemen, and their servants could not contain the troops, so I decided, on the recommendation of the captains, to retreat with the men during the night to Leipzig, where I will make a stand today. It has also been reported to me that the king's men may also have retreated to Naumburg. Tomorrow I march to Chemnitz,[2] to join with Count Gallas[3] and to probe the enemy again. I have received from the enemy more than thirty standards and flags, he no more than five or at most six from me.

[2] Chemnitz is a city 50 miles (80 km) southeast of Leipzig.

[3] Count Matthias von Gallas (1588–1647) was originally an Italian officer in Spanish service, later a Bavarian commander, and ultimately an imperial general lieutenant under Wallenstein. Together with Aldringen and Prince Ottavio Piccolomini of Amalfi, he pushed for the dismissal of Wallenstein. He took over command of the imperial forces after Wallenstein's death and led them to victory at the Battle of Nördlingen in September 1634.

46

ZACHARIAS VON QUETZ

Retrospective Account of a Participant in the Battle of Lützen

1632

During the Battle of Lützen, Zacharias von Quetz was at the side of the Swedish king Gustav Adolph as a follower and agent of Duke Franz Albrecht of Saxony-Lauenburg, who afterward was long suspected of having played a role in the killing of the king.[1] *Particularly noteworthy in Quetz's retrospective account is that rather than describe the battle and the death of the king—which he must have experienced firsthand but to which he dedicates only an emphatic half sentence introduced by "N.B."* (nota bene, *Latin for "note well")—he focuses on the advance of the Swedish troops from Naumburg and the outcome of the battle.*

November [1632]

The 3rd to Naumburg, the 5th against the enemy, and started to skirmish.

N.B. The 6th was a most unhappy day,[2] when the noble king lost his life in the battle near Lützen, but ultimately held the battlefield, routed the enemy, and on the enemy's side Pappenheim died. On this day at three o'clock in the morning Duke Franz Albrecht and Duke Bernhard [von Saxony-Weimar] and I declared the fighting to be over,

[1] Franz Albrecht of Saxony-Lauenburg (1598–1642), one of the most colorful and ambiguous figures of the Thirty Years War, was a military enterpriser, diplomat, and adventurer all at the same time. He and the troops he recruited and commanded repeatedly changed armies and fronts. Franz Albrecht had switched from the imperial to the Swedish side only a few weeks before the battle, and later he switched back to the imperial side. He was a guest of Gustav Adolph at Lützen.

[2] Quetz used the older Julian calendar to date the Battle of Lützen, fought on November 16, 1632, by the Gregorian calendar.

From Zacharias von Querz [Quetz], "Kurtze Erzehlung und Extract wie ich . . . de anno 1612, nachdem . . . [ich aus] meiner Eltern hauss uff die Universitet Leipzig verschickt worden, mein Jugend und Zeit zugebracht" ("Short Explanation and Extract How I Spent My Youth and Time after [I Was] Sent from My Parents' House to the University of Leipzig in 1612"), British Library, London, Add MS 11,660, 36v–38v.

and we inspected the dead, wounded, and miserably dying soldiers on the battlefield, and we arranged that the king would be embalmed in Weissenfels.[3] . . . At the suggestion of Duke Bernhard, Duke Franz Albrecht and I went to the elector of Saxony[4] to request that the remaining six regiments from Braunschweig-Lüneburg combine with the army of Duke Bernhard and pursue the enemy. Though we demanded this forcefully, it was in vain, and instead Duke Franz Albrecht had to stay with the elector, who negotiated with him about accepting a post as field marshal. And because after three weeks the high lords could not agree, I was finally sent back to the elector to present the duke's point of view to His Highness, whereupon the elector finally bowed to the duke's demands; thereupon the duke accepted the post, and I was granted a beautiful gold chain[5] and breastplate by the elector.

[3] Weissenfels is a city near Lützen.

[4] Johann Georg I, elector of Saxony (1585–1656; r. 1611–1656). He tried to establish Saxony as a "third power" in the Thirty Years War but was overwhelmed by imperial forces in 1631 and then temporarily allied with Sweden. In 1635, after the Peace of Prague, he switched to the imperial side.

[5] An "order chain," signifying entry into a noble order.

7

Media, Celebrity, and Death: The Cases of Gustav Adolph and Albrecht von Wallenstein

More than any war before, the Thirty Years War can be considered a media war. The war was accompanied by a gigantic expansion of all print media, from single-page broadsheets and newsletters to pamphlets and periodical newspapers. Historian Johannes Burkhardt concluded that after the period of the Reformation, it was the Thirty Years War that "gave the modern media revolution its second push."[1] However, scholars remain divided on whether and how much the media played an active role in bringing about and prolonging the war. Burkhardt and especially Wolfgang Behringer stress the special dynamic of the press as an active element in the making of the war, but they are much less definite regarding the importance of the press in the ending of the war.[2] Behringer even quotes a contemporary of the war who assessed the contribution of the *Frankfurter Postzeitung* (*Frankfurt Post Newspaper*) to the war effort to be the equivalent of twenty thousand mercenaries.[3] Another historian of seventeenth-century media, Johannes Weber, takes a more restrained position. He distinguishes between pamphlets and single-page broadsheets, which, as during the Reformation, served polemical and propagandistic aims, and periodical newspapers, whose

[1] Johannes Burkhardt, *Der Dreißigjährige Krieg* (*The Thirty Years War*) (Frankfurt: Suhrkamp, 1992), 225.

[2] Ibid., 225ff.; Wolfgang Behringer, "Veränderung der Raum-Zeitrelation: Zur Bedeutung des Zeitungs- und Nachrichtenwesens während der Zeit des Dreißigjährigen Krieges" ("Change in the Space-Time Continuum: On the Significance of the News and Information Media during the Time of the Thirty Years War"), in *Zwischen Alltag und Katastrophe: Der Dreißigjährige Krieg aus der Nähe* (*Between Everyday and Catastrophe: The Thirty Years War from Up Close*), ed. Benigna von Krusenstjern and Hans Medick, 2nd. ed. (Göttingen: Vandenhoeck and Ruprecht, 2001), 39–81.

[3] Behringer, "Veränderung der Raum-Zeitrelation," 75.

growth during the war he sees as a new development that arose from the increased demand for information and news.[4]

The deaths of famous persons and military leaders, the circumstances of their deaths, and the consequences of their deaths were perhaps of even greater interest to people in the seventeenth century than the deaths of celebrities are to people today. After all, early modern European society was understandably fascinated with the fleeting nature of life, the vanity of fame, and the culture of dying. So it is not surprising that the deaths of two of the leading figures of the Thirty Years War, Gustav Adolph and Albrecht von Wallenstein, evoked a great public response. What is of special interest, however, is how this response was molded by the contemporary media and how the different and contentious constructions of these figures in and through their deaths contributed to the creation of crucial "first moments" of memory that persisted in history and literature for centuries. The uniformly heroic representations of the death of Gustav Adolph in the Battle of Lützen thus furnish an outstanding example of the successful construction of a Protestant knight and martyr, which was even acknowledged, if somewhat critically, by the enemy side. The diverging representations of the murder of Wallenstein, by contrast, furnish a prominent example of the different and controversial portrayals of the death of a key leader.

[4] Johannes Weber, "Der große Krieg und die frühe Zeitung: Gestalt und Entwicklung der deutschen Nachrichtenpresse in der ersten Hälfte des 17. Jahrhunderts" ("The Great War and the Early Newspaper: Form and Development of the German News Media in the First Half of the Seventeenth Century"), *Jahrbuch für Kommunikationsgeschichte* (*Yearbook for the History of Communication*) 1 (1999): 23–61, here 44.

Gustav Adolph's Heroic Death in Battle

47

"Victorious before Death, in Death, and after Death"

1632

The following excerpt is from a four-page pamphlet published in Erfurt on November 22, 1632, less than one week after the Battle of Lützen. It was probably published by a member of the Swedish chancellery, which at that time was based in Erfurt, not far from the battlefield. The pamphlet is quasi-official; the title page displays the coat of arms of the fallen Swedish king, flanked by his initials.

The author describes himself as an eyewitness of and participant in the battle. It is noteworthy that he says that the battle was a God-given victory for the Protestant side and thereby declares that the death of Gustav Adolph was a hero's sacrifice for the Protestant cause. Connected with this construction of the hero—and the legacy of the king—was a political message and admonishment aimed at the Protestant princes of Germany, who were called to continue to acknowledge Swedish leadership, to remain united, and to carry on the struggle for their religious and political liberty.

Gustav Adolph's death immediately became a mass media event, and the pamphlet excerpted here was very influential. Not only was it printed in countless editions as a stand-alone publication, but it was also widely reproduced in many contemporary periodicals, sometimes with small but significant changes. The author established the image of Gustav Adolph as a religious martyr, an image that shaped the memory and history

From *Warhaffte und eygentliche Relation, Von der blutigen Schlacht zwischen der Königl. Majestät zu Schweden, etc., und der Käyserlichen Armee, den 5. und 6. Novembris deß 1632. Jahrs, bey Lützen, zwo Meil wegs von Leipzig vorgangen und geschehen. Auß Erfurt vom 12 (22) November deß 1632. Jahrs* ("True and Actual Account of the Bloody Battle between His Royal Majesty of Sweden and the Imperial Army, the 5th and 6th of November in the Year 1632, at Lützen, Two Miles Away from Leipzig. From Erfurt, 12 (22) November 1632"), Aiiv–Aiiir. Available as a digital facsimile at Herzog August Bibliothek Wolfenbüttel, http://diglib.hab.de/drucke/gl-kapsel-5-18s/start.htm.

of the king (and his death) in the Protestant world into the twentieth century.

We cannot thank the Almighty enough for this glorious and exceedingly great victory. On the enemy's side, as the prisoners attest, on the battle-field the dead lay on top of one another half as high as a man, and it is revealed that two-thirds (including Pappenheim himself and most of the other high officers) are dead and crushed, they lost all of their artillery and munitions, and the few remaining enemy soldiers were set to flight. **However, this came to nothing, considering the death of our glorious, most Christian, and in all the world highly praised king. In blessed memory, His Majesty in the first engagement was shot first in the arm, then in the back, and finally in the head. So his blessed soul was sacrificed to Lord Jesus, and his royal blood was spilled and his life and body laid down for the Protestant German electors and estates, to preserve their religion and to regain their lost liberty.**[1]

. . . The Almighty lend his grace that all the German Protestant electors and estates take this work to heart and gratefully acknowledge the glorious king's deeds and proven loyalty; and that in the future they, by combining their bodies, goods, and blood, and with God's strength, may continue and complete the holy work regarding their religion and liberty, which our most blessed king has established so well and placed in their hands; and that they gratefully acknowledge the surviving most sorrowful and pious queen, and her Swedish crown, including her high and low officers, who are resolved to give everything. However, should they separate (though may God in his mercy prevent it), and on other advice divide themselves, then it would be as His Glorious Royal Majesty prophesied before his death, namely, that our religion and our freedom would be finished . . .

In this account I cannot omit the following words, which His Blessed Royal Majesty often said, and repeated again three days before the battle to Dr. Fabricius in Naumburg:[2] "My dear Doctor, things are all good, and everything is going as hoped, but I worry, I worry, because everyone venerates me so much and, so to say, they take me for a god. God will punish me for this. But God knows that it does not please me. It is

[1] Boldface in original.
[2] Jakob Fabricius (1593–1654) was personal chaplain of King Gustav Adolph.

going as dear God wants it, I know, and he will continue things through to completion, because it glorifies his name."

This I wanted briefly to report, as much as I could observe and witness everything, as someone who was at this engagement and main battle from beginning to end, so nine continuous hours, and missed nothing of the Battle of Leipzig. May the Almighty grant my most gracious queen and the royal Swedish councilors and officers the spirit of consolation, so that they, because of this great loss of the treasure of their king and lord, may find Christian patience and divine edification elsewhere.

From all of this it is really tangible, that it is not we, but rather God, who is the master over our wills, lives, and efforts. And we can become even more patient and console ourselves that our king lost his life in the highest grade of immortal fame, because he was and remained victorious *ante mortem, in morte, and post mortem* [before death, in death, and after death].

48

A Handwritten Newsletter from Nuremberg

1632

On November 30, 1632, two weeks after the Battle of Lützen, a professional newsletter writer and agent working in Nuremberg in southern Germany sent this notice to Duke August of Braunschweig-Lüneburg in northern Germany. It was written to familiarize Duke August (1579–1666) with the prevailing mood, not only in the Protestant city of Nuremberg but also in adjacent Catholic Bavarian cities, and to inform him about the different public ways in which the death of the Swedish king was communicated and dealt with. Duke August later became the founder of the famous library in Wolfenbüttel, which in his time was the world's largest library. He was not only a great book collector but also an avid collector and distributor of news. Therefore, after the death of

From Niedersächsisches Staatsarchiv (Lower Saxon State Archive), Wolfenbüttel, 1 Z Nr. 7: Geschriebene Zeitungen (Handwritten Newsletters), 1632–33, Bl. 48. The editors thank Gillian Bepler, Wolfenbüttel, for referring them to this interesting document.

Gustav Adolph, Duke August bought numerous printed pamphlets and handwritten newsletters, which he then had copied and redistributed among people of rank.

The city of Nuremberg is still caught between hope and fear, and to demonstrate their own consciousness of their guilt [as sinners] and out of Christian condolence, the authorities have ordered that the sad death of the king of Sweden be proclaimed from all pulpits and that all citizens and residents be duly admonished to righteous repentance and penance, according to the example of Judas Maccabee. The scripture read was 1 Maccabee, chapter 9, verses 20–21: "Moreover they bewailed him, and all Israel made great lamentation for him, and mourned many days, saying: How is the valiant man fallen, that delivered Israel!"

However, in Bavaria and areas of the papacy there is great joy and jubilation. A satirical play which especially disrespects the deceased king of Sweden was performed by the Jesuits in Regensburg [Bavaria] in the presence of the bishop himself. Likewise, before a public audience the ordinary priest of Neumarkt [Upper Palatinate] compared the king with a snake that had crept into the empire but afterward was beaten with a rod or with the scourge of God, with which the Catholics had previously been beaten. It was also announced that the king, dying in agony, emitted all sorts of blasphemous words and lies against the almighty majesty of God. So there can be no doubt that God has thrown this scourge into purgatory, and now the Roman Catholic religion will bloom and prosper again. [Note in the margin by Duke August: "These are Jesuit lies, i.e., devilry."]

49

The Immortal Gustav Adolph

1633

The one-page leaflet shown on page 154 was published in 1633, only a few months after the death of Gustav Adolph. It combines a pictorial and textual message and was directed at Protestant readers and viewers who were mourning the death of the Swedish king. The image and text attempted to comfort readers and to embolden them for the continued struggle against the papacy and Catholicism.[1] *It bears the title "Der Schwede lebet noch" ("The Swede Is Still Alive").*

In the foreground of the picture, Gustav Adolph stands on a crowned rock, surrounded by an undulating sea. He strikes the pose of a victor and a bearer of peace. In his left hand is a field marshal's baton (a sign of military command), and in his right hand is a sword entwined by an olive branch (a symbol of peace). Two angels are placing a crown of laurel (a sign of fame) on his head. The angels hold palm fronds, a Christian symbol of eternal life and immortality. Next to Gustav Adolph, two other crowned rocks rise from the water, the left decorated with the Swedish coat of arms, the right with the Saxon coat of arms. This was a symbolic enunciation of the desirability of continuing the alliance between the two leading Protestant powers after the Battle of Lützen.[2]

[1] This headnote is drawn from the commentary regarding this leaflet in Wolfgang Harms, Michael Schilling, Andreas Wang, eds., *Deutsche Illustrierte Flugblätter des 16. und 17. Jahrhunderts: Die Sammlung der Herzog August Bibliothek in Wolfenbüttel*, Band 2, *Historica* (*German Illustrated Leaflets of the Sixteenth and Seventeenth Centuries: The Collection of the Duke August Library in Wolfenbüttel*, vol. 2, *Historica*) (Munich: Kraus International, 1980), 534.

[2] A short passage in the text, directed at people living on the shores of the rivers Saale, Pleisse, and Elbe (three rivers that flow through Saxony), indicates that the leaflet was probably produced in Saxony for a primarily Saxon audience.

Der Schwede lebet noch: Trawer Posten . . . Frewden Post (The Swede Lives Still: Mournful News . . . Joyful News), in *Deutsche Illustrierte Flugblätter des 16. und 17. Jahrhunderts: Die Sammlung der Herzog August Bibliothek in Wolfenbüttel*, Band 2, *Historica* (*German Illustrated Leaflets of the Sixteenth and Seventeenth Centuries: The Collection of the Duke August Library in Wolfenbüttel*, vol. 2, *Historica*), ed. Wolfgang Harms, Michael Schilling, and Andreas Wang (Munich: Kraus International, 1980), 535, image 305. Available as a digital facsimile at VD 17 (Verzeichnis der Drucke des 17. Jahrhunderts [Catalog of the Publications of the Seventeenth Century]) at www.vd17.de. Call number for the document: VD 17 1:091159x.

In the background, on the shore, two armies meet in battle. The victorious army on the left is supported by a face in heaven blowing a wind against the enemy on the right. This embodiment of God's heavenly assistance is directed not only against the routed enemy but also against the many-headed dragon of the apocalypse (in the foreground), which is crowned with papal tiaras.

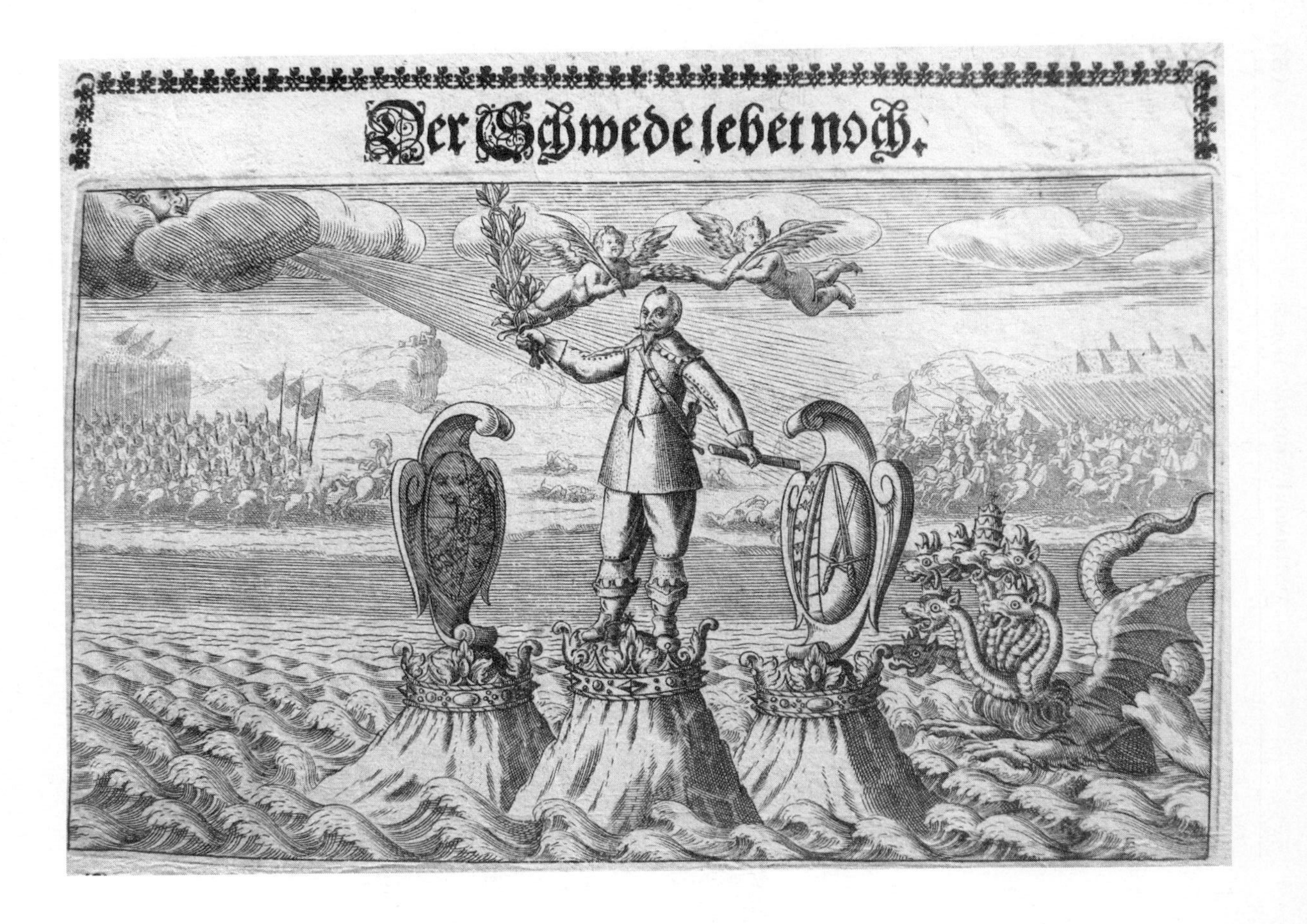
Der Schwede lebet noch.

50

MERCURY'S MESSAGE

Protestant Veneration of Gustav Adolph as Seen from the Catholic Side

1633

The article excerpted here, written by a Nuremberg correspondent, appeared in January 1633 in the Munich newspaper Mercurij Relation *(*Mercury's Message*). The newspaper represented a Catholic, pro-imperial position, and it temporarily ceased publication after the Swedes occupied Munich in the summer of 1632. This article appeared in the first issue printed after the suspension of publication. It is clear from the author's ironic tone that he disapproved of the cult surrounding Gustav Adolph that was being promoted in Protestant cities such as Nuremberg and Erfurt.*

From a Writing from Nuremberg
December 16, 1632

Everywhere here in the public pulpits they pray for the most glorious soul of the deceased king of Sweden, so that it will be accepted by the grace of God. It is also publicly announced everywhere here that the king of Sweden will be canonized and counted among the holy martyrs, because he dearly shed his most holy blood for the sake of the pure Protestant doctrine. This is why in Erfurt the entire royal court is supposed to be dressed in white, to show the great joy that he obtained for the entire Protestant side with his worthy death.[1] Some think it would

[1] At about the time the article was written, the wife of Gustav Adolph, Queen Maria Eleonore, was still residing with her court in Erfurt, where she received the news of her husband's death in battle.

From *Mercurij Relation; oder, underschiedliche Zeitungen, was nechst vergangenen Monats Decembris 1632. Jahrs sich hin und wieder zugetragen* (*Mercury's Message; or, Various News Which Happened during Last Month, December 1632*) (Munich: Verleger Niklaus Heinrich, [January] 1633), AII v. Consulted at the Institut Deutsche Presseforschung, University of Bremen, call number Z11.

have been better if it had been the color red, which is more suitable for martyrs.

Wallenstein's Assassination

51

REGULAR WEEKLY NEWS

Report of Wallenstein's Death

1634

Albrecht von Wallenstein, Duke of Friedland, was the most successful and most powerful commander on the side of the emperor during the Thirty Years War. After Wallenstein and his army lost the Battle of Lützen, however, and as he increasingly acted secretly and independently to explore the possibility of peace with their religious and political enemies, he fell out of favor with the emperor and his advisers. In a secret trial, Wallenstein was sentenced to death. On the emperor's orders, officers of Wallenstein's own army killed him and three of his closest confidants in the city of Eger (see Map 2, pages 10–11) in Bohemia during the night of February 25, 1634.

Wallenstein's assassination was widely reported in contemporary newspapers. It is noteworthy that the multiple initial statements, even by direct witnesses of the killing, especially those from Eger itself, did not assign it any political significance. The deed was termed a "murder" or, more neutrally, a "killing," and those who actually did the killing were named. No hint was given that the action was instigated by the emperor's court, not even in the Protestant-oriented newspapers, such as those published in Frankfurt, Stuttgart, Strassburg, and Zurich. This became a critical issue only in the polemical pamphlets from both sides that began to appear

"Auß Eger vom 19./29 Februarij" ("From Eger from 19/29 February"), *Ordentliche Wochentliche Zeitungen* (*Regular Weekly News*), (Frankfurt), no. 12 (publisher Johann von den Birghden Frankfurt, 1634). Consulted at the Institut Deutsche Presseforschung, University of Bremen, call number Z1/1634/12.

several weeks later. The account here, reported from Eger on February 29, appeared in the Frankfurt newspaper Ordentliche Wochentliche Zeitungen *(*Regular Weekly News*), but it was simultaneously published in almost identical form in periodical newspapers in Stuttgart, Strassburg, and Zurich.*

How it happened, with the killing of Wallenstein and the others, is to be heard: After Wallenstein came here with approximately eight hundred men, whom he quartered in the villages outside the town, he was received by Colonel Butler, from whom he expected no harm.[1] Then Count Trcka, Count Kinsky, Colonel Ilow, and Captain Niemann, who appeared willing, were invited to the castle by those favorably inclined toward the emperor.[2] On the way and at the table they discussed their agreement to the recently made resolution.[3] As it then became somewhat dark, as had been ordered before, a troop of dragoons came into the chamber, and they immediately shot down these four men in cold blood.

From there they hurried to the Duke of Friedland's quarters, and they shot down the sentinel, the chamberlain, and a page (who did not want to let them in to the duke). The duke opened the door because of the tumult, and then the commanding officer [of the dragoons] immediately stabbed him through his body. When the duke recovered and tried to reach for a gun, he stabbed him twice more, so that the duke fell down, and the blood flowed around in the room. Afterward they wrapped him in a bedsheet and carried him to the castle.

[1] Wallenstein had personally appointed Walter Butler as colonel of a regiment of dragoons.

[2] Count Adam Erdmann von Trcka, Count Wilhelm von Kinsky, and Christian von Ilow were Wallenstein's confidants. Heinrich Niemann was the captain of Wallenstein's bodyguard.

[3] At a meeting in Pilsen on January 12, 1634, Wallenstein had demanded that his officers sign a written declaration of their fidelity to him. This became known as the Pilsen Resolution.

52

REGULAR WEEKLY NEWS

A Parody of an Epitaph for Wallenstein

1634

This parody of an epitaph for Wallenstein, Duke of Friedland, appeared in the Frankfurt newspaper Ordentliche Wochentliche Zeitungen *(*Regular Weekly News*) soon after Wallenstein's death during the night of February 25, 1634. At the same time, it appeared in other German-language newspapers in Zurich and Stuttgart and also as a flyer. The satirical verse, which rhymes in the original German, was published as a message from the imperial capital of Vienna, dated March 1. Its headnote states that the "epitaph" itself was written three weeks earlier (that is, before Wallenstein's assassination), which indicates that it was part of an imperial publicity plan to vilify Wallenstein after his execution had been decided on by the emperor and his counselors in Vienna.*

The poem is a combination of a seventeenth-century memento mori,[1] *typically pointing out the transitory nature of political and military greatness, and a parody of Wallenstein's presumably well-known character traits, such as his penchant for astrology and his reluctance to wage battles and thereby risk the human and material capital of his military apparatus.*

FROM VIENNA MARCH 1.

The following epitaph of Friedland was already made and distributed three weeks ago here in Vienna:

[1] A *memento mori* (Latin for "Remember, you shall die") is a literary or artistic work created to remind people of their mortality.

Ordentliche Wochentliche Zeitung (*Regular Weekly News*) (Frankfurt), no. 13 (1634), quoted in Hans Medick, "Wallenstein's Tod: Auf den medialen Schlachtfelder des Dreißigjährigen Krieges" ("Wallenstein's Death: On the Media Battlefields of the Thirty Years War"), *Daphnis: Zeitschrift für Mittlere Deutsche Literatur und Kultur der Frühen Neuzeit (1400–1750)* (*Daphnis: Journal for Early Modern German Literature and Culture from the Early Modern Period [1400–1750]*) 37, nos. 1–2 (2008): 111–30, here 123.

Here lies and rots with skin and bones
The powerful warlord Wallenstein
Who collected great military power
But never delivered a battle:
He did grant many great good[2]
But more often he hung innocents.
Through stargazing and long-windedness
He lost much land and many people.
Too tender was his Bohemian brain,
He could not stand the ring of spurs.
Cocks, hens, and dogs he robbed
In all places where he lodged.
But he must go the way of death,
And let the cocks crow and the dogs bark.

[2] In German and English, *Gut*, or "good," can mean either something beneficial or tangible merchandise or personal property.

53

Wallenstein's Death as Treacherous Murder

1634

This document combines, like its original, text and image. It represents one of the countless newssheets that commented on Wallenstein's

From *Eygentliche Abbildung und Beschreibung deß Egerischen Panckets: Was von denen zu halten/ welche ihre Mörderische Händ an ihren Generalissimum Hertzogen Albrecht von Friedland/ General Feldmarschaln Christian vom Ilo/ Obristen Graf Wilhelm Kintzki/ Obristen Land Jägermeistern deß Königreichs Böhmen/ Obristen Tertzki/ und Rittmeister Nieman/ [et]c. gelegt/ und wie erbärmlich sie mit ihnen umbgangen; Geschehen den 15. (25.) Februarii in der Nacht/ zwischen 10. und 11. uhr/ als sie ihnen ein Gasterey hielten* (*Actual Illustration and Description of the Eger Banquet: What to Think of Them, Who Laid Their Murderous Hands on Their Generalissimo, Duke Albrecht von Friedland, General Field Marshal Christian von Ilow, Colonel Count Wilhelm Kinsky, Hunting Master of the Kingdom of Bohemia, Colonel Trcka, and Captain of the Guard, Niemann, etc., and How Pitilessly They Handled Them. Happened the 25th of February in the Night between 10 and 11 O'clock, as They Were at a Dinner, Seemingly Organized for Them in Their Honor*) [single leaf copper etching, no printer given], 1634. Herzog August Bibliothek in Wolfenbüttel, print IH 568a. The leaflet is also available digitally in the *VD17* (*Verzeichnis der Drucke des 17. Jahrhunderts* [*Catalog of the Publications of the Seventeenth Century*]) at www.vd17.de under call number VD17 23:676218X.

assassination. Some of these accounts of Wallenstein's death endorsed his killing (Document 52), but others, such as this leaflet, sharply criticized it. The four illustrations accompanying the text show, below a representation of the town of Eger, where the deed happened, the progression of the event. The upper left scene illustrates the beginning of the banquet, which ends with the killing of Wallenstein's loyal followers, shown in the upper right scene. The two lower scenes illustrate the murder of Wallenstein in his bedchamber (left) and the disposal of his body (right).

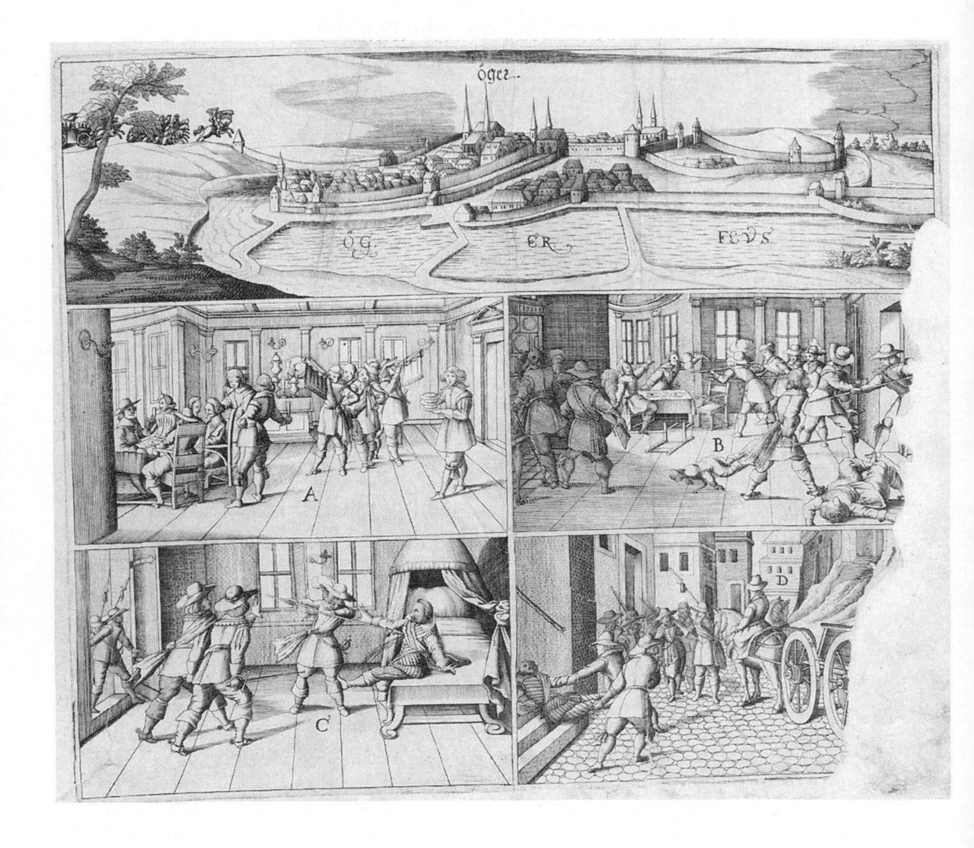

It is noteworthy that the leaflet does not place responsibility for the act on the emperor and his advisers in Vienna. Instead, it assigns guilt solely to the four men who carried out the killing, typically labeling them as

"Scotlanders," and thereby foreigners. This avoidance of any explicit criticism of the emperor indicates that the leaflet may have originated in the electorate of Saxony's sphere of influence.[1] *Saxony generally stood on the Protestant side during the Thirty Years War, but it mostly avoided directly attacking the emperor as the head of the empire.*

It is already known and lies exposed to daylight the unheard-of, unknown in all the history of the German lands, treacherous, murderous, shameful deed of the Eger bloodbath. The sun and moon, yes, the entire firmament are horrified. All men's hearts tremble. All hearty ears should scream about it. How violently contrary to God and his Word, and to the laws of all peoples, without any reason, unproven, unheard-of, unlamented, and uncondemned, Johann Gordon, Walter Leslie, Adam Gordon, and Butler,[2] who are all Scotlanders, alone out of their own volition, without command, out of jealousy, bitterness, and hate, out of vain striving for honor, for their own selfish interests, [killed] the Duke of Friedland, Count Trcka, Kinsky, Ilow, and Niemann.[3] . . . Contrary to the ways of all wild animals, they unchristianly turned the bodies of these persons into dead corpses. They also did not warn them or leave them time to pray an Our Father or to repent their sins. They laid their murderous hands and weapons on their generalissimo and general field marshal in such a way . . . as they were in no way entitled to as private persons, namely to pronounce judgment on the deeds of their superior, before they had fulfilled their own duties. They accused him of having planned to seize for himself His Imperial Majesty's crown and scepter, and to let himself be crowned as the Bohemian king, to lay the city of Vienna in ashes, and to go over to the enemy's side.

[1] Silvia S. Tschopp, "Albrecht von Wallensteins Ende im Spiegel der zeitgenössischen Flugblattpublizistik" ("Albrecht von Wallenstein's End Reflected in Contemporary Broadsheet Publications"), *Zeitschrift für Historische Forschung* (*Journal for Historical Research*) 24 (1997): 39.

[2] John Gordon was military commander in the town of Eger. Walter Leslie and Walter Butler, together with Walter Deveroux (not named here), were officers from Wallenstein's army and of Scottish (Gordon and Leslie) or Irish (Butler and Deveroux) origin. They are generally understood to have been the core group of assassins, with Deveroux as Wallenstein's killer. Adam Gordon is wrongly identified as a member of this group. He was a soldier in Wallenstein's army, but he was not actively involved in the killing.

[3] Count Adam Erdmann von Trcka, Count Wilhelm von Kinsky, and Christian von Ilow were Wallenstein's confidants. Heinrich Niemann was the captain of Wallenstein's bodyguard.

However, one knows of him . . . that this Albrecht von Wallenstein, who was previously a Bohemian nobleman, changed to serve His Imperial Majesty chivalrously in subservient honor, so that in short time he had brought peace and order to the kingdom of Bohemia and the associated lands. . . .

And because his commission [from the emperor] was absolutely aimed at making peace, which the Spanish pack and the Jesuit brood were always against, but His Princely Grace thought it was time to make an end to the calamity ruining the land, and to turn the bloody war into a blooming peace . . . therefore His Princely Grace negotiated a cease-fire.

Through the treacherous murder which has happened . . . which every day is crying for vengeance, such work toward peace has become quite uncertain, because one has the suspicion that everything is underlain with deception.

8

Peace Proclaimed and Peace Perceived: The Peace of Prague and the Peace of Westphalia

Although the Peace of Prague (1635) and the Peace of Westphalia (1648) both attempted to do little more than return to the political and religious settlements already in place before the Thirty Years War began, they represent major turning points in the history of the war. Virtually all interpretations of the war see the readiness to compromise and the realignment of alliances embodied in the Peace of Prague as marking the end of one phase of the war and the beginning of another. The Peace of Westphalia is understood not only as a watershed in the political development of Germany and the balance of European great power politics, but also as the establishment of a system of norms and a legal understanding of European international relations that would endure for centuries.

When seen through the eyes of contemporaries, however, the Peace of Prague and the Peace of Westphalia were met with skepticism and even cynicism. People whose hopes for peace had been dashed again and again did not believe that peace would actually ever come. The reality was that the everyday war, as they witnessed and experienced it, carried on unabated. Troops refused to be disbanded without fair compensation, and in the meantime they continued to appropriate their wages and their sustenance from civilians, sometimes violently. It was impossible to reconcile this reality with the seemingly meaningless declaration of peace and with the equally incongruous orders by authorities to celebrate the coming of peace. Even when the soldiers were finally gone—after an accord was reached at Nuremberg in 1650, two years after the Peace of Westphalia had been signed and proclaimed—those who had lived in fear for as long as they could remember could hardly believe that the soldiers would not come back. Although they continued to record their impressions of what was happening around them, they often found it impossible to comprehend, much less describe, what had happened over the past three decades, just as many found it impossible to begin rebuilding in hopes of a better future.

The Peace of Prague

54

The Peace of Prague

1635

On May 30, 1635, Emperor Ferdinand II and Elector Johann Georg I of Saxony signed the Peace of Prague in hopes that it would be the first step toward finally ending the war. The treaty was conceived and concluded in the wake of two important military and diplomatic events: the Battle of Nördlingen in 1634, a stunning Catholic imperial victory, and the entry of Catholic France into the war on the Protestant Swedish side in 1635. With the defeat at Nördlingen, the Swedes lost the military initiative. The time seemed ripe to break up the alliance between Sweden and the various Protestant German principalities and to negotiate a settlement. Moreover, the entry of France into the war made it both plausible and urgent for the emperor to appeal to Sweden's German allies (and even to individual German men serving in the Swedish military) to rally to expel a common foreign enemy.

The treaty was a compromise. The emperor effectively withdrew the Edict of Restitution of 1629, which had been a major bone of contention (see Documents 7–9). A new "normative date" was created: 1627, rather than 1552, meaning that the religious order would revert to what

From *Abdruck Deß Friedens Schlusses, Von der Röm. Käys. Mayt. unnd Churfürstl. Durchl. zu Sachssen, etc. zu Prag auffgerichtet: Den 20./30. Maii Anno 1635* (*Reprint of the Peace Treaty Made in Prague by His Roman Imperial Majesty and Electoral Highness of Saxony, etc., the 20th/30th of May, in the Year 1635*) (Frankfurt an der Oder: Michael Koch, 1635), Aiiv–Aiir, Axv v. Available as a digital facsimile at Universitäts- und Landesbibliothek Sachsen-Anhalt, http://digitale.bibliothek.uni-halle.de/content/titleinfo/469284. The excerpts from pages 2v–2r and 15v are revisions of the translation by Gerhard Benecke, *Germany in the Thirty Years War* (New York: St. Martin's Press, 1979), 16.

it had been in 1627. In consequence, church properties and lands that had changed hands by 1627 (that is, before the Edict of Restitution or Sweden's entry into the war) would stay in the same hands for at least the next forty years, and only those properties and lands that had changed hands since 1627 would be returned to the original owners.

The emperor also promised amnesty to most of the German princes and soldiers who were fighting against him if they would follow the example of Protestant Saxony and join his side. With the conclusion of the peace, the elector of Saxony had switched allegiances from the Protestant Swedish side to the Catholic imperial side in return for territorial concessions. Before long, several other major Protestant princes, including the Duke of Saxony-Weimar and the Landgrave of Hesse-Kassel, abandoned their alliance with Sweden to join the emperor.

Yet the Peace of Prague ultimately failed to result in a general peace. The emperor's unwillingness or inability to extend the offer of amnesty to some of his enemies—because he had already distributed their lands to his allies as spoils—only hardened their stance against him and reaffirmed their alliance with Sweden. Furthermore, the favorable resolution of an unrelated crisis in Poland allowed Sweden to move more troops into Germany. Sweden's subsequent victory at the Battle of Wittstock in 1636 broke the momentum of the Catholic imperial side, and the war would continue for more than a decade.

Let it hereby be known to all: His [Holy] Roman Imperial and also Hungarian and Bohemian Royal Majesty, our most gracious lord, as head, most eagerly attempted, and His Highness the Elector of Saxony, as a foremost pillar of the Holy Roman Emperor, loyally cooperated [to find a way] to reestablish a Christian, general, respectable, reasonable, and secure peace in the Holy Roman Empire. After so many and long-lasting wars and the misery, deprivation, and destruction suffered in them, [they wanted] to put an end to the bloodshed and to save the beloved fatherland of the noble German Nation from an ultimate downfall. Because of this unpleasant and troublesome mischief, and especially because of the continuing presence of foreign nations and armies in the territory of the empire, it would have been impossible to hold a public imperial or other general assembly. So, to such salubrious and benevolent ends, they both sent their councilor and plenipotentiaries first to Leitmeritz, from there to Pirna, and finally to Prague. For the good and honor of the empire, for the relief and salvation of the German Nation and the respective kingdoms, electorates, lands, and peoples on both sides, and for the best of the commonweal, they negotiated and concluded the following general peace.

[. . .]

Concerning all the ecclesiastical lands and properties that lay within territorial state jurisdiction and that were already annexed and held before the Treaty of Passau [of 1552] by the electors and imperial estates who are members of the Augsburg Confession [i.e., Lutherans], they shall all remain according to the clear letter and direction of the established, highly esteemed religious peace [of 1555].

However, concerning the ecclesiastical lands and properties that were territorial states in their own right and were annexed before the agreement of Passau, as well as those ecclesiastical lands and properties that fell into the hands of members of the Augsburg Confession after the conclusion of the Passau agreement, whether they lay within territorial state jurisdiction or were territorial states in their own right, we have finally agreed that those electors and imperial estates that held these lands on November 12, 1627, new style, shall have complete and free control of the same for the period of forty years from the date of this concluded agreement. And any authority that has been deprived of such lands since November 12, 1627, shall have them returned, yet without any right to claim costs and damages.

[. . .]

To achieve the long-desired pacification of our dear fatherland of the German Nation . . . each and every military occupation, recruiting and mustering, war tax, and other grievance against the laws of the empire, with which the empire has recently been burdened, is in the future to cease entirely and is never to be imposed again.

In the like manner there shall never be another particular military constitution set up within the empire, be it from the head or members, that goes against the emperor's coronation oath [or] the laws of the empire and of the imperial district administrations.

55

VOLKMAR HAPPE

Skepticism about the Recent Peace of Prague

1635

This passage is another taken from Volkmar Happe's detailed chronicle of events in and around his county of Schwarzburg-Sondershausen (see Document 17). Happe expresses his skepticism regarding whether any positive consequences would result from the peace that had just been concluded between the elector of Saxony and Emperor Ferdinand II. From his immediate, up-close perspective, the peace contained seeds of further discord and violence rather than hope for a universal and lasting peace. It is noteworthy that Happe must have written down his reaction very soon after receiving word of the peace treaty and the elector of Saxony's letter patent, that is, between the 20th and the 24th of June, 1635.

The 20th of June [1635] His Electoral Highness of Saxony sent here a printed letter patent[1] and indicated therein that His Electoral Highness had concluded a final peace with the emperor. He asks therefore that on St. John's Day [June 24] a public thanksgiving festival should be held, and one should pray that our beloved God will grant the grace that other princes and estates will accept the peace. Though we wait with fervent longing for a universal peace, right now we are more dismayed than delighted that only a separate peace with the electorate of Saxony alone has been concluded. It is therefore to be feared that thereby much more and greater warfare may result, and therefore we are more dismayed and disconcerted than delighted.

[1] A letter patent is a publicly promulgated letter.

From Volkmar Happe, *Chronicon Thuringiae* (*Thuringian Chronicle*), ed. Hans Medick, Norbert Winnige, and Andreas Bähr (electronic publication: Thüringer Universitäts- und Landesbibliothek Jena, 2008), 1:396v–97v. Available as a digital facsimile at www.mdsz.thulb.uni-jena.de/happe/quelle.php.

56

JOHANN GEORG PFORR

Perceptions of the Peace of Prague

1635

In these passages from Johann Georg Pforr's chronicle of his hometown Schmalkalden during the Thirty Years War (see Document 31), written around the time these events took place, Pforr mentions the celebration of the Peace of Prague. To this contemporary observer, the proclamation of peace did nothing to quell the everyday violence of the war.

[On] The 25th of May some imperial horsemen undertook to drive away the sheep in Weidebrun. They were chased away by the *salvaguardia* [paid guards] and the citizens, and thereby a soldier was shot and one horseman and three horses were caught.

The 28th of May was a day of fasting, repentance, and praying, because it was the conclusion of the Peace of Prague.[1]

The 14th [of June] a thanksgiving festival was held in the entire principality of Hesse and here [in the town of Schmalkalden] because of the peace concluded in Prague between His Imperial Majesty and the electorate of Saxony. Such peace helped Germany little, as the outcome revealed.

The 14th of June my godfather, Valentin Clemen, church elder, forty-three years old, passed away.

Because at the time in the local area the imperial troops were gone, on the 17th of June seven musketeers from Weimar from Brandenstein's

[1] Pforr was using the old Julian calendar, so the service mentioned took place, according to the modern Gregorian calendar, on June 7, after the signing of the treaty on May 30.

From Johann Georg Pforr, *Beschreibung etzlicher denckwürdigen Geschichden: Eine Chronik von Schmalkalden, 1400–1680* (*Description of Some Memorable Stories: A Chronicle from Schmalkalden, 1400–1680*), ed. Renate T. Wagner (Jena: Stitzius Verlag, 2008), 135–36.

regiment[2] came here, and once they were totally drunk, they started a tumult in the city. They chased people in the streets, and they stabbed to death a peasant from Struth-Helmershof.[3] Therefore the citizens came running and beat the despicable soldiers and captured them. The 27th of the same month Colonel Brandenstein had the captured soldiers picked up, but left behind the murderer, who was executed with the sword on the 5th of August.

[2] Colonel Georg Friedrich von Brandenstein (1596–1635), commander of the guards regiment of Duke Wilhelm IV of Saxony-Weimar. In June 1635, Brandenstein, who did not accept Wilhelm of Saxony-Weimar's signing of the Peace of Prague, was dismissed from the duke's army at his own request.

[3] A village approximately five miles (8 km) northeast of Schmalkalden.

The Peace of Westphalia

57

JOHANN PETER LOTICHIUS

The Relativization of Historical Truths as a Result of the War

1647

Johann Peter Lotichius was a humanist scholar, publicist, and historian who lived in Frankfurt during the Thirty Years War. For some years, he edited one of the most widely read news periodicals of the time, the Theatrum Europaeum *(*European Theater*). This remarkable passage is from Lotichius's foreword to the fifth volume of the* Theatrum Europaeum, *published in 1647, when negotiations to end the war were already under*

From Johann Peter Lotichius, "Vorrede" ("Foreword"), *Theatrum Europaei oder Historische Beschreibung aller vornembsten und denckwürdigsten Geschichten . . . Fünffter Theil* (*European Theater, or Historical Description of All Prominent and Noteworthy Histories*) 5 (Frankfurt Main: Mathaeus Merian, 1647): e v. A digital facsimile of the second edition, printed in 1651, is available at Augsburg Universitätsbibliothek, http://gateway-bayern.de/BV003815266. The digital representation is that of the second edition, printed in 1651; however, the text is identical to the first edition.

way in Münster and Osnabrück. Based on his firsthand experience of the war and his knowledge of what the historians of antiquity had written about the wars of their times, Lotichius concluded that in the reporting of complex historical events, claims of a singular truth could not be justified. In taking this relativistic position, he reflected the tone of contemporary intellectual and political discussions. Also characteristic of the times was the presentation of his argument in the form of a question.

So, then, with the short [military] operations of one or the other war (which mostly were between only two opposing parties), neither Sallust nor Tacitus[1] attained perfection in their respective works in the time of the Romans. Who would nowadays, with these frequent, intriguing, multifariously confused, and widespread wars, and more than war, [a situation] where virtually everywhere tumult and terror are normal and so many nations are in arms against each other, with so many various and muddled outrages and acts of war, who then would be allowed to presume that he would so accurately and exactly reach and attain the essential point, namely the actual truth and condition of each and every thing, action, and piece?

[1] Sallust and Tacitus were classical Roman historians who wrote about war.

58

The Peace of Westphalia

1648

The historical significance of the Peace of Westphalia is inestimable. The treaties ending the war were signed in 1648 in two neighboring Westphalian cities, Münster and Osnabrück. Indeed, the year 1648 can be seen as a watershed in the diplomatic and political history of Germany

---

From "Englische anonyme Übersetzung des IPO (1713)" ("Anonymous English Translation of the Treaty of Osnabrück [1713]"), in *Die Westfälischen Friedensverträge vom 24. Oktober 1648: Texte und Übersetzungen* (*The Westphalian Peace Treaties of 24 October 1648: Texts and Translations*), Acta Pacis Westphalicae, Supplementa electronica 1, 2004, www.pax-westphalica.de.

and of Europe. The negotiations that resulted in the Treaties of Münster and Osnabrück introduced the modern conference, or congress, system of diplomacy—that is, when the rulers of many powers, or their representatives, come together in multilateral negotiations to solve general problems—and laid the foundation for the modern European system of states. The treaties' constitutional arrangements regarding the Holy Roman Empire abolished all claims to universal power by the emperor and his rivals. They ensured continued political decentralization in Central Europe by confirming the sovereignty within the empire of individual states, which then, with their newly won authority, established themselves as absolutist states.

The following excerpts are from a 1713 English translation of the original Latin of the Treaty of Osnabrück.[1] They illustrate the Peace of Westphalia in its immediate historical context, revealing contemporaries' understanding—or at least presentation—of the causes and course of the war and the peacemaking process. Especially noteworthy is the long duration of the negotiations, from 1643 to 1648, and the emphasis on the religious nature of the war (and of the peace as well). Regarding this last point, the treaty consciously refers to previous religious settlements, such as the Peace of Augsburg in 1555 (Document 6), and expresses the continued hope that someday "the Matter of Religion can, by the Grace of God, be agreed upon." In the meantime, it promises freedom of religion, albeit freedom confined to Catholics, Lutherans, and Calvinists.

Preamble

Be it known to all and singular to whom it does concern, or whom it may in any manner concern, That after the Differences and Troubles which began several years ago in the [Holy] Roman Empire, had come to such a height, that not only all Germany, but likewise some neighbouring Kingdoms, especially Sweden and France, found themselves so involved in them, that from thence there arose a long and cruel War . . . upon which ensued a great Effusion of Christian Blood, and Devastation of several Provinces. At last it fell out by an Effect of the Divine Bounty, that both sides turned their Thoughts towards the means of making Peace, and that by a mutual Agreement made at Hamburg the 25th of December 1641[2] between the Parties, the 11th [of July] 1643 was by

[1] Slight modernizations of the spelling have been made for the sake of clarity.

[2] The dates provided here are from the Gregorian calendar. The original provides both the Julian and Gregorian dates.

common Consent appointed for beginning the Assembly or Congress of Plenipotentiaries at Osnabrück and at Munster in Westphalia.

In consequence whereof, the Ambassadors and Plenipotentiaries lawfully established on both sides, having appeared at the mentioned Time and Place. . . . After having invoked the Assistance of God, and reciprocally exchanged the Originals of their respective full Powers, they transacted and agreed among themselves, to the Glory of God, and Safety of the Christian World (the Electors, Princes and States of the Sacred Roman Empire being present, approving and consenting) the Articles of Peace and Amity, whereof the Tenour [purport] follows.

Article I

That there be a Christian, universal and perpetual Peace, and a true and sincere Friendship and Amity between his Sacred Imperial Majesty, the House of Austria, and all his Allies and Adherents, and the Heirs and Successors of each of them, chiefly the King of Spain, and the Electors, Princes and States of the Empire, on the one side; and her Sacred Royal Majesty, and the Kingdom of Sweden, her Allies and Adherents, and the Heirs and Successors of each of them, especially the most Christian King [of France], the respective Electors, Princes and States of the Empire, of the other side; and that this Peace be observed and cultivated sincerely and seriously, so that each Party may procure the Benefit, Honour and Advantage of one another, and thereby the Fruits of this Peace and Amity may be seen to grow up and flourish a-new, by a sure and reciprocal maintaining of a good and faithful Neighbourhood between the Roman Empire and the Kingdom of Sweden reciprocally.

Article II

That there be on both sides a perpetual Oblivion and Amnesty of all that has been done since the beginning of these Troubles, in what Place or in what Manner soever Hostilities may have been exercised by the one or the other Party; so that neither for any of those things, nor upon any other Account or Pretext whatsoever, any Act of Hostility or Enmity, Vexation or Hindrance shall be exercised or suffered, or caused to be exercised, either as to Persons, Condition, Goods or Security, either by one's self or by others, in private or openly, directly or indirectly, under form of Right of Law, or by open Deed, either within, or in any Place whatsoever without the Empire, notwithstanding all former Compacts to the contrary; but that all Injuries, Violences, Hostilities and Damages, and all Expenses that either side has been obliged to be at, as well before as during the War, and all Libels by Words or Writing shall be entirely forgotten, without any regard to Persons or Things; so that whatever might be demanded or pretended by one against another upon this account, shall be buried in perpetual Oblivion.

[. . .]

Article V

Now whereas the Grievances of the one and the other Religion, which were debated amongst the Electors, Princes and States of the Empire, have been partly the Cause and Occasion of the present War, it has been agreed and transacted in the following manner.

Article V, Paragraph 1

That the Transaction settled at Passau in the Year 1552 and followed in the Year 1555 with the Peace of Religion, according as it was confirmed in the Year 1566 at Augsburg, and afterwards in diverse other Diets of the Holy Roman Empire, in all its Points and Articles agreed and concluded by the unanimous Consent of the Emperor and Electors, Princes and States of both Religions, shall be maintained in its Force and Vigour, and sacredly and inviolably observed.

But those things that are appointed by this Treaty with Consent of both Parties, touching certain Articles in the said Transaction which are troublesome and litigious, shall be looked upon to have been observed in Judgment and otherwise, as a perpetual Declaration of the said Pacification, until the Matter of Religion can, by the Grace of God, be agreed upon, and that without stopping short for the Contradiction and Protestation of any one whatsoever, Ecclesiastical or Secular, either within or without the Empire, in any time whatsoever: all which Oppositions are by virtue of these Presents declared null and void.

[. . .]

Article VII, Paragraph 1

It has likewise been thought good, by the unanimous Consent of his Imperial Majesty, and all the Estates of the Empire, That the same Right or Advantage, which all the other Imperial Constitutions, the Peace of Religion, this present Transaction, and the Decision of Grievances therein contained, grant to the Catholic States and Subjects, and to those of the Confession of Augsburg [Lutherans], ought also to be granted to those who call themselves the Reformed [Calvinists]; saving nevertheless for ever the Compacts, reversal Privileges, and other Regulations which the States that call themselves Protestants have stipulated among themselves, and with their Subjects, whereby care has hitherto been taken of the States and Subjects of every place, as to Religion and the Exercise thereof, and the things that depend thereupon, saving also the Liberty of Conscience of every one.

. . . It shall not be lawful to change the Exercise of Religion, or the Ecclesiastical Laws and Customs which shall have been received formerly, nor to take the Churches, Schools, Hospitals, or the Revenues, Pensions and Salaries thereto belonging, from the first Possessors, and confer them upon those of his own Religion; and far less to oblige his Subjects under pretext of the Right of the Territory, Episcopal Right, that of Patronage, or any other, to receive Ministers of another Religion, or give any trouble or molestation to the Religion of others directly or indirectly. . . .

Article VII, Paragraph 2

. . . But besides these Religions [Catholic, Lutheran, and Calvinist] no other shall be received or tolerated in the Sacred Roman Empire.[3]

[3] For this reason, not only Jews were excluded but also Protestant sects such as the Mennonites, Baptists, and Anabaptists. Many of them later emigrated from Central Europe to North America.

59

The Messenger Bearing News of Peace

1648

The woodcut on page 176 shows a messenger astride a galloping horse, spreading the joyous news of the conclusion of peace in Münster. The eagle on his chest identifies him as an imperial mail carrier, and in the background on the left side is a post station displaying an imperial flag. The destroyed building in the background and the grave in the foreground illustrate the devastation of the war. In the upper left, the allegorical figure Fama (Fame) embodies the good news, and in the upper right the Roman messenger god Mercury delivers a large envelope. Although the name of the artist is unknown, the publisher was the Catholic Augsburg engraver and woodcut artist Marc Anton Hannas, whose name appears in the lower right corner. The woodcut, accompanied by a long celebratory prayer, was published as a single-page flyer. Such flyers were the most important and immediate means of mass communication at the time.

Freudenreicher Postilion von Münster, den durch des Allerhöchsten ohnaußsprechliche Gnad von den vornembsten Potentaten der gantzen Christenheit, daselbst den 24. und 25. Oct. 1648 ratificierten, underschriebenen und mit grossen Frewden öffentlich publicierten hochwerthen lieben Frieden bringent (*The Joyous Messenger from Münster Bringing News of the Precious Beloved Peace, Which, through the Almighty's Unspeakable Grace, Was Ratified, Signed, and with Great Joy Openly Publicized by the Most Prominent Potentates of All Christianity on the 24th and 25th of October in the Year 1648*). Colored single leaf woodcut with typeset printing by the Augsburg artist Marx Anthon Hannas (Augsburg, 1648), 370 x 275 cm, Kunstsammlungen und Museen Augsburg, Inv.-No. G20632.

AMA
BEY MARX ANTHO: HANNAS

60

CASPAR PREIS

Peace, But Not the End of the Consequences of War

1648–1649

Caspar Preis was a Catholic peasant who lived in the village of Stausebach in upper Hesse. Stausebach belonged to the Catholic enclave of Amöneburg, which was ruled by the elector and archbishop of Mainz and was encircled by Protestant territories.

Preis's chronicle, which was written at the end of 1650, especially looks back on the almost two decades of occupations and tribulations that the war brought to his village and the territory of Amöneburg since the beginning of the Swedish phase of the war. The passage quoted here is notable for its realistic assessment of the continuing burdens that the financial and logistical arrangements of the peace treaty entailed for his peasant homestead. Preis's bitter complaints about these burdens stand in stark contrast to his account of the substantial repairs and rebuilding taking place in Amöneburg, and especially on his own farm, in the aftermath of the war.

[1648]

In the year 1648 the troops moved into Bavaria, and we had a little peace here in this country and rebuilt some of the damaged buildings a bit, so that we could help ourselves to them again. Aye, you precious, merciful, good God, what a poor, torn-up, disordered village was Stausebach at that time! Oh, how we were so very poor, yes, really poor people! . . .

Now, . . . [in the year 1648] the beloved peace came, in keeping with God's beloved will, and therefore the troops were all distributed throughout the whole of Germany in cities and villages, each according to its means, so that a village got one or two soldiers, or three or four, depending on the village. We poor people had to provide for them, had

---

From Caspar Preis, *Bauernleben im Zeitalter des Dreißigjährigen Krieges: Die Stausebacher Chronik des Caspar Preis, 1636–1667* (*Peasant Life in the Age of the Thirty Years War: The Stausebach Chronicle of Caspar Preis, 1636–1667*), ed. Wilhelm A. Eckhardt and Helmut Klingelhöfer with an Introduction by Gerhard Menk (Marburg: Verlag Trautvetter & Fischer Nachf., 1998), 66–69.

to give them money, give the horses oats and hay. We poor Stausebachers had to provide for a horseman with a woman and three horses.

And in addition, before then, we had to pay a lot of money before the troops were distributed, because the Swedish first had to be paid money to leave the empire. So we Stausebachers first had to pay, for our portion of the peace tax, 36 imperial talers in one lump sum. I think it was a lot of money for each of us, because at the time in all the villages we still had very little. For myself I had to give 5 imperial talers from my savings.

So everybody was running and scraping to get his money together, and everybody thought that once we had raised the peace payment, then we would again have things in good order and peace, but the rod struck us still again. After that more troops still came and burdened us and extorted from us and tormented us still more. It cannot be said or told all the lamentations, the sorrows, and the heartache that we poor people had to suffer and endure in eighteen years. No human being would believe it, apart from those who experienced it themselves with great pain and heartache.

[1649]

The Swedish troops, as written before, lay in the countryside from January until the 8th day of December in the year 1649, and we in Stausebach, as told above, had the horseman with his woman and the three horses. We had to give every month, in money, 8 imperial talers for the horseman, three 20-kreuzer coins for provisions, [and] oats and hay for the horses, and the horseman was a great tyrant. He was a Saxon, but his woman was from Bavaria. In addition, we also still had to give, as always, the contribution to the Hessians. Aye, didn't we have misfortune and a time of impoverishment to endure?! The gracious, merciful, beloved, and true God will redeem us and help us in a fatherly way out of all afflictions and misery through Jesus Christ, his most beloved son, our Lord. . . .

In this time, the Amöneburgers again built on the mountain in their city, whoever could or wanted to. In addition, they bought the shabby old buildings in all the villages, as they could get them. The buildings that they now made into houses, before they would have hardly been taken for pigsties. But this was no help to us. We have enough experience, yes, of what our doing and not doing is worth, when dear God pulls back his kind hand from us.

In this year, that is in the year 1649, I rebuilt two buildings and then the house that stands behind our farmstead, which belonged to Hans

Bornman's widow and which I had bought from her. As one can easily imagine, it cost a lot in a time that is as bad as the present, in which we have so very little. The carpenter labor cost me 40 guldens. It was done during Lent.

In this year, as I already said above, there were again eighteen houses in Stausebach. God grant further good fortune and his holy blessing. In this year twelve plows again went into the fields around Stausebach, but pulled by mere oxen and cattle. There was still not a single horse in the village. There also hadn't been any which had belonged to the villagers for nine years. Earlier there were sometimes far too many horses here, but to our ruin and great loss. I myself again had two large draft oxen and also two small ones, which we harnessed together, and a cow, a bull, and a calf, eight pigs, large and small, a rooster, and five hens. God be praised and thanked. It is again a good start. God bring us good fortune and blessings again.

61

HANS HEBERLE

The Uneasy Peace and Its Aftermath

1648–1650

Hans Heberle was the cobbler, peasant, and self-taught writer in the countryside near Ulm (Swabia) whose reflections on the ominous appearance of the comet at the beginning of the war are provided in Document 4. In this passage from his chronicle, which runs all through the war, he contrasts the experience of the peace celebrations that the city authorities of Ulm ordered and held at the end of 1648 with his own family's experience at the time, when they once more had to flee their home in

From Gerd Zillhardt, ed., *Der Dreißigjährige Krieg in zeitgenössischer Darstellung: Hans Heberles "Zeytregister" (1618–1672). Aufzeichnungen aus dem Ulmer Territorium. Ein Beitrag zu Geschichtsschreibung und Geschichtsverständnis der Unterschichten* (*The Thirty Years War in Contemporary Portrayals: Hans Heberle's "Time Register" (1618–1672). Records from the Territory of Ulm. Regarding the History Writing and Historical Understanding of the Lower Classes*) (Ulm: Kommissionsverlag W. Kohlhammer, 1975), 224–27, 235–37.

the countryside to seek refuge within the walls of the nearby city in order to escape approaching French troops. Heberle was vividly and painfully aware that the mere proclamation of peace hardly changed conditions in the countryside.

The 12th day of November [1648],[1] after the peace had now been concluded, and the soldiers were supposed to be evacuated, we again fled to the city of Ulm with wife and kids, horse and cow, on a Sunday. It was at just this time, Monday, the 13th day of November, that the authorities in Ulm announced to the whole country that a celebration of thanksgiving and peace should be festively carried out, with sermons, holy communion, and diligent praying—this we diligently and festively did, having taken refuge in Ulm. One celebrated this festival primly and exuberantly, just like Holy Christmas always is.[2] And praise and thanks be to God, we were happy to flee this time, because it was the last flight, the twenty-ninth or approximately thirtieth or even more, all of which could not possibly be described. These flights [each recorded by Heberle in his chronicle], and still others besides, to other destinations, I could not write down at the time on account of being sorely distressed. For often one village or hamlet fled to another, and vice versa. There were also a lot of times that people fled into the thickets and forests, so that it is impossible for anyone to describe them all.

In sum it was such a pitiable affair that even a stone would have taken pity, not to mention a human heart. We were hunted like game in the woods. One was caught and cruelly beaten, the other was hacked and stabbed, the third was shot, and the last one robbed of his bit of bread and his clothes. Therefore we cannot praise God enough for the sublime peace that we have experienced. What have we endured in these thirty flights just to the city of Ulm!? One happened in the dark of night and in bad weather, another in snow and bitter cold, a third in peril because of the soldiers, so that we often risked poverty on the way—indeed, risked life and limb.

The 28th day of November we and the entire countryside joyously went home again. We cleaned up our houses and put them to right,

[1] By the older Julian calendar used by Heberle; November 22 by the modern Gregorian calendar.

[2] The peace celebration took place in Ulm on Monday, November 18 (old Julian Calendar), 1648.

because some of them were quite badly damaged, especially the windows, stoves, and doors.

[. . .]

This year, 1649, is a happy chosen year of joy and celebration. Even though peace was made in 1648, the peace has not been fully concluded. Yet God alone in heaven be honored and praised for having made peace in our Germany and throughout the [Holy] Roman Empire under the emperor, the Swedes, the French, and all kings, princes, counts, and cities, villages, hamlets, farms, and cottages, whether rich or poor, young or old, woman and man, wife and child altogether, including the dear cattle and horses, have everything to rejoice and the peace to enjoy. Yes, also the dear soil and the fields, which have long been neglected and lain fallow, will once again be properly plowed and sown, so that we miserable children of man can again grow our sustenance, and so we can make good the harm that we have suffered so that our sorrows can be healed again. And also that we may again carry on our crafts and manufactures, so that we may endure the riders billeted on us and be able to pay the peace tax [for demobilization], and finally bring to an end this great burden.

On the 6th day of January [1649] a regiment of Swedish riders was billeted in all the hamlets of our Ulm district, and we had to pay a mighty great sum of money.

Now that peace has been concluded at Münster and everybody has left there, there was another meeting of the same lords this year in Nuremberg, which lasted more than a year. They concluded the peace fully and with good unanimity.[3]

The lords negotiated with one another and reached an agreement among themselves regarding how and when each of their regiments should be paid off and dismissed, so that their soldiers would not mutiny, rob, plunder, and so on in the empire. Most of the soldiers [here] are wholly bad and audacious, like almost all soldiers are, and it took a long time to negotiate, and the whole time we had to pay exorbitant sums every month, even weekly and daily. But God be praised and thanked, at last the orders arrived here in the Ulm countryside for our regiment on the 11th day of October (in the same week as the consecration of the church of Holzkirchen), and the soldiers were paid off and marched away in good order and without any further damage.

[. . .]

[3] Heberle is referring here to the final Nuremberg Accords for the Implementation of the Peace of Westphalia of June 16, 1650.

These seven imperial regional administrative districts of the empire have been ordered to pay the Swedes and their armies 5 million Reichstalers in three installments. The first installment will be 1.8 million imperial talers in cash. . . . And everyone will have to meet and work out his share of the 1.8 million taler assessment. And that was the decision that they reached at Nuremberg and that concluded the peace.

The 24th day of August [1650], on St. Bartholomew's Day, there was a thanksgiving and peace celebration in Ulm and in all the villages in the countryside with sermons, songs, prayers, and Holy Communion. It was joyous, because the soldiers had now left all their quarters and locations, and everywhere and in every place this was celebrated, and we now had the whole, total, and general peace for which we had prayed and begged God and his noble potentates. So the following fine prayer was composed especially for the occasion and spoken from all the pulpits:

> Thank you, gracious Lord, that after we have long endured turmoil and war you have granted us peace and tranquillity, and that you have turned our pain into joy and our suffering into good days. We thank you for pulling us like burning wood out of the fire and that we have come away with our lives as booty. Oh merciful Father, how can we sufficiently repay this great kindness, that you have so graciously looked upon us and heard our prayers and have done for us, who are not worthy to raise our eyes to you in heaven, what we have asked from you in our prayers.
>
> Oh Lord, you have indeed treated us with all of your mercy, so that our city and country, which had been full of fear and terror, are now full of joy and happiness. We most humbly beseech you, we who have been saved from the sword and survived, that you will continue to grant us mercy to let our grain grow again, so that we may multiply and bear fruit again. Rebuild us, Lord, so that we may live securely, each under his fruit tree and grapevine, so that the places that were torn apart and destroyed will be newly occupied and rebuilt, and the countryside that was abandoned will be plowed again, and all people will see that you are the Lord who builds what was destroyed and plants what was laid to waste. Oh God, thou lover of peace, grant us henceforth peace, and let us occupy our boundaries and houses in peace and tranquillity, so that the voice of the war messenger does not terrify us nor the man of war harm us.[4]

[4] Heberle took this thanksgiving prayer from a printed flyer distributed by the religious authorities of Ulm.

62

The Experience of War, Anxiety regarding the Future, and the Will to Reconstruct

1647

This notation in a family Bible from the village of Gerstetten in the Swabian Alps (in southern Germany), dated January 17, 1647, was discovered by the folklorist and historian Angelika Bischoff-Luithlen. The anonymous author, who lived in a region of Central Europe that was especially devastated by the war, expresses the experience and attitudes that resulted from the war's long duration and impact.

They say the terrible war is now over. But it still doesn't feel like peace anywhere. Everywhere there is jealousy, hate, and worse things—the war has taught us such. The old people have grown old with godlessness—how could they still change before their end? There are only a few cottages left in the village. We people live like animals, eating bark and grass. No person can imagine that something like this has happened before us. Many people say it is now certain that there is no God. In the last couple of days foreign people moved in, they say from the mountains. They speak a strange language.[1] Seem to me to be capable workers, anyway. Want to stay here, since they were driven out because of heresy. Benckheler, Heinzmann, I, and one of the strangers got together today to see whether we couldn't make a couple of the crumbling cottages habitable again. The others all say it's not really peace, the soldiers will surely come again, and there's no point in doing anything. But we believe that God has not abandoned us. We all must stand together now and get to work, inside and out.

[1] The author is referring to the Protestants, who at the end of the war were forced to emigrate from the territories of the archbishop of Salzburg, now part of Austria. They found vacant farmsteads on which to settle in the villages of the Swabian Alps and other areas of Central Europe that had been devastated by war. They spoke German, although their dialect was "strange" to the local residents.

Quoted from the original manuscript in Angelika Bischoff-Luithlen, *Gruorn: Ein Dorf und sein Ende* (*Gruorn: A Village and Its End*) (Stuttgart: Schwäbischer Alb Verein, 1967), 83.

A Chronology of the Era of the Thirty Years War (1608–1650)

1608 *May 14* Protestant Union established.

1609 *July 10* Catholic League established.

1617 *June 26* Ferdinand II crowned king of Bohemia.

1618 *May 23* Defenestration of Prague sets off Thirty Years War.

September–November Comet appears in night sky.

1619 *March 20* Holy Roman Emperor Matthias dies.

August 19 Bohemian Estates depose Ferdinand II.

August 28 Ferdinand II elected Holy Roman Emperor.

November 3 Frederick V, elector of Palatinate, crowned Frederick I, king of Bohemia.

1620 *November 8* At Battle of White Mountain, Catholic League army under Tilly defeats Protestant Bohemian army.

1623 *June 3* Ferdinand II commissions Wallenstein to raise imperial army.

1625 *June* Denmark enters Thirty Years War.

1626 *June 9–10* Imperial troops storm town of Münden.

August 4 Town of Wernigerode negotiates "contribution" to occupying imperial troops.

1627 *April 3* Soldier and chronicler Peter Hagendorf enlists with Pappenheim's imperial troops.

1629 *March 6* Ferdinand II issues Edict of Restitution.

May 22 Denmark withdraws officially from the war.

1630 *July 6* Sweden enters war when Swedish troops led by King Gustav Adolph land on Baltic coast.

August 13 Wallenstein dismissed as imperial commander.

1631 *May 20* Imperial troops storm Magdeburg.

September 7 At Battle of Breitenfeld, Swedish Protestant army commanded by Gustav Adolph defeats Catholic imperial army commanded by Tilly.

December 9 Jesuit priest Liborius Wagner killed near Schonungen and thereafter venerated as martyr.

1632 *April 14* Wallenstein reinstated as imperial commander.

September 7 Protestants occupy Cathedral of Erfurt.

November 16 At Battle of Lützen, Swedish Protestant army defeats imperial troops commanded by Wallenstein; Gustav Adolph killed.

1634 *February 25* Wallenstein assassinated in Eger.

September 6 At Battle of Nördlingen, a combined imperial and Spanish army under the joint commands of Archduke Ferdinand of Austria (who later became Emperor Ferdinand III) and his cousin Prince Ferdinand of Spain and Portugal, Archbishop of Toledo, defeats the Swedish Protestant army under Gustav Karlsson Horn, count of Bjöneborg, and Duke Bernhard of Saxony-Weimar.

1635 *February 3* During widespread plague and famine, Michael Lebhardt reports cannibalism in Agawang.

May France officially declares war on Spain and directly intervenes in Thirty Years War in Central Europe; Peace of Prague concluded between Holy Roman Emperor and Saxony.

June 14–17 During thanksgiving festival to celebrate Peace of Prague in Schmalkalden, deadly "tumult" breaks out between residents and newly arrived Swedish Protestant troops.

1636 English diplomat William Crowne journeys through war-torn Germany.

September 15 Schmalkalden town council seeks to expel local Jews.

1637 *February 15* Holy Roman Emperor Ferdinand II dies; succeeded by Ferdinand III.

1640 *May 30* Swedish troops attack town of Sondershausen.

1643 *July 11* Peace negotiations begin in Münster and Osnabrück.

1648 *October 24–25* Peace of Westphalia concluded in Münster and Osnabrück.

November 12 Chronicler and cobbler Hans Heberle flees for the last time from his home to escape rampaging troops.

1650 *June 16* Nuremberg Accords for the Final Implementation of the Peace of Westphalia concluded; troops at last compensated and discharged.

Questions for Consideration

1. Consider the historical consciousness of the people who lived through the Thirty Years War. To what extent were they conscious of the significance of the events happening around them? How well did they understand the larger geographic, historical, religious, and political contexts of the events they witnessed or participated in? How did they understand when the war began, how its course changed, and how long it might last?
2. To what extent were people in the war conscious of social rank and honor? To what extent did this awareness influence their perceptions of the people they encountered? How did concern about their own place in society—and that of their associates—motivate their behavior and attitudes? Consider especially Documents 29–33, 37, and 53.
3. How conscious of religious difference were people during the war? To what extent did they identify themselves and others in confessional terms? Consider especially the documents in chapter 2.
4. To what extent did people look to God as the cause of their problems, or the solution?
5. To what extent did religion motivate soldiers and civilians? What other factors influenced their thoughts and deeds?
6. How did people avoid violence, or defend themselves against violence, during the war? How much was violence (or the threat of it) countered with violence (or the threat of it)? To what extent were people able to deflect or avoid violence through nonviolent means?
7. What role did gender play in shaping the experience of soldiers and civilians during the Thirty Years War? How did wartime experiences affect relations between men and women? How did sexualized violence against women affect their honor and the honor of their male associates? See especially the documents in chapter 3.
8. How did people's experiences of the war change their attitudes toward authority figures—heads of household, local officials, military officers, and rulers? To what extent did they look to authority figures to remedy

problems, and to what extent did they lose faith that the authorities could solve problems?

9. How did people survive the Thirty Years War? What strategies did they use to increase their odds of survival for themselves and for their families? How much were these strategies planned, and how much were they only identified in retrospect? What role did women and children play in these strategies of survival?
10. Considering that the war featured relatively few spectacular battles, how and why did the destruction of Magdeburg and the Battle of Lützen become so associated with the war in cultural memory? See the documents in chapter 6.
11. How were news and information spread by mass media during the Thirty Years War? To what extent were people informed by the press, and to what extent were they skeptical of it? Consider especially the documents in chapters 7 and 8.
12. What problems for civilians and soldiers were raised by the transition from war to peace?
13. From the perspective of people's everyday experiences at the local level, what seem to have been the climax years of the war in respect to human suffering and death? Consider the division of the war into political-military phases by historians and compare the perspectives and experiences in the ego-documents collected here based on these phases.

Selected Bibliography

Arndt, Johannes. *Der Dreißigjährige Krieg, 1618–1648* (*The Thirty Years War, 1618–1648*). Stuttgart: Reclam Universal-Bibliothek, 2009. This brief introduction to the Thirty Years War reflects the current state of the field. It emphasizes the war's origin in a conflict over the political and religious constitution of the Holy Roman Empire, but it also stresses the war's broader European ramifications. Arndt presents both military and civilian perceptions of the war and the war's reflection in the contemporary press.

Asch, Ronald G. *The Thirty Years War: The Holy Roman Empire and Europe, 1618–1648.* New York: St. Martin's Press, 1997. In this introduction to the political and military history of the war, the Bohemian Rebellion of 1618–1620, the Edict of Restitution of 1629, and the Peace of Prague of 1635 are treated as the starting and turning points of the war. Asch sees the dynamics of the war progressing from a conflict located within the Holy Roman Empire to a widespread European war. Especially remarkable is a final chapter on the problems of war finance and their influence on the changing structures of warfare.

Berg, Holger. *Military Occupation under the Eyes of the Lord: Studies in Erfurt during the Thirty Years War.* Göttingen: Vandenhoeck and Ruprecht, 2010. This pioneering and intensive examination of the perceptions of wartime events in contemporary sermons and chronicles uses the special focus of a local study to investigate the religious dimension of these perceptions and their dynamics.

Brady, Thomas A. "The Thirty Years War." Chap. 17 in *German Histories in the Age of Reformations, 1400–1650*, 375–404. Cambridge, U.K.: Cambridge University Press, 2009. This succinct and engaging chapter on the war concludes a book devoted to the multiple and often unpredictable paths of German history in the age of the reformations and Counter-Reformation. Through analytic acuity and skillful writing, Brady integrates the political and military dynamics of the war with its socioeconomic conditions and consequences as well as its human dimension of suffering and death.

Burkhardt, Johannes. *Der Dreißigjährige Krieg* (*The Thirty Years War*). Frankfurt: Suhrkamp, 1992. This crucially important systematic analysis views the Thirty Years War less as a conflict between states and political powers and more as a "war of state formation," in which the problems of emerging modern states and their contests for universal hegemony were acted out in bellicose ways. A condensed version of Burkhardt's argument is available in English:

———. "The Thirty Years' War." In *A Companion to the Reformation World*, edited by Ronnie Po-Chia Hsia, 272–90. Malden, Mass.: Blackwell, 2007.

Bussmann, Klaus, and Heinz Schilling, eds. *1648: War and Peace in Europe, Münster-Osnabrück, 24.10.1998–17.1.1999*. Vol. 1, *Politics, Religion, Law and Society*. Münster: Veranstaltungsgesellschaft 350 Jahre Westfälischer Friede, 1999. This volume of scholarly essays on the political and social history of the Thirty Years War was published as the first of a three-volume catalog documenting a 1998 exhibition in Münster on the occasion of the 350th anniversary of the Peace of Westphalia.

Flint, Eric. *1632*. Riverdale, N.Y.: Baen, 2000. This is the first in a recent series of historical novels set during the Thirty Years War that demonstrate the continuing cultural memory of the war at the turn of the twenty-first century. The story transports modern West Virginian coal miners through space and time to Thuringia in 1632, where they form an army and join the Swedish Protestant side. They ultimately shoot Wallenstein and make Gustav Adolph "Emperor of the Confederated Principalities of Europe" and "Captain General of the United States."

Grimmelshausen, Hans Jacob Christoffel von. *Simplicissimus: The German Adventurer*. Translated by John C. Osborne. With a foreword by Lynne Tatlock. Knoxville: University of Tennessee Press, 2008. Available at www.lib.utk.edu/newfoundpress/osborne/. This is the classic fictional work set in the world of the Thirty Years War. The first edition appeared in Nuremberg in 1668, although it carried the imprint of 1669. Written as a first-person narrative, the novel has often been mistaken for an autobiography and therefore considered and used as a document reflecting the harsh realities of the war. However, its poetic mode of presenting the wartime adventures of its picaresque hero transcends the representational mode of an autobiography. The widespread distribution and reading of *Simplicius Simplicissimus*, especially since the nineteenth century, have done much to shape the cultural memory of the war. Osborne's unabridged translation of the first edition is highly recommended, as is Tatlock's insightful discussion of the history of the text (and of its translations) in the foreword.

Grimmelshausen, Johann Jakob Christoffel von. *The Adventures of a Simpleton: Simplicius Simplicissimus*. Translated by Mike Mitchell. 2nd ed. Sawtry, U.K.: Dedalus, 2005. Mitchell's abridged translation is recommended as a very readable modernized version of the novel.

Hartmann, Peter, and Florian Schuller, eds. *Der Dreißigjährige Krieg: Facetten einer Epoche* (*The Thirty Years War: Facets of an Epoch*). Regensburg:

Friedrich Pustet Verlag, 2010. This volume is the proceedings of a conference, with contributions mainly by historians of politics. Interesting attempts at new assessments of leading protagonists such as Maximilian I of Bavaria, Tilly, and Wallenstein are accompanied by more traditional efforts to assess the politics of the war. Some of the essays are devoted to the historical anthropology of the war and the epochal assessment of the peacemaking effort of 1648.

Helfferich, Tryntje, ed. *The Thirty Years War: A Documentary History*. Indianapolis: Hackett, 2009. This collection of documents emphasizes diplomatic correspondence and official texts. Two extensive excerpts from the personal accounts of the soldier Peter Hagendorf and the cobbler Hans Heberle provide an overview of two contrasting wartime experiences.

Kampmann, Christoph. *Europa und das Reich im Dreißigjährigen Krieg: Geschichte eines europäischen Konflikts* (*Europe and the Empire in the Thirty Years War: History of a European Conflict*). Stuttgart: W. Kohlhammer, 2008. This interesting analysis of a political historian presents the war as a conflict among European powers from the beginning. Kampmann's thesis is that it was not the bellicosity of the involved powers that acted as a motor propelling the enduring conflicts of the war. On the contrary, it was each one's search for an "honorable peace."

Krusenstjern, Benigna von, and Hans Medick, eds. *Zwischen Alltag und Katastrophe: Der Dreißigjährige Krieg aus der Nähe* (*Between Everyday and Catastrophe: The Thirty Years War from Up Close*). 2nd ed. Göttingen: Vandenhoeck and Ruprecht, 2001. This collection of articles from European and American historians views the war from both micro- and macrohistorical perspectives.

Medick, Hans. "Historical Event and Contemporary Experience: The Capture and Destruction of Magdeburg in 1631." *History Workshop Journal* 52 (2001): 23–48. This article draws on contemporary ego-documents and media to examine the storming and destruction of Magdeburg as a "defining event" of the Thirty Years War.

———. "The Thirty Years' War as Experience and Memory: Contemporary Perceptions of a Macro-Historical Event." In *Enduring Loss in Early Modern Germany: Cross Disciplinary Perspectives*, edited by Lynne Tatlock, 25–50. Leiden: Brill, 2010. This study of ego-documents investigates contemporaries' understandings of the war and their influence on the later cultural memory of it.

———. "Wallensteins Tod: Auf den medialen Schlachtfeldern des Dreißigjährigen Krieges" ("Wallenstein's Death: On the Media Battlefields of the Thirty Years War"). *Daphnis: Zeitschrift für Mittlere Deutsche Literatur und Kultur der Frühen Neuzeit (1400–1750)* (*Daphnis: Journal for Central German Literature and Culture from the Early Modern Period [1400–1750]*) 37, nos. 1–2 (2008): 111–30. This study explores Wallenstein's death as a media event.

Medick, Hans, and Norbert Winnige, eds. *Mitteldeutsche Selbstzeugnisse der Zeit des Dreißigjährigen Krieges* (*Central German Ego-Documents from the Time of the Thirty Years War*). Jena: Thüringer Universitäts- und Landesbibliothek Jena, 2008. Available at: www.mdsz.thulb.uni-jena.de. This collection makes available as digital editions four previously unpublished ego-documents (including the documents from Volkmar Happe and Hans Krafft presented in this book). The documents are available as digital facsimiles of the original manuscript and as verbatim transcriptions annotated with rich hyperlinked information. Included are numerous research and search features that are easily accessible and usable via the Internet.

Mortimer, Geoff. *Eyewitness Accounts of the Thirty Years War, 1618–48*. Basingstoke, U.K.: Palgrave Macmillan, 2002. This first systematic study of eyewitness accounts of the Thirty Years War is valuable primarily for its analysis of civilian perceptions of the war.

———. *Wallenstein: The Enigma of the Thirty Years War*. Basingstoke, U.K.: Palgrave Macmillan, 2010. The most up-to-date biography of Wallenstein.

Paas, Martha, and Roger Paas, eds. *The Kipper and Wipper Inflation, 1619–23: An Economic History with Contemporary Broadsheets*. New Haven, Conn.: Yale University Press, 2012. This original work is an analysis of the inflation accompanying the initial stages of the war and propelling its dynamic. The main part contains a rich documentation of contemporary reactions to this inflation from German broadsheets with the German texts and their English translations.

Parker, Geoffrey, ed. *The Thirty Years' War*. 2nd rev. ed. London: Routledge, 1997. This important collaborative overview and study was mainly written by Parker, with contributions by other leading historians. It sets the war in the context not only of power politics but also of changing military practices and the economics of warfare.

Polišenský, Joseph V. *The Thirty Years War*. Translated by Richard Evans. Berkeley: University of California Press, 1971. This interesting study by a Czech Marxist historian is an early attempt at uniting a macro-historical and a micro-historical study. It views the war as the culmination of the great struggle for hegemony between the Protestant and Catholic powers of Europe and investigates the repercussions of this struggle for the small domain of Zlin in western Moravia.

Rabb, Theodore K. *The Struggle for Stability in Early Modern Europe*. New York: Oxford University Press, 1975. This brilliant and wide-ranging analysis takes the form of a large essay. It shows how a general desire for order and stability and their permanent institutionalization emerged from experiencing the war as a cultural, religious, and social crisis.

Schroeder, Peter, and Olaf Asbach, eds. *Research Companion to the Thirty Years War*. London: Ashgate, 2013. This volume with contributions from German, English, Estonian, French, and American scholars offers an innovative survey of the different theaters, factors, protagonists, and periods of the war.

Theibault, John. *German Villages in Crisis: Rural Life in Hesse-Kassel and the Thirty Years' War, 1580–1720.* Atlantic Highlands, N.J.: Humanities Press, 1994. This is an important pioneering study of the effects of the war in a rural region of central Germany.

———. "Landfrauen, Soldaten und Vergewaltigungen während des Dreißigjährigen Krieges" ("Rural Women, Soldiers, and Rape during the Thirty Years War"). *Werkstatt Geschichte* (*Workshop History*) 19 (1998): 25–39. This is one of the few innovative articles on gender relations during the war.

Wedgwood, Cicely Veronica. *The Thirty Years War.* London: Jonathan Cape, 1938. A classic work of narrative political history, this book has been published in many editions in English and other languages since it first appeared in 1938. A 2005 edition published by the New York Review of Books includes a foreword by Anthony Grafton, which puts the book in the contemporary historical context before the Second World War in which it was written and published, and an introduction by Paul Kennedy.

Whaley, Joachim. "The Thirty Years War, 1618–1648." Chap. 7 in *Germany and the Holy Roman Empire.* Vol. 1, *From Maximilian I to the Peace of Westphalia, 1493–1648.* Oxford, U.K.: Oxford University Press, 2012. This clearly written chapter on the war is part of a book by a political and constitutional historian devoted to the complex history of the Holy Roman Empire from the Reformation to the Peace of Westphalia. It essentially portrays the Thirty Years War as a constitutional conflict within the Holy Roman Empire about the shape of the "German Polity," into which foreign powers intervened, but in the end did not play a dominating role. Only one contemporary ego-document (by William Crowne; see Document 36) is mentioned, but not extensively quoted; however, it becomes clear that Whaley's perspective stands in an interesting contrast to that of our book.

Wilson, Peter H. *Europe's Tragedy: A History of the Thirty Years War.* London: Allen Lane, 2009. This is a masterful work of political history. Wilson's thesis is pointed: He sees the causes of the continued ferocity of the war not in the religious motives of the belligerents, but in the dynastic ambitions and political fissures within the Holy Roman Empire, which in later phases of the war drew in other major European powers as contenders.

———. *The Thirty Years War: A Sourcebook.* Basingstoke, U.K.: Palgrave Macmillan, 2010. Wilson's sourcebook follows the pattern of his monograph on the war, referenced above, and lays out in chronological order sources dealing primarily with the political and military history of the war.

Acknowledgments (continued from p. iv)

Figure 1: Matthaeus Merian, copper-etching, "The Comet of 1618 over Heidelberg," from Johann Philipp Abelin, Matthaeus Merian, *Theatrum Europaeum* [1617–1628] (Frankfurt 1635), p. 119. Herzog August Bibliothek Wolfenbüttel, Sign. A: 70.A Hist.2. Reproduced with permission from the Herzog August Bibliothek Wolfenbüttel.

Figure 2: The Peasants' Revenge, plate 17 from "The Miseries and Misfortunes of War," engraved by Israel Henriet (c. 1590–1661) 1633 (engraving) (b/w photo), Callot, Jacques (1592–1635) (after) / Grosjean Collection, Paris, France / The Bridgeman Art Library. Reproduced with permission from the Bridgeman Art Library.

Figure 3: Daniel Mannasser, *Ware Contrafactur der Statt Magdenburg*; engraving, 1631. Bayrische Staatsbibliothek München, Einbl. V,8 k. Reproduced with permission from the Bayerische Staatsbibliothek, Munich.

Figure 4: Jan Asselijn (1610–1652), King Gustavus II Adolphus of Sweden in the Battle of Luetzen. 1634. Oil on oak, 89.4 x 12.8 cm. Herzog Anton Ulrich-Museum, Braunschweig, Germany / bpk, Berlin / Hermann Buresch (photographer) / Art Resource, N.Y. Reproduced with permission from Art Resource, N.Y.

Documents 1 and 2: *Quellen zum Verfassungsorganismus des Heiligen Römischen Reiches Deutscher Nation, 1495–1815* (*Sources regarding the Constitution of the Holy Roman Empire of the German Nation, 1495–1815*), Hanns Hubert Hofmann, ed. (Darmstadt: Wissenschaftliche Buchgesellschaft, 1976), pp. 150, 151, 152–53. Reprinted with permission from Wissenschaftliche Buchgesellschaft, Darmstadt.

Documents 4 and 61: *Der Dreißigjährige Krieg in zeitgenössischer Darstellung. Hans Heberles "Zeytregister" (1618–1672). Aufzeichnungen aus dem Ulmer Territorium. Ein Beitrag zu Geschichtsschreibung und Geschichtsverständnis der Unterschichten*, Gerd Zillhardt, ed. (Ulm/Stuttgart: Kommissionsverlag W. Kohlhammer, 1975), pp. 85–87, 93–94, 224–27, 235–47. Reprinted with permission from the Haus der Stadtgeschichte - Stadtarchiv Ulm.

Document 10: Bartholomäus Dietwar, *Chronik. Leben eines evangelischen Pfarrers im früheren markgräflichen Amte Kitzingen von 1592–1670, von ihm selbst erzählt. Zugleich ein Beitrag zur Geschichte des 30jährigen Krieges in Franken. Mit erläuternden Zusätzen herausgegeben*, Gerd Högner, ed. (Kitzingen: Self-published, 2009), p. 48ff., p 52. Reprinted with permission from the editor.

Documents 12 and 37: Maurus Friesenegger, *Tagebuch aus dem 30jährigen Krieg. Nach einer Handschrift im Kloster Andechs*, Willibald Mathäser, ed. (Munich: Allitera Verlag, 2007), pp. 17ff., 48–59, 60–72. Reprinted with permission of Allitera Verlag/Buch und Medien, Munich.

Document 13: Wolfgang Lenz, oil painting, 1974, *Liborius Wagner, Ascending to Heaven*. Reproduced with kind permission from the artist, Wolfgang Lenz, Würzburg.

Document 14: Nürtinger Blutbibel, Württembergische Landesbibliothek Stuttgart. Order Number: B (deutsch 1627 03), here p. 229. Reproduced with permission from the Württembergische Landesbibliothek Stuttgart.

Documents 18, 23, 33, and 41: Peter Hagendorf, *Tagebuch eines Söldners aus dem Dreißigjährigen Krieg*, Jan Peters, ed. (2nd rev. edition, Göttingen: V & R Unipress, 2012), pp. 104–5, 135–39, 145, 146, 148, 151, 170, 173, 175. Reprinted with permission of V & R Unipress, Göttingen.

Document 19: Augustin Güntzer, *Kleines Biechlen von meinem gantzen leben: Die Autobiographie eines Elsässer Kannengießers aus dem 17. Jahrhundert*, Fabian Brändle and Dominik Sieber, eds. (Cologne, Weimar, Vienna: Böhlau Verlag, 2002), pp. 237–39. Reprinted with permission of Böhlau Verlag, Cologne, Weimar, Vienna.

Documents 20 and 21: "Kriegstagebuch des Rüthener Bürgermeisters Christoph Brandis (ca. 1578–1658) über die hessische Einquartierung 1636," in *Sterbzeiten: der Dreißigjährige Krieg im Herzogtum Westfalen; Eine Dokumentation*, ed. Horst Conrad and Gunnar Teske, (Westfälische Quellen und Archivpublikationen 23) (Münster: Landschaftsverband Westfalen-Lippe, Archivamt), pp. 309, 310. Reproduced with permission from the Archivamt Landschaftsverband Westfalen-Lippe.

Documents 25–28: Fritz Wolff, "Feldpostbriefe aus dem Dreißigjährigen Kriege. Selbstzeugnisse der kleinen Leute," in *Hundert Jahre Historische Kommission für Hessen 1897–1997* (*Veröffentlichungen der Historischen Kommission für Hessen* 61), Walter Heinemeyer, ed. (Marburg: N.G. Elwert Verlag, 1997), 509ff. Reproduced with permission from the president of the "Historische Kommission für Hessen," Marburg.

Document 29: Johann Georg Maul, "The Burdens of Contribution," in Gottfried Staffel, Justinianus Wolff, and Justinus Heinrich Wolff, *Notabilia: Naumburger Denkwürdigkeiten aus dem 17. Jahrhundert 1608–1623, 1680–1683, 1695–1702, ergänzt um Johann Georg Mauls Diarium 1631–1645*, Siegfried Wagner and Karl-Heinz Wünsch, eds. (Naumburg: Uder Verlag, 2005), p. 118. Reproduced with permission of Uder Verlag, Gladbeck.

Documents 31 and 56: Johann Georg Pforr, *Beschreibung etzlicher denckwürdigen Geschichden: Eine Chronik von Schmalkalden, 1400–1680*, Renate T. Wagner, ed. (Jena: Stitzius Verlag, 2008), pp. 139, 147, 135ff. Reprinted with permission from the editor.

Document 32: Complaint from Three Jewish Heads of Household from Dülmen 1626, ms. of document in Landesarchiv Nordrhein-Westfalen Abteilung Westfalen, Fürstbistum Münster-Landesarchiv 39.3, Bl. 11–12. First printed in *Der Dreißigjährige Krieg und der Alltag in Westfalen: Quellen aus dem Staatsarchiv Münster*, Leopold Schütte, ed. (Münster: Nordrhein-Westfälisches Staatsarchiv, 1998), pp. 166–67. Reprinted with permission from the Landesarchiv Nordrhein-Westfalen.

Document 35: Johann Daniel Minck, "The Plague as the Scourge of God, 1635," in: *Südhessische Chroniken aus der Zeit des Dreißigjährigen Krieges*, Rudolf Kunz and Willy Lizalek, eds., *Sonderband der Geschichtsblätter des Kreises Bergstrasse* (Heppenheim: Verlag Laurissa, 1983), 254–55. Reprinted with permission from the president of the "Arbeitsgemeinschaft der Geschichts- und Heimatvereine des Kreises Bergstrasse."

Document 39: Asmus Teufel, "Report of Massacre of 1626 at Münden," manuscript in Stadtarchiv Hannoversch-Münden, A 2/2001 Nr. 688 – M 1/Sch 2/21. The transcription of the document and the headnote was made available to the editors by Thomas Kossert, Göttingen/Hannoversch-Münden.

Document 44: "Brief und Hilfsgesuch Albrecht von Wallensteins an Feldmarschall Pappenheim von November 1632 (mit Blutflecken)," Heeresgeschichtliches Museum, Wien, Inv. Nr. NI1773. Reproduced with permission from the director, Heeresgeschichtliches Museum, Vienna.

Document 46: Zacharias von Quetz, "Account of a Participant in the Battle of Lützen." British Library, London, Add MS 11,660, 36v–38v. Reprinted with permission from the British Library.

Document 48: "A handwritten newsletter from Nuremberg, 1632. " Niedersächsisches Staatsarchiv, Wolfenbüttel, Sign.: 1 Z Nr. 7: Geschriebene Zeitungen, 1632–33, Bl. 48. Reprinted with permission from the Niedersächsisches Staatsarchiv, Wolfenbüttel.

Document 49: "Der Schwede lebet noch." Staatsbibliothek zu Berlin, Stiftung Preussischer Kulterbesitz, Berlin, Germany / bpk, Berlin / Benjamin Marschke (photographer) / Art Resource, N.Y. Reproduced with permission from Art Resource, N.Y.

Documents 50, 51, 52: *Mercurij Relation*, Decembris 1632, München 1633 (call no. Z.11), Ordentliche Wochentliche Zeitungen No. 12, Frankfurt 1634 (call no.

Z1/1634/12), Ordentliche Wochentliche Zeitung No. 13, Frankfurt 1634 (call no. Z1/1634/13). The reprints in this volume are made from copies of contemporary originals in the collections of the Institut Deutsche Presseforschung, University of Bremen. Reprinted with permission from the Institut Deutsche Presseforschung, University of Bremen.

Document 53: "Eygentliche Abbildung und Beschreibung des Egerischen Panckets," single leaf copper-etching. Herzog August Bibliothek Wolfenbüttel, Sign.: IH 568 a. Reproduced with permission from the Herzog August Bibliothek Wolfenbüttel.

Document 59: Marx Anthon Hannas, single leaf colored woodcut "Freudenreicher Postillon von Münster, den Frieden verkündend, " Augsburg 1648, 370 x 275 cm, Kunstsammlungen und Museen Augsburg, Inv.-Nr. G20632. Reproduced with permission from the Kunstsammlungen und Museen Augsburg.

Document 60: Caspar Preis, *Bauernleben im Zeitalter des Dreißigjährigen Krieges: Die Stausebacher Chronik des Caspar Preis, 1636–1667*, Wilhelm A. Eckhardt and Helmut Klingelhöfer, eds. (Marburg an der Lahn: Verlag Trautvetter & Fischer Nachf., 1998), pp. 66–69. Reprinted with permission from the editors.

Document 62: Quoted from the original manuscript in Angelika Bischoff-Luithlen, *Gruorn. Ein Dorf und sein Ende* (Stuttgart: Schwäbischer Alb Verein, 1967), p. 83. Reprinted with permission from the descendants of Angelika Bischoff-Luithlen.

Index